Rising Tall

Kemi Nelson

ISBN: 9798892831109

Library of Congress Control Number: 2024912759

Contents

Introduction

For a long time, the thought of this book was in the back of my mind. I felt the need to tell the story and was driven to share and help many others who silently go through similar struggles, believing themselves unworthy due to life's circumstances. It's one thing to suffer, but it's far worse to feed the enemy with our own feelings of unworthiness and unfulfillment.

The best champions rise from the toughest situations. They are never defined by their struggles but by their resilience.

This book comes from a place of deep personal experience and reflection. Life's trials shape us and mold our character in ways we may not see immediately. Through my own journey, I've come to understand that the most profound growth comes from the twists and turns in our lives. It is in these times of despair that our true strength is revealed.

You too can stand tall. You have the strength to face each challenge and rise above whatever comes your way. You have the right to rewrite your story, assert your worth, and find your joyful fulfillment.

This book is your experiential reminder of light and hope.

Yes, go ahead, determine today you'll be known in the history books as one constantly RISING TALL amidst all storms. I give you permission. My name is Folakemi Nelson and I approve this message. ☺

Some names have been changed to protect identities of those in my life story.

Foreword

I am only ever certain of a few things in life and this is one of them. This was a story worth being told and I am more than convinced that this book will change the lives of many others out there. It is with such profound joy that I write this foreword for "Rising Tall."

The moment I laid my eyes on the pages of this book, I felt an immediate connection to Folakemi's journey—a journey of heartbreak and incredible faith. This memoir is more than a collection of memories; it is a vivid portrayal of the strength and courage that reside within each one of us.

"Rising Tall," is a world of raw emotion. Folakemi opens her heart with overflowing honesty, sharing experiences that many would find too sore to revisit. In her vulnerability, there is immense strength. She teaches us that confronting our past can transform our pain into power and our wounds into wisdom.

There is a journey laid out in these pages, one full of transformation. Folakemi's life, filled with both challenges and glorious moments, is proof of the human spirit's capacity to overcome and to stand tall. Her story is a lamp for anyone who has ever felt the weight of darkness. It's remarkable how the book shows us that even in our darkest times, there is a path forward, lit by hope, faith, and perseverance.

What struck me the most about this book is Folakemi's relationship with God. She prays, and hopes, and her faith grows, despite the hardships. It is not only inspiring but also humbling. She reminds us that no matter the trials we face, there is an inherent strength through God that can guide us through. Her resilience is a powerful example of how we can all rise above our circumstances.

This book is filled with candid storytelling. Her story is a call to each of us to find our own strength and to rise tall in the face of our struggles. She beautifully illustrates that our stories, no matter how difficult, are worth telling and that our voices, no matter how quiet, deserve to be heard.

For those who have felt marginalized, overlooked, or silenced, this book is to give them hope. "Rising Tall" is more than just a story of survival; it is a guide to finding purpose amidst life's challenges. It is an invitation to embrace your own narrative and to discover the power that lies within you.

In reading this memoir, you will find not only comfort but also a renewed drive. The experiences resonate deeply. Her words remind us that we are not defined by our hardships, but by how we respond to them. We all can rise, heal, and transform our pain into power.

May "Rising Tall" inspire you as it has inspired me. As you find your way through your own journey, may you find the courage to face your challenges with the same strength and grace that Folakemi has so poignantly shared. This book is proof of the power of the human spirit, and I am honored to have the opportunity to share in its message.

With deepest admiration,

Mary Lee Mason.

Founder/President & Director

New Heart of Texas Ministries

Dedication

This book is dedicated to Joyce Meyer and other victors of childhood trauma from intimate abuse. Those sheroes and heroes who successfully relinquished their fights for Justice in the place of divine purposefulness.

Acknowledgements

To the immortal, invisible, the only wise God. The one who says in Jeremiah 29:11, *"I know what I am doing."*

I knew the time was ripe to tell my story. It was the right time to bless souls and reap the incremental and exponential rewards of seeing hearts read it and gain healing from the pain I bore. I unreservedly embarked on finding someone who could write the story for me. Someone who would take the monumental task off my hands and tell it all. I searched high and low, but no one met my set standards. No one could tell this story that was mine. My standards were high and my experiences unique. Yet my story offers inspiration and hope for many to embrace universally as theirs.

Though I couldn't find a surrogate or ghostwriter, I found someone even more valuable—an editor, a sister, and a friend. Someone with exactly the same name as mine, Folakemi. She, like me, proudly embraced her full name. We were born in the same month, and she was the first Folakemi I had ever met. Her insights gave ground to my story and she challenged me in more ways than one. She became a worthy skilled writing tutor and editor, a listener, and a sister. With her persistent encouragement, she has become a big part of my story. Folakemi, thank you for believing in me and in this story. Your support has been invaluable.

To Dr. Anita, Oana, Peace, Dupe, Morenike, and all my alpha and beta readers, thank you for your candid and glowingly constructive feedback.

Carol Lempert, Lauren Underwood, Christy Haskell, and Dawn McClelland, your support has meant the world to me. Thank you for being part of this journey.

Beth Moore, I bless you for being a signal to God's LOVE during a time that mattered nationally.

The impetus for my memoir was originally birthed during the Christmas holiday of 2007, while vacationing with my bookworm sister in Hemel Hempstead, England. I discovered Joyce Meyer's *Beauty for Ashes* in my sister's library and couldn't put it down until I finished it. I couldn't fathom the sexual abuse she suffered from her parents... But she found her voice, and so have I, and so will everyone reading this book who needs to find theirs.

To my siblings, nieces, and nephews, you put a dance in my life story. You have my deepest gratitude.

To my Favour and Praise. You lived through the pains and the incredible triumphs. Yet, you have only seen a bit of the treasures planned for you in championship. No eyes have seen what the LORD has planned for you, my baes!

My gratitude also goes to everyone who has been a part of my life story. For the pains and the victories, you have all played a role in shaping who I am and in the creation of this book.

And to you, the reader, thank you for taking the time to embark on this journey with me. May this story bring you hope, healing, and the courage to embrace your own story, no matter where it may lead.

CHAPTER 1

Yet He Knows
The Way I Have Taken

Heart thundering, threatening to burst out of my chest as I sat at the edge of the seat, feeling smaller than I was. The windows were rolled all the way up in the back of the car, and only a little bit of air reached me from Mom's half-cracked window in the front. Yet, it felt like I was drowning in an ocean of air.

My lungs filled up and up and up and never seemed to be able to contract. I was hyperventilating, petrified. The car was a prison, and I felt like someone being driven to the gallows to die.

"Quit shaking the seat." Mom's stern voice came to me. She was driving, her hands tight on the steering wheel, and she did not look back as she snapped her order at me.

But she needn't have looked back. I knew what her face would look like. Tight, contorted in anger, bewildered. The same look she had when she'd caught me eating the forbidden fruit.

The car was now careening towards our destination, a little, almost non-descript church that we'd passed a thousand times before. The pounding of my heart graduated, swelled, and crescendoed into a full-blown panic. I finally exhaled the pent-up air in my lungs, but for the very life of me, I couldn't draw another breath. I had forgotten how to breathe.

"Stop that," Mom said again, "Stop that, now."

I opened my mouth, trying to catch any errant air so that I could fill my lungs. What came out of me instead, was a shriek, a small shriek that collected, encapsulated, and manifested the despair that I so deeply felt inside.

The day had started innocently enough and gave no indication that I'd be here now, being taken to be spiritually diagnosed; and over something as simple, and as stupid as a half-eaten *agbalumo*. That was the forbidden fruit.

In Nigeria, the African Star Apple is known by many names. In my world, it was (and is) called agbalumo, a fruit with a very complex taste. Depending on how mature it is, it can be terribly sour or amazingly sweet. The ripe agbalumo is savory-sweet and tart in flavor, sometimes as sweet as honey. I loved the tartness and the sweetness and the flavor that exploded on my tongue when I bit into a perfectly ripe fruit.

As a child, I'd give my right arm and eye for a delicious African star apple; the only problem was that Mom hated them.

Mom was soft, and kind, and beautiful, and all the tender things that mothers are. She was a very passionate woman who loved with all of her being. She would give her life for her kids.

However, when she was Mom the disciplinarian, she seemed to forget to exit that role. None of us children had the temerity to look our firebrand mother in the eyes or ever built up the courage to openly disobey her word.

Mother was the epitome West African disciplinarian, much revered and feared, whose children were always to be nothing but their absolute best. And that, all five of us children were. Always at our best. Best in life manners, best in educational classes, best behaved. Eating fruits did not fit the mold.

Meals were structured, had to be eaten according to a roster of meals, and at the dining table. As a child, I ate what was placed in front of me without question, and did not (was not allowed to) have a preference. And God protect the child that dared ask "why?" I wasn't privy to Mom's thought processes, nor learnt from her decision-making approach at that early age. All I knew was that Mom was lord, queen, mayor, governor, and president, and you'd be crazy to question her.

My mom was an advanced nurse; our meals were generous, healthy and nutritious, but eating times had so much rigidity that it wasn't as joyful as a child desired.

I also loved mangoes, even though the only ones allowed were the ones Mom or Dad got from the elite International Institute of Tropical Agriculture (IITA), but agbalumo was an absolute no.

I was barely five years old, insanely curious about the world, eager to take a bite of everything and be acquainted with new flavors. And clever enough, I thought I could explore those flavors surreptitiously without crossing Mom.

So, walking along the dusty Ibadan roads, I'd find half-eaten treasures – half eaten agbalumos – on the roads. Sometimes, but not quite often enough, I'd even find perfectly whole African star apples under trees. These discarded fruits (perhaps even sweeter because they were discarded and forbidden) took me to the sweet gates of heaven and back each and every time. I'd pick a few and secretly hide them away in my school bag, in the compartments that nobody checked.

And when I was done with homework and chores and had some free time to myself, I'd sneak off to the woods behind our house. We had large mature trees in that backyard that seemed to be made just for my hiding. I'd slide down the smooth trunk of one of them and feel at peace, away from the foreboding presence of Mom or other adults that may suspect my disobedience.

That blisteringly hot afternoon, I'd done exactly what I'd done a hundred times in the past. I hurried through my homework and chores. With Mom engrossed in a medical book and my siblings gathered around a board game in the girls' room, I escaped with my backpack.

The kitchen door had a creakiness to it that announced your departure or arrival, but I had grown to master it. I braced it with my slim shoulders, raising it a little over its hinges before sliding open the deadbolt. The creakiness was muffled.

When I was sure no one had heard me, I fled across the courtyard and into the large-treed yard. At the base of one of the trees, I sat, opening my backpack to three pieces of half-eaten agbalumos. I didn't know whether they had been eaten by diseased people or one of the many crazies that walked the streets. I didn't know if a child like me had eaten them and tossed them out of their parent's car. I knew nothing, except that these were about the most extraordinary thing I'd tasted up to that point in my life.

Gingerly, wanting to savor the experience for as long as I could, I picked one of the seeds (dripping with juice) and placed it in my mouth. Welcome sourness, tinged with a little bit of sweetness, exploded on my tongue. I closed my eyes.

I've always loved to daydream and plan, often imagining a beautiful future and family as my natural family was not at that moment. That afternoon, I daydreamed again; closed my eyes, and was no longer a little girl hiding from her mom's fury behind a tree. Rather, I was seated around the dining table with Dad, Mom, and siblings. We had a tray of fruits – everything under the sun – apples, oranges, grapes, mangoes, grapefruits, fruits I didn't even know existed, and of course, a plethora of star apples. Mom had a massive smile as she passed the fruits of our choices to each of us. Her smile was dazzling, her eyes dancing with light, her teeth perfectly straight and white.

"Aww, Mom. You are so kind, so beautiful, so loving. I love you so much."

"Folakemi. Are you nuts?" The words that came to me didn't come from my imaginary mom. Instead, they came from my real-life mom, who was now suddenly standing over me in the place that was supposed to be my sanctuary. And instead of light and love, her eyes were filled with menace and fury.

For a little while, I struggled. Suddenly yanked from my perfect dream world and thrust back into the real world. My secret found out, I didn't know what to feel. I hit the real world, hit reality with a hard bounce. I staggered to my feet, forgetting to hide the stolen pleasure I had in my hand.

"What are you doing, talking to trees?" Mom dragged me up by the scruff of my dress, and because I was already halfway to standing myself, the dress tightened against my neck and almost cut off my breath.

"And what have you here?" Her voice was low, not loud, but because it was filled with so much fury, it sounded louder than a thousand drums. She let go of me and turned to my bag instead. She picked the first half-eaten agbalumo, holding it up like it was vermin.

"Where did you get this?"

I struggled to find the words to explain myself. The words rose in my belly, rose to my throat, and then died without being uttered.

"I said, where did you get this?" She asked again. Now, she had the fruit in one hand and me in the other hand.

I tried speaking again, but only a garbled "Roadside, Ma" came out.

We made it to the house somehow. All the while, I felt not like myself but like I had a stranger inhabiting my body. I felt like an onlooker, a petrified onlooker.

As the hour passed and the interrogation intensified, the confession came out in bits and pieces. My voice came back to me, but not entirely, and I no longer felt discombobulated from my body as I spoke. Haltingly, I told on myself, of picking throwaways, of finding solace behind the house, of eating the forbidden fruit, time and time again.

"And speaking to trees. I caught you speaking to trees." Mom insisted, wanting me to add this last one to my litany of offenses.

I agreed with all she said, but not this. Because I had not been speaking to the trees. I didn't even know that trees talked or that you could talk to them.

"I wasn't speaking to trees, Mom." On this, I was adamant, would not budge.

"You were calling a tree 'Mom.'" She spat out at me.

We were in the living room, she in a chair, me kneeling in front of her. My siblings, three older ones and a younger one, had taken refuge in a nearby room. Like me, they feared Mom. In times like this, it was better not to be involved, to take shelter somewhere else, let the storm pass, and later, when it was safe, comfort the sibling on the receiving end.

I knew their hearts were with me, but how I wished they'd come into the room, make all this go away.

"I know what I saw. I know what I heard. You are possessed, must be. There is no other explanation."

A woman of strong convictions, once this explanation happened upon Mom, there was no turning back. To her, there was no other tenable explanation. My behavior was out of the norm, so there had to be something out of the norm pushing me to do what I had done. I was possessed, plain and simple.

Now a mom myself, with an overwhelming abundance of love for my children, how I would have asked *why*. How I would have knelt on one knee and raised my child's face so that her eyes met mine. How I would curl up in bed with her, cuddling her, stroking her head. How I would be what I know best to be. Curious, intentionally curious to learn my child's heart, to know why she had snuck the agbalumos. To explain to her the health and safety risk she exposed herself to by picking half-eaten fruits off the ground to eat.

I have no doubt my mom's furious response was born from love. Love to see me safe. Love to make sure this sickly child did not eat an allergen that would precipitate yet another anaphylaxis attack (although always mild). Love to shield her from the gross lack of hygiene her behavior involved, and the exposure to debilitating diseases like pneumonia. Love to keep her from yet another asthmatic episode that would surely land us in the hospital. I have no doubt Mom's fury was her love-speak, although too complex for a child to interpret accurately, and translate into anything but a total fear of authority.

And so here we were, in the car that felt more like a prison, driving to a church that scared me from the tips of my hair to the soles of my feet.

The priest (or pastor or exorcist or whatever she was) met us at the door, and I immediately felt a chill like I had never felt before. My stomach, which had been hot before we got here, suddenly felt like it had been dunked in an ice bath. The cold spread from my insides to my extremities, and I felt myself shaking.

"She is possessed. There is no other explanation." The exorcist told Mom.

"Ogbanje ni omo yii; o lo nba igi soro ni."

I remember the fright that bunched my chest up and the hard-knocking of my heart. I was frightened, but I was suddenly mute again. All I wanted to do was get Mom's attention and have her return me home, away from this place of loud prayers and ringing prayer bells. But her back was turned to me, her arms folded across her chest.

I will never forget those words. *"Ogbanje ni omo yii; o lo nba igi soro ni,"* meaning "this child is possessed with the most dangerous spirits. She's been talking to trees as her peer spirits."

My heart broke inside of me because I knew this wasn't true.

In Yoruba folklore (and many other African cultures), an ogbanje is a reincarnating spirit that causes grief or pain. They're most often children that die stillborn or children that die very young. They are the children that exhibit strange signs and don't fit in with society.

Yes, I was young, but I had heard of ogbanjes, and to be labeled as one, to be diagnosed as speaking to trees when I was not, broke my heart.

I loved Mom with the whole of my being, but at that moment, standing in that prayer house and with her believing such a deathly strange verdict about her very own daughter, the five-year old child felt lost and unloved by mother. I was also filled with sadness and grief, bewilderment and pain. Wasn't this person supposed to be my number one advocate in life? Weren't parents meant to protect their children at all costs and not sell them out?

I had no evil reincarnating spirit living inside of me. I was simply Folakemi (Busola) Ajayi, an innocent young girl who wanted nothing more than to be gathered up in her mother's arms and loved. I wanted to be asked why the secrecy. I wanted to be home. I wanted to be away from here.

I wanted to say something, to refute the claims of this so-called prophetess. But I was not allowed a word. Each time I tried to speak, "holy water" was forced into my mouth, this in their minds to cast out the evil spirit. But there was no evil spirit. All there was, was a little girl who was frightened out of her mind.

The agbalumo/*ogbanje* incident marked a turning point in my childlike innocence and led to more secrets. We would have our family life together, and then I would have my separate life, where all my secrets were mine, held close to the chest. Some of these secrets would sting and burn and smother and follow me into adulthood like a bad smell, but I would never share them.

***

Unique in life! There was something different, something about me that was not quite *Ajayi*.

It started from long before I was even born. You see, my older siblings are British-born, and I am not. For the longest time, this was a sore point for me. I thought they were fortunate, that they had something that I didn't, that they had been born more privileged than I was. And in later years, my younger brother would also gain an American permanent residence, while I managed to just narrowly miss out on that too.

It is funny how we label ourselves disadvantaged when we are really not, often because we do not know of God's word or fail to bring to mind our Father's commitment that all things work together for the good of those who love Him, or because we simply want it now, our way, our timing. Now, I know that the way you come into the world and the initial circumstances of your life may affect the trajectory of life's opportunities, but none of those can ever remove you from God's predestined purpose. I didn't always know this, and didn't fully understand it until recently.

My parents were both born and bred in Nigeria, the country of wet and dry and harmattan seasons. They are learned people, in love with education, and from a young age, they knew that life prospects outside the country were much more promising than inside, both for themselves and for their future progeny.

They relocated to the UK in the 1960s to study, and later settled and had their first three children there. First came a set of identical twin boys, named Dele and Ayo. Then came an adorable little girl they named Ronke. According to UK laws, all three received British citizenship at birth. Armed with dual citizenships, they could be British when they pleased and Nigerians when it suited for a better purpose. Wherever they went, they would always have this advantage.

My story was different.

More than a decade after my parents left Africa, they decided to go back home to Nigeria for what was supposed to be a brief visit. It wasn't brief as planned, and I came into the world on a beautiful hot August day, counting four decades ago. Conceived and born in the land of my origin, a dark-skinned, dark-haired, dark-eyed girl, very much loved by God and destined for great things in life. Only, for a long time, I didn't know that I would come to bear my name; *Oluwafolakemi*: The LORD pampers me with all round fulfillment and success.

Dad settled in as a head pharmacist at The Polytechnic, Ibadan. At that time, The Polytechnic was still a fledgling school, having been founded in March 1970. Similar to other polytechnics in Nigeria, it was established to provide an alternative higher education to universities, particularly in technical skill acquisition. Mom worked at the IAR&T clinic (Institute of Agricultural Research & Training).

My earliest memories are of Dad waving us goodbye as he went to work in the mornings. Mom would follow suit not long afterward.

My parents were always hardworking people and had a slightly different schedule from the typical 9-5 schedule. Getting back from work, Dad would head over to his retail pharmacy shop to put in another shift and wouldn't get back home until 10 pm. If he was at the shop, Mom was home. Sometimes, Mom stood in for him so that he was home while she was at the shop. As children, we were expected to work just as hard, to always put in our best. Performance mattered.

I was becoming more independent, and loved preschool with a passion. Our lives had started to settle into a routine until my parents gave us all an amazing bundle of joy, the gift of my younger brother, Sean. One thing about siblings is that you never know you were missing them until they arrive; this was true about Sean.

I became a doting elder sister who loved this new human being and wanted to do anything for him. The closeness I shared with Sean as a baby followed us into adulthood. Today, we remain close friends.

I also had an amazing friendship with my older sister. Being the only other girl in the family, she was my confidante, my go-to person, the one person I could fall asleep with my head on her lap, not worried about anything.

As siblings, we were very close, all five of us. And we all had a common love-fear relationship with Mom because we all scuttled at her heavy-handedness again and again and again.

We shared the terror at the bellows of her voice. When she called your name from another room, you started to quiver in your boots, even before you knew what you had done wrong, or if you had even done anything wrong.

Closeted in one of our rooms, we'd giggle and laugh and then clamp shut each other's mouths so that the giggles stayed trapped inside as we recounted something funny about Mom. We'd giggle silently, holding our sides until they hurt. We loved our Mom and would give up our lives for her in a heartbeat, but we were also in mortal fear of her.

I am no longer that little girl who lived her life in fear of Mom. Our relationship grew and evolved into an understanding of each other and a deeper love for one another. Mother was a beautiful, doting grandmother before she passed on. As an adult, I now value my natural family like never before. I feel blessed that Mom had been chosen to birth and raise me, fully aware that God is a God of intentions and never makes mistakes.

He knows the end from the very beginning. The latter part of Jeremiah 29:10-11 in The Message translation says, *"I know what I'm doing. I have it all planned out—plans to take care of you, not abandon you, plans to give you the future you hope for."*

This, I now know.

***

Childhood was not all about discipline, even though discipline and performance played a huge part.

My childhood was also filled with beautiful memories of fun and family. It was innocent. It was everything childhood should be. I remember the happy child I was and feeling cocooned by the presence and love of family. I remember that Sundays were particularly special.

We had *iyan* (pounded yam), which was prepared the traditional way. Yam was boiled in huge pots, and when the slices were nice and tender, they were pounded to a soft, slightly draw-ey, delicate consistency with a huge mortar and pestle. Mom would cook vast pots of *Egusi* soup (that was the standard fare). Sometimes, she made her signature spinach vegetable mix.

These Sunday lunches were a feast, with lots of family around. We had many "adopted" siblings that lived with us, as my parents were fond of raising extended family members and children of some community members that were at financial disadvantage.

After lunch came the practice dance in advance for school. The dance times were light-hearted and fun, and we competed against each other in the friendliest ways. I was always the star, and at this point in my life, I loved being the center of attraction. In later years, after life had interjected and taught many hard lessons, I would become a true introvert. But in the innocence of childhood, there was nothing I loved more than being with family, eating my fill of the family feast every Sunday, and dancing *ijo-ibile* until my feet hurt, and my heart soared in triumph.

These were my memories of early childhood. The precious memories of life before my consciousness was overtaken and overwhelmed; the little child unsuspectingly pushed by fear and "discipline" into the arms of an abuser.

These were my beautiful memories until the rape.

CHAPTER 2

The Biology Of
An Ironing Board

I t hurt like fire.

The place that was supposed to be mine, exclusively mine; it hurt like a thousand cuts of broken glass. It had been violated.

Doubled over, the pain shooting from my private parts into my belly where it ballooned and crushed against my heart, I thought I was going to die. Everything ached; my back, my head, my arms (which had been tightly gripping the bathroom door), my chest, and of course, that private place.

He had left me in the bathroom to clean up. As he left, he'd had an odd look in his eyes; a half-smile tinged with menace. This was a half-smile I had come to know, to learn, to hate. When I had first met this young man, his smile had been like a sun; shining, brilliant, soothing. Not anymore.

When he smiled at me now, terror filled my heart, and my mouth filled with spit at the panic of it all. To everyone else, he was soft-spoken, warm, and sincere. To me, he was now a menace.

It is incredible how human neuropsychology processes trauma. I was about twelve years old, had been raped repeatedly since I was almost eleven, and this would continue for another year.

I heard the slam of a door. Biting back on the tears that flooded my eyes, I listened intently. It was the door to Mom's room, and the very knowledge that she was unexpectedly back from her outing catapulted me into action.

With the back of my hands, I dried my giveaway tears and hurriedly pulled myself together. I still hurt and ached and throbbed, but I emerged from the bathroom with all normalcy; like nothing had happened, like I had not just been raped for the umpteenth time right in my own home by a supposed family friend, and without the knowledge of anyone else in the home.

I was petrified of being found out. Would everyone think it was my fault if I ever spoke up? Would all the adults think that I had led him on? Would everyone think I had tricked him into the abuse as he threatened they would? Would they take sides with him? Would Mom cart me off to another prayer house to be delivered from the ogbanje spirit she believed plagued me?

As much as she loved me, could she ever understand me? How was I to explain what had happened to me? How do I begin to make them see me? How was I to make sense of all the convoluted feelings in my heart and soul? How do I explain to God that this wasn't my fault? Or was it?

How was I to explain to anyone that I was truly a godly child that loved doing the right thing, loved to be called good, loved to get it right with God and please Him with my very soul and being? How could I make sense of what was happening to me?

He said it was all my fault. He said little girls weren't to ask questions about things. But wait, didn't *he* initiate the questions and asked me if I wanted to know the answers?

There were too many questions I couldn't answer, too heavy a burden that I carried alone, but one thing I was sure of. All that was happening had to be my fault and I had to keep the secret. Not a soul could know of the horror that was being visited upon me.

And so the rape became as a sin that I would carry deep within me, in secrecy, for decades. Alone.

There are many emotions that are tangled with being a rape victim. Hopelessness, like there is no way out, no end in sight. Aloneness, like you are the only one left in the world. Muteness, like no one can hear you. Unseen, like you have gone up in smoke and are invisible. You feel hot and you feel cold. You are afraid. You are ashamed.

And after a while, you become numb.

***

The taste of childhood rape is the taste of life-long trauma, if unresolved. The acrid, pungent taste may fade and lessen as one grows older, but it seems to have a permanent lodge in the soul of the afflicted. But for divine intervention, it is as an unrelenting psychological kyphosis to carry and to bear.

I remember the events that precipitated my ordeal.

"Folakemi, get me my purse from my room?" Mom asked one dark evening.

I was about ten years old; old enough to run such a simple errand; and young enough to be terrified of the dark; petrified to cross our beautiful open courtyard architecture by myself. That was all that stood between me and Mom's room. In the daytime, the courtyard held no terrors of fear. It shone in all its glory with beauty and nature. In the evenings, however, ridden with electric power blackouts, the same beauty of nature suddenly throbbed with darkness as my imagination came alive with the worst of possibilities. There were robbers and murderers and ax men lurking in the shadows, waiting just for my ten-year-old self to cross the courtyard so that they could pounce on me, with death and torture at their hands.

There were snakes from the beautiful plants, big enough to swallow the entire house. Vivid enough in my child heart to torment. Yet my curious analytical mind; the futuristic dreamer we met earlier, lacked the mental maturity to hold forth and simply use the same power of logic to disprove those fiery darts of evil imaginations.

Because of my very fertile, yet immature imagination, I didn't cross the courtyard all by myself in the dark if I could help it. I became pretty adept at circumventing the place and avoided it as best as I could.

However, I dared not say no to my mom's beckon. As an African child, you were supposed to obey your parents without question.

That dark, starless night, I hearkened to Mom's beckoning, shoving my fear deep down my throat and into my abdomen. My reverence of Mom trumped the fear of crossing the courtyard and I made that trip more often than you could count. I never said no to Mom, never told her about the fears I carried.

And then, we had a guest.

"This is one of my friends' nephews, and he will be staying with us while he pursues his degree here, okay?"

It was a cool morning when Dad introduced my would-be-abuser to the family. I remember staggering out of bed, still sleepy-eyed, to meet this new, not-planned-for family member. He had arrived from his destination in the most Northern part of Western Nigeria, and so early too.

School was out of session for us kids, and we were home. I was ten years old and had just finished my first year of secondary school.

He had a great smile, and as he was introduced to each of us, his smile never died. He seemed nice and pleasant enough. And there was nothing to be worried about (at least at that point). My parents often had many people come and go; ours was a house of extended family members and friends and "adoptees." All the "aunties" and "uncles" as they were to be called, brought us the joy of community...until now.

Like others, this was a great adopted uncle during that holiday period.

"Hey, Folakemi. You should hear this new joke," he'd say.

I'd sit in the chair opposite the ironing board from him as he ironed (he had a love affair with crisp shirts and pants). He didn't talk down to me. He didn't bark orders at me. He didn't treat me like a ten-year-old. Instead, he treated me like an equal, like someone who had things to say, like someone who should be heard.

He was equal parts funny and engaging. He told fantastic jokes that had you cracking up. And when the occasion demanded it, he listened ever so intently, wanting to know what things were bothering you. He also gave great hugs.

He settled seamlessly into our family.

"Folakemi, dear," Mom said to me one late night, "The car keys...get them from my room, will you?"

We were in the living room, watching the late-night news. Dad was still at the pharmacy shop, and because his own car was in the repair shop, Mom had to go get him home.

Sighing but under my breath, I rose to my feet. So did my new "uncle."

"I'll go with you."

The fear took a backseat as he walked with me across the courtyard.

"Hey, the stars kind of look pretty amazing this night, don't they?" He asked.

I didn't want to look up at the sky. I just wanted to lunge across the courtyard as I had done so many times in the past. But he made me stop, pulling my hand until I ground to a halt. And then slowly but carefully, he tilted my face, and held my chin so that I was staring into the sky, despite myself.

As my heart quieted, I was indeed struck by the beauty of the sky; the deep dark blue that was broken up only by the dazzling lights of the stars.

"Not so terrible, is it?" He smiled at me, and my fears went away.

He waited at the entrance to my parents' room while I retrieved the car keys. When we walked back across the courtyard, my heart did not pound as hard as it used to.

He was my savior. He would later become my tormentor, but this night, he saved me from my fears and my imagination and I got to enjoy the beauty of skylight from our enchanting courtyard architecture for the first time. Ever.

***

And then came the day when my older siblings returned to school and I was left behind.

I had been in the Federal Government Boarding College and completed my first-year there. Moving into the second year, however, all second-year students were mandated to temporarily hold off on return resumption due to ongoing constructions that were delayed beyond planned timing. The wisdom of school administration was that this group had the least at stake from such a shortening of their full year programming.

My sister was in the same school and in a higher grade. She went back as previously planned. My older brothers, who were in another but similar boarding school, also returned after that summer vacation ended.

The only "support system" left would be my abuser. A man that seemed to read my mind and understood the turmoil inside. "I'm here for you, I am. I will take good care of you."

It felt natural coming from him.

And so, I began to lean more on him. His presence comforted me. I missed Sister Ronke, my older sister, but my newly acquired uncle filled the void.

***

As an adult who has had time and the hindsight to revisit this period, I now know that this trusted uncle took me through the six stages of sexual grooming, all in plain sight, yet without the knowledge of other adults. Statistics show that 92% of sexually abused children know their offender. A relationship in some form is often established beforehand.

My abuser was a young man seemingly always by the ironing board, ironing a shirt, or maybe a pair of pants. He'd inquire, and I'd tell him about school, church, friends; about everything and anything really.

I formed a bond with him because he had gained my trust. He had taken the time to understand my needs and somehow knew just how to fill those needs. He gave me what I was missing; attention and affection in the way an eleven year old understood so. He offered consistent companionship. He didn't even need to give me gifts. He didn't make me feel there was something he gained from me. He was an uncle through and through.

The sex talk started there at the ironing table. The ironing board would later become a symbol of hatred and self-loathing, and it took so long to understand why I so detested ironing until my healing began, and I started to revisit this dreadful period of life. The puzzles suddenly came together during trusted dialogue one day and I connected the dots. It had nothing to do with a chore. Ironing had all to do with what had been treacherously planted in the neurobiology of the 11-year-old child.

I cannot remember how we somehow went from an uncle's advice and innocuous friendly banter to sexually suggestive, talks that quickly progressed into sexualized behaviors. It continued to feel innocent for a long time, with just a little more edge each time. When I instinctively expressed suspicion that it felt excessive, "Uncle" quickly reassured me that this was normal. That I was unaware because of my nerdy tendencies for books only, coupled with a strict upbringing. He confidently told me that he, like all uncles about his age, did the same with my Dad's friend's children, from whom we knew him; and older girls that I greatly loved and respected.

He "accidentally" walked in on me changing clothes or in the bathroom. We played secret games that included wrestling and tickling and touching each other in places that no else could see.

"It feels great, doesn't it?"

It didn't feel great. Of all the adjectives to describe feelings, "great" was not on the list of how I felt. Dirty, unclean, confused, but not great. By this time, I was petrified of "Uncle" who deftly navigated threats and compliments. I knew what Mom's reaction would be if she heard either from me or from him. It was easier to give in to this torture that Uncle called "education," than it would be to revisit an experience like I'd had with the African star apple incident.

This was a secret worth keeping.

And then the touching progressed. "You are a sexual being, Folakemi," he'd whisper as he touched my privacy, "and you are very special to me. We are special to each other. You are lucky to have found this joy as a prepubescent eleven year old girl."

"But I shouldn't be that surprised," he'd continue. "You are really a smart girl, and special to God."

I was reading in my bedroom the day he came in and asked me to follow him to his. My parents were at work. That was the first time he penetrated me.

I died. At least I thought I did because I blacked out the entire time. Darkness swam across my vision, and I experienced myself floating in a deep, dark place. When I came to, he was standing over me, an idiotic grin across his face, and he was naked from the waist down. I brought my knees up to my chest and the pain that tore through me and the stench of his bodily fluids was how I knew what had happened to me.

"We made love," he said. "And this must always be our secret. You must never tell a soul."

I blacked out many more times and eventually crawled into the bathroom. I scrubbed my skin so hard it almost fell apart. I had to wash away the stench of him, the touch of him, and if possible, the very essence of him.

The sun, shining brightly overhead, when I stepped out, seemed a betrayal of sorts. Innocence had been stripped from me. What right had the sun to shine? What right had the day to continue its unfolding?

Yet that first time was not the last.

There was secrecy and blame. There were threats and manipulative coercion. He maintained a strong control over me for all of the two years he lived with us.

***

During the holidays, when my big sister was home, the abuse abated. In those times, my laughter was a little bit more from the heart. The light shone more from my eyes. The darkness and silence were silenced just enough as Sister Ronke and I laughed together and made new memories.

But I never told her. She would never know this until she met Jesus face to face.

I could not bear to see the horror on my sister's face if she ever knew. Of all the people in my life, I wanted her love most of all and couldn't bear for her to see me as a tainted person, which uncle said I was. He had told me of his full intention to paint me as the instigator and my young mind had been too immature to rationalize that no one would believe that an eleven-year-old had seduced a 20-something-year-old man!

Deep within, I knew it couldn't really be my fault, but I blamed myself nevertheless, convinced that I was the one who had done something wrong, that I had invited the rape, that I hadn't done enough to stop it. Older and wiser, I now know that this sort of thinking is natural and typical of rape victims.

Statistically, as many as 90% of rape survivors never report their abuse to law enforcement, and more than 30% never report their abuse to anyone. This is despite the fact that 14.8% of women and girls have been raped at one time or the other in their lives, and that 15% of sexual assault and rape victims are under the age 12. If you are the parent of a daughter, brother or sister to a female sibling, or uncle or aunt to a niece, read that again...slowly. And let it sink in.

After I was a married adult with children of my own, children that I would lay down my life for, children I would kill for, I began to unravel my childhood as they each approached the age my innocence was stolen. I began to process the clouds that pressed me down. The weights that crushed my shoulders. The weight of the secret I had never told anyone.

I knew that I would take on a thousand afflictions if it would spare my daughters from rape. I wonder if Mom ever felt the same about me. I wonder now, as an adult, what she would have done if I had told her what our adopted uncle did to me. But I never mustered courage to tell of the sordid tale, and certainly not to Mom.

CHAPTER 3

A Mother I Adore!

Mom's life story started like everyone else's. Just a little different. Fit for purpose.

It is true even in Ilesha, Nigeria, that the showers of April bring the flowers of May. So on a beautiful May day, Mama Eleyele was appointed to push two babies into the world. The first was my mom, a perfectly healthy, beautiful baby girl. On her heels was another beautiful bounty, a twin they hadn't known existed until then. She was a perfect replica of Mom. In everything, they were the same, only that Mom was alive, and this twin was dead. In those days, medical science was very rudimentary in developing countries like Nigeria, so there was nothing anyone could have done to save my aunt. Thank God for the advances of the 21st century and the millions of babies that have been saved from unnecessary death.

What had begun as a routine delivery turned out to be anything but.

The night before, Mama Eleyele had gone into labor. This wasn't her first pregnancy, and it definitely wasn't her first delivery, but this labor was different. The contractions were fast and furious and left her gasping for breath. The pain did not let up, not even after the midwife was called to minister to her.

My grandfather, Josiah, who had a weakness for his wife, grew even weaker in the knees and patrolled the hallways. He was rendered in half again and again by his wife's screams.

Early in the morning, before the sun had moved center stage into the sky, Mom slipped out of the birthing canal after a huge contraction. Unaware of another baby, the midwife cut the umbilical cord and waited for another contraction for the placenta to be delivered.

In agony, grandma pushed and pushed. The contractions rippled across her belly and arched into her back, and she kept saying that she was dying.

"This is confounding; this has never happened to me before." The midwife could be heard saying again and again. With a flat palm, she pushed against Mama's rippling belly one more time.

And then out slipped not the expected placenta, but a perfect replica of Mom; alike in every way but life. She was blue and still.

They buried her that same day and took Mom home to love on.

She was the last child of her father, and the fact that she had lost the person who was supposed to be the closest to her in life made her father love her more than his own life.

***

Baba Josiah Fadugba was my maternal grandfather. I never got to meet him. Even more unfortunately, his daughter (Mom) knew him for just a fraction of her lifetime.

Despite never meeting him, I know a lot about Josiah Fadugba and the greatness that he exhibited and taught. For the love of country and community, he was thrown into jail in the 1940s, and his freedom was later fought for and won by the Ijesha people in the historic Ilesha riot. This is documented in The University of Ife archives. Although, as Winston Churchill would say, "History is written by Victors." Luckily, Mama Eleyele, ever so proud of her husband, joyfully narrated the story to her second-generation progeny on VCR recording before she left Earth. I choose her version.

Social responsibility runs in our veins, and you will find all of my siblings ministering one way or another to others for the betterment of our communities and future generations. This brings us so much joy, both as we remember the past and project into the future.

A man of many wives, Mama Eleyele was Baba Josiah Fadugba's youngest, and he seemed to favor her greatly. Any offspring of hers immediately inherited this love. Before Mom, there were two older sisters. These older sisters had been showered with his fatherly love and cherished all their lives.

And when Mom came, one half of what should have been twins, Baba Josiah fell irrevocably in love. Mom was precocious and funny and spontaneous and beautiful, and everyone loved her, her father most of all.

Mom recounts many happy memories from her childhood, how her father often gave her the choicest pieces of meat from his plate, how she sat on his lap and felt the stubble of his chin on her neck. In her times, men were not exactly openly affectionate towards children (and girl children in particular), but her case was an exception. Baba Josiah loved passionately, and he was not afraid to wear his emotions on his sleeves.

Sadly, Mom couldn't forget her twin. By culture, she was not allowed to.

"It's Taiwo and Kehinde's birthday today." She woke up on her fifth birthday to the same kind of celebration she had woken up to four years in a row.

A huge breakfast of tender beans cooked with chili and palm oil, and a life-sized wooden carving (called *sigidi ibeji*) of her twin. She was Taiwo, her dead twin Kehinde. Kehinde was dead, had never even taken a breath, but she was very much alive and would remain so until the day that Mom met Jesus Christ.

"Eat your breakfast, Love." Mom was told. "You know you are a deity. *Ẹ̀ jìrẹ́ ará ìṣokún. ... Ọ́-bẹ́-kẹ́ ṣé-bẹ́-kàṣà, Ó fẹṣẹ̀ méjèèjì bẹ sílé alákìísà; Ó salákìísà donígba aṣọ. Gbajúmọ̀ ọmọ tíí gbàkúnlẹ̀ ìyá...*"

The Yoruba panegyric was loud and clear, and Mom knew the *oriki* front to back, and back to front by the time she was five. She danced to the hand-clap rhythm of her dad and her mom, reveling in the love they had for her, and in the love and companionship of her dead identical twin.

✳✳✳

Growing up, I noticed that Mom went into a dreamy state anytime we had chicken. Sitting at our huge dining table, meal times were often business-like. We ate neatly and quickly, and then took the dishes to the kitchen, where they were immediately washed and drained.

The only time I knew Mom to linger was over a piece of chicken. You could see the pleasure in her eyes as she ate. One day, I asked why.

She looked taken aback for a while, and then she sighed.

"Chicken ...eating it, I mean, reminds me of my father."

I loved hearing stories about Mom's childhood because they made me feel close to her, made her more accessible and open.

Sister Ronke was in the process of standing up from the dining table because she had finished her food, but she sat back down. Every one of us loved hearing about Mom's childhood. Mom's huge eyes got even bigger, and a smile came to her face and stayed put there.

"I loved chicken so much, but in those days, chicken was for festive occasions...Christmases, weddings, and the likes... But my father noticed that I had a special liking for it. And so, he bought a live chicken every Saturday, not for anyone else, but me..."

She smiled and sighed at the same time as she was transported to good times. "And so every Sunday, I had a lunch of rice and chicken. Sometimes, it was Amala or pounded yam and soup, but with huge pieces of chicken inside. Of course, I couldn't finish a whole chicken by myself, so my elder sisters also got to eat...Mama too... Each time I eat chicken now, I remember the love of a dad for his little girl. I remember Baba."

A lone tear formed at the corner of her eyes, and she whisked this away with a quick movement of her hands. In reciprocation, because I loved Mom so much and whatever hurt her hurt me, my own tears also formed. Like her, I also quickly cleaned them away.

***

She was seven when her dad died, and she experienced real heartbreak for the first time in her life. She had loved him the way she hadn't ever loved someone (except for her twin, maybe), and to have him stripped from her, never to be seen again, rendered her heart in two.

I remember the longing in her voice when she spoke of her dad, when she spoke of the happy memories they'd created in the seven years they had together.

Within a year of her dad dying, his physical place was taken by her uncle, her dad's younger brother, who married Mama Eleyele. The biblical concept of a kinsman redeemer was so visibly alive in Ijesha customs. There are rumors, till today, that my grandpa's death had not been a natural one, that he had been killed by a close family member. Invalidated rumors, but they are out there.

Baba Josiah had been gentle, graceful, feisty only for what was godly. His brother was seemingly brash and always ready to pick a fight.

Life settled into a new normalcy. Mama Eleyele had a boy who was promptly named Idowu, the name traditionally given to the child that comes after twins. Mom fell in love with her younger brother, his arrival soothing the hurt in her young heart.

I remember the fierce love I had for my own little brother, Sean, and the way I wanted to protect him from the whole world. Seeing me, Mom would smile and nod her head, "that's how I felt about Idowu when we were children."

My uncle was in my life, still is, and is a great uncle. A dad in many ways.

He was the brightest spot in Mom's life after her father died.

***

Mom was stunning. She was long and tall and lean and was a vision to behold. She had skin the color of caramel, and her white eyes shone so brightly it was like looking perpetually into a light source.

Even after five children, she remained every inch as beautiful. When I close my eyes today, and the image of Mom forms behind my eyelids, the memories that come to me are of her regality, the way she stood with her back straight, the way she walked like she owned the whole world.

Dad agrees.

They met through one of Mom's cousins and were introduced just casually. But what they felt between them, what they parlayed into a relationship, was anything but casual.

"Her smile..." Dad reminisces up till today. "She had such a brilliant smile, it was like the sun peeking from behind dark skies. And she was the perfect complement to me, helping me grow fully into the person I would become."

Couple years after they met, they were married.

Through their sojourn in the UK, and then back in Nigeria, and then back to the UK, they were the closest couple in purpose that you'd ever meet. When it came to raising godly progeny, when it came to giving all and making sacrifices for children, when it came to moving mountains, kicking down walls of resistance, or tearing down lies that stood in the way of fulfilling life's purpose, these two were an unmatchable pair. Even when Dad was away in Saudi Arabia for years and Mom was in Ibadan, they fell into each other's arms when reunited. And I remember always looking away in embarrassment at two parents who acted like they were teenagers.

***

Mom was a people lover. She loved community, and made sure the ones around her thrived.

Growing up, our house had other children who were not us, but who were not treated any different than us. They enjoyed the same love and the same discipline. They loved and feared Mom just like we did. They were children of relatives and of friends. They came from church and from workers in Dad's livestock farm. Many were children who needed help attaining a good education or good discipline, and they became part of our home. We ate at the same table, prayed at the same altar.

When she was done raising all of us, Mom proceeded to help each raise our own children. Always a busy person, a career woman through and through, yet one that never failed to drop all to play the role of a true mother in Israel.

By the time the grandchildren arrived on the scene, you'd be hard pressed to believe Mom once was the toughie. Like most grandparents, she had mellowed for the grandchildren.

She was the most doting grandmother, ministering not only to the newborn but also to the newly-minted mother time and again.

When I pushed my first daughter into the world, she was there all twenty hours and more of labor. She was midwife. She was comforter. She was support and stay. She was doctor, she was nurse. My sage ObGyn, younger by couple decades than the sage midwife in Mother, even gladly learned a thing or two. What a team they played!

Without Mom, my first daughter may not be here today.

A glorious summer day it was, the weather perfect just like I liked it. I sat at the dining table over a cup of tepid tea. I'd just finished reading a book I hadn't had time to read in forever and was filled with contentment from the inside out. I was just a few days from my estimated due date, and Mom had arrived dutifully from the UK. First-born children like to come on their own terms, she'd said. Don't all children make the terms of their parenting?! Because Mom was a medical expert who knew her stuff, and to whom the best of doctors bowed in midwifery, I had but nothing to worry about.

But like the excited new mom I was, I was filled with a low-throbbing need to see this child I had carried within me for nine months, to hold her in my arms, to become a mother in the fullest sense of the word.

Mom was reclined on the sofa, half asleep, her Bible on her lap as always, and a devotional book with it, about to tumble to the floor (I inherited both Dad and Mom's love for books). Smiling to myself, I stood slowly to my feet, intending to right the book.

The light sleeper she was, as I neared her, she came awake. She blinked, adjusted her glasses and sat up slowly. In an instant, her eyes turned from placid to a dark shade of worry.

"What's that on your wrapper?"

For the sake of convenience, I often tied a wrapper loosely around my waist when I was home. It made the huge weight of the pregnancy a little easier to carry. I looked down and turned back to see the back of the wrapper now. There was a brownish-grayish semi-thick liquid on it. I shrugged with non-knowing.

With a deft finger, she plucked a little bit of the material off my wrapper and held it to her nose.

"Meconium." She said in a whisper. "We need to get you to the hospital. Now!"

I shook my head. I didn't want to go to the hospital. I didn't even want to as much as call the kind Dr. Jennifer again. A number of times in the previous weeks, I had called, thinking I was in labor only to be affirmatively told that what I was experiencing was Braxton Hicks and that I would know when it was the real labor. The doctors and nurses were nice enough, but I didn't want to gain the "troublesome, attention-seeking woman" label.

"The baby is coming, Folakemi. Go get dressed and let's go or call your doctor now."

Reluctantly, I went to make the call, but it was without enthusiasm, and I told Dr. Jennifer that much. The true Texan she was, yet sage with cultures, Dr. Jennifer told me to hearken to Mom, and just stop by the hospital. She assured me that I could return home once a labor & delivery nurse tested the stain and found it negative for meconium.

Mom, who was a left-side driving UK citizen, took on the big American city road, courageously driving on the right side. Later, she would talk of speaking in tongues and prayers behind the wheel to keep faith.

We arrived at the hospital not a minute too soon because although I was barely two centimeters dilated when the nurse checked, it was meconium through and through, and the nurse said we had all of 24 hours maximum to delivery time either by nature or assisted. And it was like the labor pains had waited for me to set foot on the threshold of the hospital before beginning.

When the pain started, it wouldn't stop. Yet, the pain didn't seem to be progressing to delivery. After more than twenty hours, I had only dilated three centimeters. Playing the champion mother, I took the pain with grit and grace; determined not to succumb to relief by an epidural injection. Hebrew women didn't take that in the days of Moses.

The ever so wise godly Dr. Jennifer suggested an epidural did not take away from my womanhood. In fact, even a caesarian section didn't. But she warned that the latter would become the only available option in an hour or two, if progress remained delayed.

Speaking to my analyst heart, she added, "I did see an article in the Ob journal recently where some women contract so tight, they cannot release except their body gains relief from feeling the contractions." She said this was true for barely 0.02% of birthers but proceeded to say, "You and I wouldn't be surprised if that is you." Uniquely purposed by God in every way.

I trusted Dr. Jennifer enough to agree. I took the epidural and 45-minutes later, felt the urge for a bowel movement.

My overseeing nurse thought that was unusual. She said, "if you told me this in a few hours' time, I might actually think the baby is here. But it's been only an hour since I checked you last at 3cm. Let's check anyways before I help you to the bathroom."

A moment later, she gasped at seeing the baby's head, paged Dr. Jennifer (who in the shower after a long day, wondered which patient it could be, and was blessedly happily surprised to learn who).

My child, the one who turned me into a mother, came into the world close to thirty hours after Mom had first noticed the meconium on my wrapper. Joy was wrapped in both her own feces and cord. What a miracle birth is!

Mom had saved the day, in many ways.

When she was not raising the grandchildren, she was helping others raise theirs. Mom passed on to glory in 2018; the tributes were overwhelming and continue to be a source of comfort for all. They were raw and pain-filled. And with each read, I realize anew that Mom had not been just Mom to her biological children and grandchildren. She was a mom to hundreds of others.

Neighbors turned daughters. Church members turned family. You were not a cousin or a nephew or a niece or an in-law. You were a child. And you knew you were loved.

***

"No child should ever have to do without." Of all of Mom's mantras, that was the one that stuck the most with me, because she lived her convictions. Mom was a diehard giver.

"It's just money." She often told Dad, who was a little bit more frugal.

"I don't see how that is necessary." Dad would grumble, but then he'd shrug and let Mom have her way. Of the two, he was the quieter one, the one who didn't like confrontations and conflicts. And when Mom was convinced about something, Dad got influenced over.

Food, clothing, school fees, shoes, everything and anything; Mom gave it all. And she gave it with grace and love.

The benevolence and generosity that my siblings and I display towards others today was learnt at our mother's feet. This is just one of the many beautiful qualities I have my mom to thank for.

***

It does matter how a child comes into the world, how that child begins life. However, it matters more what happens at the end of that child's life and what he or she does with the life and circumstances he or she was given.

Mom's story may not have started out as the cleanest, straightforward story, but my mom lived well and had a fantastic life. When I think about Mom's life and mine, I often remember Psalm 139: 14: *"I praise you because I am fearfully and wonderfully made; your works are wonderful, I know that full well."* We are special to God, and when we give Him center stage, it all makes sense in the end.

She was an ardent follower of Christ, a faithful soldier, strong in faith, prayerful and passionate about soul-winning. It seemed that any darkness from her childhood had been bleached out of her and that she was infused with the comforting light of Christ. Just as the blood of Jesus promises to do.

As a young girl, I was terrified of her. As she grew older, I saw the soft and welcoming and radiant side of her. Mom's smile, which I'd had peeks of as a child, seemed to come out in its full glory. In fact, her giant smile could light up and fill up any room. Her heart was genuine and caring and compassionate.

Even in the face of challenges, health and otherwise, her smile never faded. Her faith never wavered. She had a faith worthy of emulation, remaining strong in faith despite adversity and always trusting the Lord Jesus Christ for victory in every situation.

For Mom, prayer was often warfare. She would grasp each prayer request with extreme zeal and enthusiasm. She would not let go, would dig in with her heels until the answer came. Beyond prayer, she was also a compassionate evangelist. One of the tributes at her funeral spoke of how she was on the streets of Manchester, England, still evangelizing, even with mobility restrictions.

The Sunday before she would pass on to glory, she was in church.

Her life had finally come full circle.

CHAPTER 4

Broken For Beautification

He was vibrant and on fire for the Lord. He was unashamed of his faith, and when he spoke of Jesus, he always knew the Bible passages to use. No wonder his nickname was "Oga Bible," translated "Master of the Bible."

I felt God imprinting on my heart that he would be my husband someday. He appealed to my fifteen-year-old self, that self that had attempted to capture the fractured parts of herself and put them all back together.

Chronologically, I was no longer fifteen. I was 23 years old, and was in my final year at the university, coming into my own and peering out at the world through the eyes of a woman, no longer the eyes of a child.

Yet, Akin struck a chord with my fifteen-year-old self.

We all have pivotal years that our minds cast back to now and then, that year that we start to become. Mine was fifteen. That was the year my body started to bloom. That was also the year that I sought God like I hadn't done before. It was the year of many changes.

I still held the secret of my rape to my chest, a secret that tormented and burned me but that I couldn't bring myself to share with anyone.

For reasons I didn't understand at that time, but that I get now, my body didn't flower the way those of my age mates did. Most girls typically start filling out their sports bras from the time they turn ten (or even earlier), but not me. My body just plain refused to budge. Even through the two years that I was continually raped, I was flat-chested.

I was not only flat-chested, but was also on the short and skinny side, such that I was always first or second in line when we lined up according to our heights on the school assembly ground.

It would take me years to understand, to have it fully sink in, that rapists are rapists not because of how we look or what we do or how we act or how developed our bodies are. They are rapists because they are simply evil. It definitely wasn't my burgeoning body that had drawn the evil that was visited on me for two years, because there was none to speak of at that point.

So ages ten through fifteen, I was skinny and short and would have passed for a little boy were it not for my long hair. It was my one testament to being a girl. But what I lacked in height and womanly parts, I seemed to make up in brains.

Like Mom and Dad, and like the older children before me, I had a knack for mathematics and logic. I loved to sit and ponder, levels of intellectual curiosity well beyond my years. My mind always yearned for new knowledge, and because we lived in a home filled with books, I devoured them like food. And I loved it all; I loved the sound of big words when

I spoke. I loved to figure things out myself. I loved that eureka moment when the puzzles fit together and everything just clicked.

At school, I was easily one of the best, even though I never put my mind to studying as much as others did.

I was almost fifteen years old, and in the fifth form in secondary school.

Two years before then, the Nigerian government had passed a new law for secondary schools that was currently being tested out in select colleges. Before the new law, secondary school education was accomplished in five straight years. The new law broke secondary schooling into two three-year parts, which meant students had to spend six years in school instead of the previous five. Federal government colleges were the renowned institutions of secondary education and became the guinea pigs. They were the first to hop on board, and every single one of my siblings attended federal schools, thought to be better than their state-run or privately-run counterparts.

My older sister was in the very first set of students to experience the new system, and it was to be my turn two years later. But Mom had other plans.

"That will not be happening, Folakemi," she said. "Perhaps I will see it down the line, but at the moment, I don't get it. Ronke did the sixth year as required, but did it make her any better educationally or improve her prospects for university?" She shook her head. It was actually a rhetorical question, and I didn't have an answer either, but I knew Mom had my back. She would extinguish fire off the wildest forest if it was meant to rescue her children. She said so much to the effect herself.

We were seated in the pharmacy shop Mom ran with Dad. I had started helping out in the shop during the holidays when I turned fourteen, and by the time I turned sixteen, I would be responsible for managing the sales attendants and pharmaceutical contracts. That particular afternoon, it was Mom and I in the shop.

I stepped away from attending to a customer and faced Mom. I agreed with her. I knew that I was blessed with the gift of a keen mind, and it didn't make sense to waste another year in school. Sister Ronke had told us that the added year was pretty much to summarize all the things learned in the previous two years. I could summarize by myself. I could do reviews on my own. Why waste a child's full year of life on that?

"You are right, Mom. Why waste such precious time?"

And so we came up with a plan. Dad was away in Saudi Arabia; this was a mom and daughter thing, one of the then few but exhilarating moments where we drew together in total agreement.

***

I went to school with a doctor's note. I had been quite the sickly little child anyways, but I had grown out of most of these illnesses and was mostly fine and rarely malaised with breathing episodes any longer.

But we were going to resurrect something to get me excused from school while I prepared for GCSE exams, which were an alternative route to the university. You didn't have to show evidence that you'd completed six years of secondary school before you could sit for the exam, so the plan was for me to write GCSE and go straight to the university if I passed. That way, I would skip the now mandatory sixth year form where my school was one of the select pilot testers.

I needed time to study, and going to school every day to prepare for another year of school that I didn't plan to be a part of didn't make any sense to Mom and me.

So we resurrected asthma. As a child, I'd spent many a time gasping for breath and only getting respite from a rescue inhaler. This was a well-known nuisance sometimes on assembly lines during school-wide student meetings. It had been documented in previous school records and the school knew what to do in case I had a severe attack. I, however, had not had an asthmatic attack in a while.

But we had a plan. I would stay home and return to school after the exams, armed with a doctor's report that the asthma had returned and kept me back. I don't regret the move that would later get me into the university on time, but I do regret that we lied to do so.

I have since taken hold of the word of God as an adult and appropriated my healing. I have overcome bad health by His grace in many, many areas. Asthma, though, is a sore point on which I still have to consciously enforce my understanding of the scriptures. Never give the enemy a yard. He will take an acre.

The Bible says that all things work together for good to them that are called according to His purpose. I believe God has a reason for my creation, a why for my presence here on Earth. In His infinite wisdom, He knew I needed that year at home to confront the devils of my past and to forge me into the woman I would later become.

I truly, really needed that year at home.

My fifteen-year-old self, while blooming physically, also had to bloom emotionally and come to grips with the rape I'd suffered as an eleven-year-old.

***

My torment at the hands of the rapist was because I was home alone, lost without my sister and brothers, who at the point were away in boarding schools. A year after the rape stopped, I went back to the boarding house and only went home for holidays, just like my siblings.

My pending GCSE exams were why I would be home all by myself again.

The rapist was long gone, but he seemed to be everywhere I turned. When I crossed the courtyard that had scared me so terribly as a child and that he had taken me by the hands to cross, I smelt the scent of him. I heard the thud of his footfalls. When I went into my room, I saw him superimposed upon everything.

Until that point in my life, I had been a scared little girl. I had been afraid of shadows (mine and everyone else's). I had been afraid of strange noises, of dark places, of sudden movements.

As I again confronted the smells and images of the rapist, I slowly began to lose my fear as it morphed into a wave of slow, burning anger. No longer was I the timid Folakemi who cowered at threats. My fifteen-year-old became an angry person.

I was mad at the rapist. I was angry at the life circumstances that had made me good fodder for a rapist. I was mad at Mom for not intuiting that something had gone wrong and for not coming to my rescue. I was mad at Dad and Sister

Ronke for being gone, for not saving me. I was mad at all men.

And I was mad at me.

"How could I have allowed this to happen? How did I allow myself to become a statistic?" My fifteen-year-old would stand in front of the mirror, beating myself up along with every other person who had let down the younger me. But I was yet too passive to show the world my anger.

I was angry, but I was privately so. Like the secret of the rape, the secret of this blossoming anger was something I would bear all by myself, a secret I would harbor within myself for years, except the times it exploded by itself.

The one person I could not be mad at was God. Somehow, our teachings from Bible study and my personal study sessions let me know that He wasn't responsible for the rape, that He hadn't vacationed while it was happening. I knew God was God and that He was good. I wasn't mad at Him, but fear billowed over my heart anytime I thought about Him. Or was I mad at Him and too scared of His omnipotence to admit it? Time would later tell.

"You like it as much as I do, Folakemi. Admit it." The abuser had told me again and again and again, and I had somehow come to believe that the rape was not just his fault, but mine as well. I had allowed it. I had somehow brought the evil upon myself.

And so, I was scared that God hated me. I feared this Holy God who was spotless and blameless. I feared that He would strike me down at some point in my life for having allowed the rape. My entire life at that point became one of pleasing Him. Perhaps He'd be less angry and wouldn't strike me with leprosy or something worse if I pleased Him just a little bit more.

It would be years down the line that I would encounter the Father heart of God. As a fifteen-year-old, I loved Him, mostly out of fear, and wanted to please Him. But love driven by fear cannot be true love. It would be much later that I would meet God as a father. But for years, I worshipped Him out of fear.

***

My life in the fifteenth year soon settled into a routine. Prep lessons for my upcoming exams. Quiet evenings at home or behind the counter at the pharmacy shop, my head stuck in a book. Nights dressing down and getting into bed, the sleep not coming.

And then I'd get on my knees and pray. I prayed for hours on end. I prayed for Dad and Mom. I prayed for my siblings. I prayed for the people around me that I knew needed God's hand in one area of their lives or another. And I prayed for myself, for my soul.

I cried bitter tears because I didn't want to go to hell. I wept hot tears because I felt that my soul was damned. My virginity, which was supposed to be exclusively mine until I gave it as a gift to my husband on our wedding night, had been taken, and I had allowed it to be taken.

It didn't matter that I asked God for forgiveness every day. The next night, I'd be on my knees crying for forgiveness again. The truth was that I felt dirty. Yes, I was a child of God, but I couldn't ever feel clean enough.

My fifteen-year-old wanted to be holy, wanted to be chaste, wanted to be pure. I wanted to please God with and in everything, but I somehow knew, just knew that He couldn't be pleased with me. That He wasn't entirely happy with me. As I said, I hadn't yet met the Father heart of my Savior.

It was my fifteen-year-old self whose spirit would connect with Akin's several years later. My soul inside of me saw a man who was as close to God as I had ever seen, a man who seemed to live and breathe for God, a man who wouldn't violate me as the rapist had done, a man who loved this God that I so wanted to love desperately too.

Akin also had the poverty to go with it, seen often in Christian circles as godliness. It was this fractured fifteen-year-old self whose soul immediately knit with Akin's.

***

It was also in that fifteenth year that God started to prepare me for motherhood, arming me with the godly skills that I would so desperately need in the future when I became a single mother.

Mommy Faje was such a blessing in my life, and she exemplified what motherhood was all about. She was the kind of mother I wished I had and the kind of mom I wanted to grow up to be.

I believe she was placed in my life for a purpose, to show me how things were supposed to be between a mother and the children she loved, to plant in me the seeds that would later soften my heart so that God's fatherly love would bloom therein down the lane.

Mummy Faje's first daughter, Buki, and I were peers at FGGC Oyo. Classmates and fast friends, we also had a relationship outside of school. As we both began for various exams, we took preparatory lessons at Pious, one of the most acclaimed prep centers in Ibadan at that time.

The parents rotated drop-offs and pick-ups. This meant that if my mom or dad took us going, the Fajes would bring us back. And if the Fajes took us going, my mom or dad got us back home in the evenings. This was sensible since Mr. Faje also worked at the polytechnic, and his family lived in the staff quarters like we did.

In the Fajes' car, in the utter chaos of children talking and laughing and being children, I always felt at peace when the matriarch was at the wheel, like this was how a family was supposed to be, like this was home, like I could tell Mommy Faje anything and would be disciplined but would not be castigated or ostracized.

No conversation was off-limits between Buki and her mom. This was a woman with six children, and I could see that each one of them was special to her. Each had a special place in her heart, and she would drop everything just to listen.

In that car, some conversations were light-hearted and funny. Some conversations brought tears and then comfort. I knew without a doubt that Buki wouldn't, couldn't keep it a secret from her mom if she had been raped as I had been. The door to conversations with her mom was always open, and I saw her go through this door, again and again, harboring no secrets, baring her soul before her mom every single time.

In bed at night, hugging my pillow for comfort, I sometimes wished I had been born into the Faje family. I have told my children repeatedly now that I learned how to parent from Mommy Faje, from watching how she made it all about the child, from seeing how the whole world fell away as she graced her child with her attention and love.

Mommy Faje was firm and scolded her children when necessary. But she was also quick to forgive, and her arms were always opened wide for embraces.

She asked all the questions in the world. Silly questions, deep questions. There was no depth or breadth that she would not plumb to find out how her children fared. She asked them (and I) all kinds of questions about school and life and love and hurts, and it didn't ever feel strange or awkward filling her in on our days.

I had to catch myself again and again from telling her about the rape that had been inflicted upon me. I came very close, but I never told.

***

My fifteenth year was a year of discoveries.

I learned how to study and propel myself into my future.

I learned how to pray for myself and others, seeking the face of God for the first time in my life.

Unbeknownst to me, the fifteenth year was the year I resolved no human being would ever again take advantage of me. It was the year the fighter in me was born. It was the year I wished for life that I had fought the rapist to save my younger years of the past.

It was the year that elicited the fierce motherly love I had seen modeled as the way I would later parent.

My fifteenth year was also the year I promised God that I would marry a godly man if I ever got married.

CHAPTER 5

A Passage Of Necessity

Akin was the Bible study secretary of the Christian Union Fellowship to which I belonged. We had been in the group together since he joined the university, and I was in year two. However, we had no connection in the large group of students. I laid low.

Yes, I was only a member of the fellowship, but I absolutely loved it there. I was utterly dedicated to the things of the spirit and wanted to just soak in everything that had to do with Jesus. Somewhat a rebel at heart but lacking the courage to express some of my dearly held truth. For that, I admired my dear friend, Sade, a true rebel for Christ. The fellowship instituted such "holiness" rules as head coverings and would offer you a scarf if you were a female that approached the entrance without head covering. Many a-times, I would return to my dormitory to get my own scarf, in fear of head lice and in fear of being labelled a rebel. Many such times, I was already late from class. For the fear of man, I chose to return to the room and be that much later for fellowship with God whom I valued.

More than once, Sade, in the same predicament, went to the fellowship sans head covering, and rejected the offered scarf at entrance. She repeatedly stated, "Folakemi, no one died for me. Only Jesus did. The fellowship people didn't die for me. The fellowship exco (executive body) is not who died for me. Jesus is the one who died for me. He is the only one that gets to set my rules for living in love with Him." What maturity!

Akin was in year three when we met through a village evangelism event, and I was in year four. I had spent the last three years in school pouring myself out for the Lord, so the fellowship was like a second home to me.

Poverty was written all over Akin, and he had only one dress shirt and one pair of dress pants that I and others could tell of. The shirt and suit were routinely carefully laundered and ironed, and he seemed to wear them with pride. Not the pride of the flesh, but like he was proud of who he was and was pretty well settled in his identity.

He often joked of breaking long fasts with *gari* (a powdery substance made from cassava) and prophesying protein into the pure carbohydrate gari because there simply was no way to eat a balanced meal. He was that poor.

I sensed that God was speaking to me to marry him, and looking back now, I cannot differentiate if it was really God that spoke, or whether the fifteen-year-old in me found herself a worthy cause. Perhaps this young girl just wanted to lift this brother out of poverty and into a better life.

Regardless, God is all-powerful and intentionally purposeful. Even if in error, all of it was used for divine plan and purpose and Jeremiah 29:11 in The Message Translation is 100% truth. I am too precious to God for Him to have watched me go wrong while in sincerity seeking to please Him. Same is true for a reader of this memoir.

Your mistakes, however, how assuredly in error you were, are not sufficient enough to remove you from the ardent, fiery reckless love God has over you. There's no shadow He won't light up, no Mountain He won't climb up to come after you. There's no wall He won't kick down, no lie He won't tear down, coming after YOU.

I do not for one day regret marrying Akin. There was a reason, and although we know and understand only in part on this side of heaven, now I know a part of that purpose and will know more in heaven.

***

I was shy, and even though I had grown less wary of people, I was not one to go about sharing my deepest feelings with others. So, I thought a lot about Akin but kept my fondness of him a secret from my year four (and his year three) all the way to my year five (his year four).

When he spoke of Jesus, I was riveted. When he sang, I heard his voice above every other person's. That unique timbre of voice that was his and his alone.

After one year of waiting for him to come to me, to start to see me in the same light that I saw him, I was finally frustrated enough to speak with Brother Jide, the president of the fellowship from the previous year and a dear, dear brother to me.

"I feel like God is imprinting on my heart to marry this man," I told him directly. In front of my mirror that morning, I had practiced and practiced and re-practiced how I was going to tell Jide about what was in my heart.

I was naturally an introspective person, and I didn't like sharing feelings. And I had no romantic past to speak about whatsoever, so I didn't know how one approached these things, how one was supposed to.

But I didn't want to wait and waste. I had to know that I wasn't growing crazy, and I also needed to find out if there was another woman in his life. Part of me would have been happy to hear that, because I would have been saved from marrying a poor man for Jesus. But whatever the answer would be, I didn't want to keep waiting with bated hopes for something that may never be. I was on the heels of departure from Nigeria to pursue better things.

Brother Jide had an amazing smile that warmed your heart. Such a fatherly brotherly figure, all in one. He knew the Jesus He believed in to the very end. The day he passed away in a car accident was very bittersweet. It was the same day my toddler gave her life to Jesus Christ, so his memory lingers forever.

When he smiled at me that afternoon, his chin dimpled. He sighed a little sigh and then smiled again.

"God is a spectacular God, a God of intentions. We must never forget that, Sister Folakemi," He said.

I waited for him to unravel the meaning of what he'd just said, and thankfully, I didn't have to wait for so long.

He continued, "What if I told you that this same man, this same Brother Akin came to see me last month..." He allowed his words to trail off, and I wanted to fall off my chair in anticipation.

"Well, he came to see me..." A wayward bee had flown into the office where we sat, and this distracted Jide for longer than necessary.

I wanted the bee gone, and the conversation continued. I was usually a very patient person and often waited for news to come meet me where I was, but I was anxious this evening, couldn't help it. The bee finally settled on a windowpane and quieted.

Jide went on. "As I was saying, he came to see me, and he told me...'I kind of like Sister Folakemi. In fact, I feel God impressing on my heart that she is my future helpmate, my wife and the mother of my future children.'"

My heart fell all the way to my feet and stayed put there, beating, it seemed, against the soles of my shoes. Exhilaration tore through me, but you wouldn't know it to look at me, because I maintained the same inscrutable straight-faced demeanor people had long come to associate me with, unbeknownst to me.

"One thing though." He added, raising his hand. My throat went dry. "He doesn't know how to come to you, how to broach the subject."

I wanted to ask why, but at the same time, I couldn't bring myself to.

"Well, he did tell me that he is scared of what you'd say, how you'd respond. I recall him saying something like...how could he measure up to you, seeing that you are one of the richest girls in the fellowship...and him about the poorest."

I shifted in my seat, wiping the sudden sweat that had beaded all over my face.

Jide went on. "And to be perfectly honest, I see his point. You drive a sleek car, the likes of which some of our lecturers cannot even afford. And you are easily the best-dressed female in the fellowship. He is intimidated by your wealth."

My mouth sprang wide open. I knew my family was a little better off than the average family, but I had never really considered myself rich-rich. The Mercedes Benz was not mine, but Dad's. It had originally belonged to my parents, but Dad was away, working in Saudi Arabia, and Mom had relocated to the US with my younger brother. My older ones had also all returned to the UK to live their lives. I was the only Ajayi living in the country and had full access to my parents' belongings, hence the car.

I did not know a car was going to be a problem.

To think that I had somehow measured myself against Akin and found myself wanting because he was "up there" spiritually, brought me pause. He was the kind of Christian I wanted to be, and I'd felt that perhaps he'd looked at me and concluded that I was not spiritual enough for him.

Just goes to show that we humans often forget that we are loved by God as we are, chosen by Him, and perfect in His sight. And so, we go measuring ourselves against others, always falling short by a contrived measurement all our own.

I didn't know what to say to Jide, so I chose the next best thing: silence.

He allowed the silence to ricochet around the room, like he wanted me to think about what he'd said. In the periphery of my vision, I saw the bee lift off again. I heard the buzz buzz of its wings, the slow creak of the slow fan...and my heart, thundering away.

Jide sighed. "Do you want me to introduce..." He shook his head at his choice of words. "Don't mean introduce. I mean, do you want me to bring you together? He's said he likes you and senses God spoke to Him, and you've also told me you sensed God spoke to you, so..." He shrugged.

I was horrified and shook my head no. "No, no..."

He squinted at me. "So, what do you want me to do?"

"Nothing." I got the word past my throat somehow. I didn't want him to do anything because I didn't want any human pollution of what it seemed God should do. If God really wanted us to be together, Akin would find his way to me somehow. And I didn't want to seem desperate.

***

I held the phone fast to my ear, the rope wound tightly around my fists. My heart would slow down, then it would jackhammer back to life.

"Hi, Folakemi." His voice still had the same timbre, still sounding like honey being poured over ice cream. It was warm and low and all the right things.

One year had not dimmed my feelings for him, and to have gone our separate ways after graduation and now be contacted by him brought shivers and tremors into my body.

We had graduated the previous year, and up till the time that we did, we had remained nothing beyond acquaintances. We said the obligatory hi and hello when we walked into each other, when we had projects to work on together in the fellowship. But it was never more than that.

I walked around with the knowledge that I felt something for him, and that he felt something for me. I walked around with the mild anxiety that the bridge between us couldn't be bridged.

When he called me for the first time, I knew things had come full circle, that the time which hadn't been right before was now right. I was the last one of my family in the country and was actually preparing to go back to the UK. In the meantime, I lived with Pastor Oludiran and his family. He was my childhood pastor but was in every way like a dad.

Akin called me on Pastor Oludiran's home phone.

"Hi, Akin." My voice was high and girly, and I had to tell myself to tone it down.

And so the phone calls began. He called very often, and I would smilingly wonder if he was trying to cram the past year into the new, trying to make up for lost time.

"I want to marry you." He finally said one warm evening. This was not a phone call but something that felt like a date. He was in town, had come over to say hi to me and Pastor Oludiran's family, and had asked me if I wanted to take a stroll with him.

We meandered through the bustling streets and somehow ended up in a saner, quieter portion of the city. We sat on a bench, watching the evening breeze strip some trees of their less hardy leaves.

"I can't see my life without you, Folakemi. I can no longer see my future without you."

I had gotten the inkling in my spirit more than a year ago that I would marry this man, but now that he had finally come out to say it, I felt the reluctance take over me. Why had he waited for so long? Why had he allowed so long to pass before ever mentioning of his love for me? My circumstances hadn't changed; I still had more means than he did. So, what had changed for him? If anything had changed for me, it was a relief that I obeyed God, or had at least tried to do so. And now I could be free to perhaps marry a British or American born citizen when I moved away, and that without the judgement of God.

I swept my gaze over the gently swirling leaves. I didn't know what to answer. He had decided not to do anything for so long. Did I want such an indecisive person to journey with through life?

And so, I didn't respond. I took the answer I would have given and pushed it deep down into my belly.

"Say something, please." He had dark eyes that were as piercing as mine, but I wouldn't look into them.

***

For months, Akin kept asking me to be his wife. And I kept saying no.

"Why wasn't it a priority one or two years ago, and now it is?" I asked him one day.

He shook his head, "You are right. But marriage was way back, all the way at the back page in my life for a long time. But now, it's on the title page. It is the title page. The Holy Spirit is impressing upon my heart the need to marry...and not just anyone, but you. Marry you, and that's what I want to do."

Each time Akin spoke as he did now, my heart thrilled. But I still didn't say yes.

Life settled into somewhat of a routine, even though I waited with bated breath for several things to happen. I was preparing to move to the US. I was also waiting to say yes to

Akin. I knew I was going to say yes, at this point, mostly out of godly fear.

I asked Akin questions. I wanted to know all about his childhood, what had forged him into the man he now was. I wanted to know about his present and his hopes for the future. I wanted to know all about him.

***

I had gone to family in the UK, needed to renew my passport, and had returned to Nigeria. And now I was preparing to relocate to the US.

On the day I would leave the country for the US, I went to the airport to check in my luggage early in the morning to have time to spend the last evening uninterrupted with my friends. My very good friend and courageous daughter of Jesus, Sade, and her parents lived at the Ikeja Barracks, close to the international airport. That was the spot we picked to gather.

Somehow, Akin ended up as part of our group.

We had take-out dinner, played a game of Scrabble, and talked long and hard as the day waned.

I was in quite an emotional frame of mind. I was going to miss my friends. I was going to miss this country. I was going to miss a lot of things, including Akin. And it dawned on me for the first time that I didn't want to miss him, that I didn't want to lose him.

He seemed to read my mood correctly because he slipped his hand into mine, something he had never done before. My palm was hot and dry, his cool and slightly moist. As we made this first-ever physical contact with each other, my shakiness quieted.

"Can we talk, in private?" He finally asked.

And so we found a little corner where we could be alone. Our friends were a stone's throw away but we were, in essence, in a world of our own.

We talked at length; we spoke about the important things in life – how many children we wanted, how we were going to achieve our dreams, how we would grow old serving the Lord. And we spoke about the stupid things – how I hated the sound of chirping crickets, how he could cross his fingers in an insanely shocking way.

We spoke for hours.

And then, same as he'd now done many times in the past, he asked me again, "Will you marry me, Folakemi?"

And with shimmering tears in my eyes, less than twenty-four hours to the time I was to start a new life in a new country, I said yes.

CHAPTER 6

O'er The Land Of The Free And At The Home Of The Brave

A special song arouses stinging eyes whenever I hear it played, with a tear drop or two:

This land is your land, and this land is my land

From California to the New York island

From the redwood forest to the Gulf Stream waters

This land was made for you and me

As I went walking that ribbon of highway

I saw above me that endless skyway

Saw below me that golden valley

This land was made for you and me

I roamed and rambled and I've followed my footsteps

To the sparkling sands of her diamond deserts

All around me a voice was sounding

This land was made for you and me

When the sun come shining, then I was strolling

And the wheat fields waving and the dust clouds rolling

The voice was chanting as the fog was lifting

This land was made for you and me

This land is your land and this land is my land

From California to the New York island

From the redwood forest to the Gulf Stream waters

This land was made for you and me

When the sun come shining, then I was strolling

And the wheat fields waving and the dust clouds rolling

The voice come a-chanting and the fog was lifting

This land was made for you and me

***

I stepped out of the plane into a white, white world. It was mid-January, and winter was in full swing.

The cold sting of nature's razor-sharp air sliced away at my face as I exited the door from the confines of the warm plane. Yet, there was warmth in my heart, a billowing joy that I was here, in the land of the free, that I was about to take on yet another chapter of life.

Life lay before me, filled with hope and a swollen expectation of good things to come. Three days ago, I was back in Nigeria, looking forward to the soon-coming migration for my studies in the US. At that time, I had been single and unattached. And here I was, just three days later; not just following my dreams for graduate studies, but also embracing the new phase of life with open arms and a heart filled with overflowing love for the fiancé I had just gained.

The snow was thick but soft, and my boots went through the slush, causing me to walk a little unsteadily. I had been out of my native country several times before this time, most of the time to the UK, but because I almost always went on holidays and merrymaking, I always arrived in a new country to blue skies and a warm sun.

To arrive in a cold-swept land was a new experience.

It was a relief to locate the family members who had come to pick me up, and as we waited for my luggage to come rolling in on the conveyor belt, all felt right with the world. There was a calmness in my heart, and I knew that this was where I was supposed to be, that God had orchestrated everything for my good.

It was late in the evening that I had my first look at New York. The buildings were dizzyingly tall, covered in a patina of snow, yet shimmering with all kinds of light. The city felt big, like a vast unexplored land, and yet it felt small like it was holding out its warm hands to me.

This was a whole new adventure to me, and as I curled up to bed that night in a strange bed, my belly full of warm soup, I was transported, flung back into the past.

My life, I realized, just like it is for every yielded child of God, was not left to chance and the fates. Even when I didn't know He was, God was always in control. He truly was the master orchestrator for good, even when things hurt and chaffed and stung. There was and is absolutely nothing that has ever happened to me, good or bad, that God has not redeemed and used for His glory.

As a child, I was exceptionally bright and had carried the torch of this brightness with me into adulthood. Everyone in my immediate family was intellectually gifted. Dad was a pharmacist and Mom a nurse, and every child found a calling in the medical line. But not me. I just didn't have the nerves for biology and all those slimy, wet, bloody factors that made up a human body. I liked some abstract, and I loved objective provable logical facts. Anything mathematical or analytical stole my fancy. I had wanted to study accounting for a first degree, but it didn't sit right for some reason. My dad also did not want me to go that route, and neither did my uncle. With the wisdom of the clan, engineering became THE better choice for me.

I had an almost photographic memory that froze-framed facts, formulas, and diagrams, and lodged them where they would never be forgotten. I went for the most "mathy" of the engineering disciplines, the one closest to math and logical reasoning: electrical engineering. I had graduated with a first-class, a rare feat considering that I had never had a need to study near as much as my counterparts did. God could seem positively unfair sometimes!

A year before graduation, I got an internship at Mobil (ExxonMobil) in Lagos, Nigeria, and it was this internship that would lead me all the way to that snowy January day in the US.

God places people in our lives for a purpose, and one of the greatest disservices we can do to ourselves is not to recognize the helpers of destiny placed in our paths or to underestimate the impact of relationships. I cannot remember what Mr. Otori looks like now. He had made such a brief appearance in the story of my life, but he had had an overwhelming amount of clout.

That summer internship, Mr. Otori was a Mobil engineer. He was an unassuming strong presence. Quiet but full of life. And a wealthy expatriate to Nigeria, howbeit a Nigerian. One afternoon, as I placed a file requiring his attention on his table, he smiled up at me and slipped me a $100 bill. "You're a very bright girl. I want you to study in the US someday. When you land, use this money to buy yourself a meal or whatever."

It was a random sentence, and it was very much unexpected. But then Otori often did unexpected and shocking things.

It was the first US bill I ever held in my hands that was completely mine. I rode in excitement all the way home and showed the money to my paternal cousin Rotimi whose house I lived in at that time.

Perhaps that statement from Mr. Otori had been a sign from God that I hadn't picked up as soon as I should have. I don't know. But God has a way of beating us over the head with a double whammy when He wants us to listen.

During the same internship, I got a little close to one of the other supervisors. His name was Chukwu, and he was boisterous and gregarious. He had a hoarse laughter that you would hear even long before you stepped into his cubicle of an office. And he had this massive gold ring that he was almost always fingering.

One afternoon, I pushed myself to ask him a question that had swirled around in my mind for a while. "Where's that from?"

His face lit up, and I knew this was an important subject for him. I wasn't wrong. "It's my class ring from UTA. It's massive, isn't it?" He asked, with not a small amount of pride.

I nodded, agreeing to its enormity, but I had other questions. "Where is UTA?"

He cocked his head and looked at me with a sideways glance like everyone should know what UTA was. After a while, he responded. "The University of Texas, Arlington. The best school in the world." He had graduated from UTA, was very proud of his Alma mater, and couldn't hold himself back as he spoke of the school. He spoke of the lush, green fields of the school. He spoke of something called the maverick experience and then some unforgettable wild tales about his dorm room.

"You should go there someday." He concluded.

That day, I sensed in my soul that I was one day going to attend the University of Texas at Arlington, and this dream would come true two years later. It felt surreal, like this was my life but at the same time, not exactly my life. Like I was an actor and at the same time, a viewer of what was unfolding.

***

The journey to the US had not been smooth and easy sailing, filled instead with bumps and turns and disappointments. And on the other side of the frustration, appointment and joy.

Four years before I would arrive in the US, before the Mobil internship, my dad had won the Green Card Lottery. He was away working in Saudi when this happened, and I recall that he had played the Green Card Lottery specifically because of me and my younger brother, Sean. Of all five children, we were the only two without dual citizenships.

Holidays to the UK, of which our elder siblings were citizens, were not always a hassle, but there were times they were. Because the older children were citizens, they didn't need visas, could go and come as they pleased. Not the same case for Sean and me. We had to renew our visas when they expired, and there was no guarantee for those renewals.

The Green Card Lottery, if won, was supposed to even things out, put us on the journey to be at par with our siblings, and the idea was for me to use that platform to study for my masters, which was all a good and fine idea on paper. Things would turn out differently.

The day I got the call from Dad that he had won the lottery, and that I would effectively be on the same win, was an absolutely delightful day of dreams come true.

On the day we eventually visited the US embassy in Lagos, everything had seemed all right with my world. A beautiful, sunny afternoon, and then the consular decision that would pierce my dreams.

"I'm so sorry, Mrs. Ajayi," the consul began. I was right by Mom's side. "I have good news for you and your son, and bad news for you regarding your daughter's application..."

The floor reeled slightly under me. He went on.

"She turns 21 in just a few days and is no longer a minor. She will not be able to attend any US school as a citizen. It would have to be another way."

And so I missed out on becoming a US permanent resident. I did not appreciate the early birthday gift that was actually not a gift. It was very disappointing, to say the least, but God has a way of changing disappointments into appointments.

When Dad visited the US, his first order of business, after regularizing his permanent residency stay, was to file for me as an adult child of a green card holder. That immediately changed my future designation on US immigration matters to that of an "Intended Immigrant." This was before I would later apply for a non-immigrant student visa. As a designated intended immigrant, the embassy shouldn't have approved my application for a non-immigrant visa for studies. Routinely, the US embassy in Lagos, Nigeria declined applications that were seemingly qualified on paper. Mine should have been a very straight forward decline, BUT GOD! Somehow, I was offered this highly coveted study visa. And this, despite the fact that I was honest and transparent with my visa interviewer. I let him know of my intentions not to return to Nigeria because I didn't have direct family left there. I told him that I was hoping to stay in the US if I was able to get a job there after my studies. These were flags that consular interviewers did not like to hear, known factors that got the applicant an X stamp against your visa application.

The decision to award me one astounded me and left me in awe of God. Because it shouldn't have happened. We had applied with a little faith and a lot of hope. But God, who is a God of purpose, aligns the world to favor His own.

And so I got my visa in December of 1998 and arrived in New York that cold January 1999 night.

✳✳✳

I fell in love with Nedderman Hall the first day I set foot on UTA campus, just like Chukwu had said I would. I had spent a few days in New York with family and family friends before flying to Texas all by myself. Texas was different from New York. More wide open spaces and the people seemed friendlier somewhat. I stood in awe. This was true – everything is big in the heart of Texas.

I was not one to make friends very quickly, but friendship at UTA came easily to me because everyone just seemed to want to be your friend, and I had reckoned that I would need help adjusting to a completely new environment. Turned out I did need the help, in more ways than I could have thought.

Nigeria uses the British educational system. An A began at 70% and sometimes at 65%. In my new life, one had to earn at least 90% before being awarded an A. I knew that I would not be able to breeze through school as I had done in my undergraduate years, that I would have to put in effort and study to earn this graduate degree. Where on God's earth did I and my Nigeria college mates hear the common rhetoric that US academics was a walk in the park? Why did we think because the study materials were heavily synthesized, fun, and easy to digest, that it signified easy work? If there are easy academics in the US, it must only be at the Bachelor level and below.

I had never done an overnighter to study while in UI, no matter how challenging the class was. I had attempted it once, but bailed out at 10 pm. I simply couldn't do it. I got up, packed my books, walked to my car, and drove back to the dormitory. Sade, my friend, came into my dorm room smiling the following day.

"You couldn't do it, could you?"

I smiled back at her. "You know me so well."

I never tried pulling any other overnighters throughout my Bachelor's degree in UI, but they became a common thing for me at UTA. I was petrified of failing and was overwhelmed by the fact that I had to score 90% for an A.

God is faithful for every season! He gave me the strength I needed to study long and hard, and my results showed His favor. All papers came back with an A, except for one 80% grade that I got. That one nearly devastated me, and I had to relearn that I was more than my grades. That I was more valuable than my cognitive intelligence.

It was in UTA that my relationship with God evolved from "I can do it if I tried enough" to "I have to be intimate with Him on a regular basis."

At the end of the day, I did well at UTA. Other than that 80-something, I had an A in all my classes. Out of more than 45 credit hours taken at UTA, that was the only non-A class that resulted in a 3.89 graduating GPA from UT Arlington.

***

The standards for an "A" were not the only thing I needed to get acclimatized to. I emigrated from a country that spoke and lived British English and American English was definitely not the same.

Compulsory was not compulsory, but mandatory.

It wasn't a schedule clash but a calendar conflict.

And it definitely wasn't maize, but corn.

"And your maize, please. One cob would do just fine."

The waitress at this restaurant, a true Texan loud, boisterous, and warm, fell silent. She sidled up to me and cleared her throat, prompting me to repeat myself.

I was about to repeat the request when I realized that she was feeling second-hand embarrassment and confusion on my behalf. I laughingly realized the variance and quickly corrected myself. "One corn on the cob, please."

She patted me on the back and went back into her loud and warm persona. When the corn came, I had it packed to go, feeling like everyone had overheard me when I made my faux pas. A laugh for their evening, I was happy to offer. As for me, I was learning almost an entirely new lingua franca.

Angry would now be mad, autumn now fall, bank notes now bills, biscuits now cookies, car bonnet now hood, boot now trunk, chemist now pharmacy store, curtains now drapes, dummy now pacifier, dustbin now garbage can, rubbish now trash, flat now apartment, ground floor now first floor (and don't press the "1" button on the lift, sorry, elevator, if you meant to go to the next floor up for ground).

If you're mad, you're different from a crazy person who is British mad. You're just upset. And if you're driving, be sure to look for the freeway, not a motorway. Change the baby's diaper, what's a nappy? And take a peek, not a peep. And it's in the UK that you are not allowed to talk about your pants in public. Yes, go ahead and talk all about your pants in the US because, hey, they are equivalent to the British person's trousers. Toilet? How gross. Say bathroom and look fine. But don't get all fancy and ask for the queue. Just join the line. What's a sellotape? You mean scotch tape? A round-trip ticket is better than one-way, but what's a return ticket? And make sure to respect your school faculty. Don't call them staff. Get an apartment with walk in closets, not a flat with wardrobes.

Epitome is pronounced with a very soft "t" rather than a hard one. It took years of me calling it the British/Nigerian way and for Americans looking at me with raised eyebrows before I finally got the difference.

The list is endless.

But what lesson did I take away from my transplantation experience? I learned the importance of community, the importance of family. Immerse yourself into your new home and surround yourself with family, whether born of blood or of heart, and this family will make the transplantation experience a little easier, if not a lot easier. Assimilation is definitely quicker when done hand in hand with a safe and loving family.

***

My stay at UTA was also the perfect time to grow the relationship with Akin. I called often, and he would rush to the phone each time. It was cheaper and more practical for me to do the calling, although not without sacrificial expenses for a mere student as I.

The conversations were long and were often the fuel to carry me through the next week. We talked about school, his work in Nigeria, and the friends we shared in common. More often than not, we spoke of our intended future together in the land of the free. He had never traveled out of the country before, but he seemed to have fallen in love with America just like I had.

And so it was the love of God, the hope of a future with Akin, and the friendliness of my colleagues that kept me going for the 18 months that my master's degree lasted to a brilliant completion.

CHAPTER 7

From Loss To Loss

I left work on Thursday night, after a day of feeling caught between a rock and a hard place. I was the "leader," the stakeholder manager. I will not lie; my integrity means the world to me. Diplomacy was not my natural language either. I rather wished people did the right thing and held to the corporate values proclaimed and embedded into a proclaimed drive for culture change.

I had gotten accustomed to working the many extra hours, so that I could hold my head up high and maintain integrity. I wouldn't play the dirty game, wouldn't lie, and wouldn't throw anyone under a fast-moving bus. I would cover up for perceived under-performers and gently coach them off the "fire him" ledge, despite repeated calls to do so. But today, this Thursday, it was obvious that the same one being gently helped was not helping themselves or their work. More so, their own lack of mutual commitment became an exposure where my own integrity was questioned. Laughably, I worked hard to keep my cool, survived the meeting where a counterpart ordered their subordinate to silence me, unbeknownst that their side dialogue was off the subordinate's unmuted shared zoom call.

My counterpart was someone who had feigned love to my family, a mere acquaintance who would randomly show up in my house with gifts, of whom another colleague had warned me not to feel cozy. This was someone who, having experienced a loss themselves, I had stood by them and become Facebook friends with them in the process. Deep in reflection, I had thought, "how about reaching out on Facebook?' And off I went online, but I had been blocked. How scummy humans can be! That was another experience of loss. Perhaps the final straw.

Have you heard about the Law of the Garbage Truck?

In the late 90's, while riding in a New York City taxi, international keynote speaker and positive psychology leader, David J. Pollay, narrowly escaped a life-threatening car crash. The driver who almost caused the accident started yelling at David's cab driver, but the inoffensive cab driver simply waved the dangerous driver a smile with best wishes. David was shocked. They had just narrowly missed death by inches. On inquiring why his taxi driver had been so friendly when the other guy had almost ruined his car and their lives, his driver went on to teach him "The Law of Garbage Trucks" - an important life lesson for all.

Most people are like garbage trucks, full of garbage, frustration, anger, and disappointment. Once the garbage has piled up and has no other place to go, they need somewhere to dump all that trash. David J. Pollay had said, "If you let such people, they'll dump their trash on you. When someone wants to dump on you, don't take it personally. Instead, just smile, wave, wish them well, and move on. You'll be happier because you did."

Friday morning came and I felt like THAT garbage truck, at its peak.

Burden after burden after burden, human frailty can only drown under the weight of the heavy load borne. Yet there would be more. I knew that much. The weekend hadn't even started yet, as I had yet to navigate the airport and its Covid-19 protocols, had yet to arrive in DC and give her my final respects.

***

When I was done and seated, I felt my face flush. I was running out of air but would not give in to tears because I was simply not the kind who did so.

I am a loyal Delta flier. All of us in the family are. The children bemoan being just silver. We, the parents are platinum and my husband is a million miler. We enjoyed the perks that came with that. But you'd never know it, not from pride nor from boasting. We got to the airport and enjoyed smooth global-entry-identified security passage, and we got on and off planes without fuss. We said bless you and thank you to flight attendants and pilots and represented Jesus with pride. But not today. Being kind and a heaven-representative was not even on my mind. I just had to get there.

The gate agent said the cabin luggage dockets were full. Our luggage would have to come on a later flight. For that I flipped. The garbage truck just up and dumped it.

"What do you mean the plane is full? Ma'am, I'm a platinum flier." I said, uncharacteristic arrogance pulsing in my veins, "and I need my luggage to come with me on this flight. I am heading to DC to bury my best friend and maid of honor and you are not going to add to my stress."

I was hyperventilating and demanded that she go ask the flight crew if there was any space at all. We routinely get upgraded to business class, so class of service was not an issue.

The flight agent returned and insisted the bags be checked in to their destination. After asking her name and detailed employee information, I told her I'd have her job if as much as a scratch happened to our luggage.

This wasn't me. I never said things like that. Never lost my composure in public. I can handle extremes gracefully and even lend grace to the offender. I was never one to need a venting partner at work. Yet, on that Friday morning before Father's Day, I knew that I meant every word I spoke. I would have written to Delta Airlines and asked for the gate attendant's job, but God.

***

Settled in and logged on to Gogo Wi-Fi mid-flight, I sent a text message to my siblings. As I typed, the tears started to flow. My heart felt frozen still inside my chest.

"Pray for me, fam. I feel like the garbage truck today, angry and impatient. My heart is so heavy I almost can't breathe. Please pray for me."

"Relax. Sis, just rest. That is grief. Don't be hard on yourself." Sean's response hit my phone and calmed me some. Others also sent messages and many prayers to heaven. They knew I'd need it much this weekend. My older brother, Ayo, texted me Isaiah 53:4.

The rest of Friday was uneventful except for the realization of why we came to DC.

Last time I saw her, she was absolutely fine and in good health. She'd been her beautiful and her elegant vivacious self, our conversations as quick and engaging the way we always did them. She was not born of my mother, but Yomi was my sister through and through. She knew me and saw my heart the way it was as I did hers. We loved each other despite all.

But she was gone.

Saturday was to be the burial. I woke up three times that Friday night with confusional arousal. Tumbling out of sleep at 2 am, engulfed with panic. "We have to go; we will be late for the funeral. Let's go now, please. We're running late."

My two daughters knew this was the number seven loss in two years, and the last two had been the closest to home. They must have been worried about the state of my mind and weren't sleeping deeply either. They jumped from their beds into mine with arms around me. "It's not yet time, Mommy. It's 2 am."

Their words soothed my soul. I knew I had just done something weird, but I didn't know exactly what. My brain had maxed out its trauma capacity.

So I went back to sleep, comforted by the presence and love of my daughters. I would wake two more times before morning broke, each time in a cold sweat, each time thinking we were late.

Morning came and we made it to the funeral. Yomi was there in the casket. But my heart didn't want to believe it. I felt like

I was swimming through molasses, like I was having an out-of-body experience.

Yomi was my best friend. The last month had been an overwhelming one. I had just come back from London where I went to bury my sister. What a cruel joke.

*****

My sister, Ronke, had been diagnosed with lupus when she was 24.

A relatively common disease with black women 20 to 45 years old, it came completely unexpected. The indefatigable Ronke had suddenly been easily fatigued, felt stiff and swollen at the same time, especially in the joints. The butterfly-shaped rashes were a give-away.

Even though we were separated by distance, we fought the disease together. We prayed together. We prayed our hearts out.

The systemic lupus never went away, but it never dominated her life. She lived with it, triumphantly. Her prognosis was that she would never have children, but she did. Jemima was born around 30 weeks, and Samuela barely made 26 weeks' gestation because of the lupus. But in spite of it, they lived and survived.

She was my hero, the one I longed to emulate, the one who always had my back, the absolute of FAITH impersonated.

My sister's faith brought forth her children. Her faith gave her the life she desired. When I think of the Hebrew 11 hallmark of faith fame, I cannot help but see Ronke's name included, if she had lived in bible days. When she took hold of God's word, she held onto it for all that it was worth. She was not a doubter, not one that wavered. She was the true picture of Ephesians 3: 20: *"Now to him who is able to do far more abundantly than all that we ask or think, according to the power at work within us."*

And then at 36 years old, one beautiful August day, she had a seizure. The UK emergency 999 was called and she was taken to the hospital.

After living as a conqueror with lupus for 12 years, she would be diagnosed with Hodgkin's lymphoma of the brain. Not an uncommon progression for systemic lupus erythematosus.

"They say I've got only months to live, but we are not taking that for an answer. My life here on Earth is not done, and no one has the power to take me home but God, and I know He is not ready to. I just know it."

The news was devastating for all. I didn't want to lose my sister. For most of our adult lives, we had lived in different countries, separated as it were by millions and millions of miles. But we were close. She was my sister, friend, confidant, and prayer partner. I couldn't bear to lose her. I connected with Bill Johnson ministries, whom my daughter and I had come to know and love. Bill and Beni were heading to the UK for a revival meeting. "Bill, would you please pray for my sister when you get there...here is her phone number."

"Sis, guess who I just spoke with." I could hear her excitement from the other end of the phone line. "Bill Johnson. He called me and prayed over me."

Even that was a miracle!

I piggybacked on Ronke's faith because mine was pretty low. But she was so verbal about hers and her testimony struck so many people, made them feel the warm embrace of the Father. Her neurologist, for one. She told him point-blank, "No, I'm not going to die. I have a word of life."

After brain surgeries and several months of battling, she was fine, just like she'd said she was going to be. The day she was discharged and allowed to go home, I wept tears of joy and gratitude to the good Lord who'd spared her life.

It would take the doctors a few years to admit her healing and tell her she was in remission, a fact she'd been telling them since day one. The brain cancer was gone, and she could go ahead and live life, enjoy her life.

Sister Ronke was a firebrand, and she warmed our hearts, lit up the room, charged the atmosphere with her light.

She went back to work, the feisty no-nonsense pharmacist that she was. She went back to her normal full schedule, to life. She lived as she had always done, thoroughly and zestfully. Leading healing sessions in church and sending off church teenagers to college with pocket money to spend.

And then, in February 2013, she had a stroke. I was pregnant and devastated.

Just the day before, we'd spoken on phone and jokingly, she had tried to encourage me to breastfeed this baby while I insisted I would not. It was a happy call as she begged and begged. She had not been able to breastfeed her babies because of her lupus medications, and I wanted this shared experience with her.

"I will feed her *ogi*. She will drink *eko* from day one. No breastfeeding. I paid my dues on that one with her sister."

Ogi and eko are the same thing, a Yoruba meal made from corn, sans protein.

I wouldn't learn of the stroke until three days after it happened. Because I was going to give birth anytime soon, the family was reluctant to tell me, as the doctors had put the possibility of her surviving at 0.1%. This news hit me the same way every bad news about her health had hit. Even after I piled heaps and heaps of blankets over myself. I couldn't get warm.

My sister could not speak, so I couldn't speak with her. But how I wanted to talk to her. How I wanted to hear her voice telling me that it would be okay.

***

When my new baby was three months old, the entire family made the trip to London to see sister Ronke. By then, she was out of the hospital and in a recovery home. She hadn't died like the doctors said she would, but she was not the same Ronke as before.

She held my new daughter, her newest niece, in her arms, and her eyes lit up. It was serene, at peace, and my heart quieted within me for the first time since I learned of her stroke.

She had aphasia and couldn't speak, but her eyes were bright. Her eyes shone with an intensity that was uplifting. She started singing. Not loud but clear as a bell, and the surprise rippled through me. This was a woman who had had aphasia for months, who was, as they said, locked in her own world, and here she was singing and praising God.

That was the first of many songs. For the remainder of her battle, my sister didn't speak well because of the aphasia, but miraculously, she could sing. And she sang in gratitude to God.

When we returned to the US, I'd call her over the phone. Sometimes, she could say a few words, but most of the time, she was unable to.

But scriptures flowed from her. I don't know how her brain was able to hold so many scriptures and how her mouth, which could no longer speak normal words, could speak such beautiful scriptures, healing scriptures. She sang and she prophesied scriptures. She sang newly released songs which let me know her brain was still functional to learn. "You are great, yes, you are holy one...everything written about you is great..."

**

My sister had been ill longer than my daughter had been alive, but the two of them just had this incredible bond for the seven years they had together.

All the way from London, borne by the connections of telephone lines, my sister sang to her niece. My sister quoted scriptures to her niece and loved her like her mother.

And then, almost eight years after that first stroke, sister Ronke had a second, and this time, the neurologist gave a zero chance of survival. Medical statistics show a 0% chance of an SLE patient surviving brain cancer and surviving one stroke. Now two?

"It's better to do a compassionate exit." He advised my brother. In the UK, doctors reserve the right to withdraw resuscitation towards euthanasia without the consent of the family. However, he was extending professional courtesy to my brother, a consultant psychiatrist and a colleague. My brother wouldn't have it.

This was sister Ronke, a woman who had fought long and hard all her adult life, who had overcome insurmountable mountains. We weren't going to give up on her, because she wouldn't ever give up on any of us.

"We'll do all we can to keep her alive." My brother insisted.

"You know we can't go in for another surgery."

"That I understand." My brother asserted. "But still, we'll let her go in her own time."

Much to the neurologist's surprise, she didn't up and die as he'd expected. Day by day, she grew stronger and a few weeks after the second stroke, she was given the all clear to go into a recovery home.

"There is something about your sister that I quite can't place my finger on. She shouldn't be alive. She shouldn't be regaining strength, but she is."

My brother smiled, "That would be Jesus."

And indeed it was Jesus. Sister Ronke had once again beaten the odds.

***

She was supposed to be in the recovery home for two weeks and then go on home.

She never made it back to her earthly home, but she did proceed on to her most worthy home.

On March 8, 2020, Ronke choked on dinner and within twenty-four hours, was visited at the pearly gates of heaven.

Since the second stroke, we had prayed every day for her healing, and we had joined our faith with hers. This was just going to be another test of faith, we believed. She was going to come out on the other end. But she didn't, at least not in the way we humans understand. It pleased Jesus to take her home to Him because her work was done, her life fully lived despite the fact that it had not been as long as we had hoped.

It was a hard, hard pill to swallow. She had survived two strokes, crushed cancer, and had sung consistently despite her aphasia. And to be felled by something as innocuous as choking. Everything had felt on course, like she was going to be okay, and then she choked? On dinner?

***

Covid 19 was still ravaging the world, and we had ourselves a whole new universe no one really understood. As the world banded together and grieved over those collectively lost to the pandemic, I went through a private tragedy of mine. I had held out hope that my sister would be fine, and then she was gone.

I wanted to go to the UK immediately to be with her in the morgue. I lamented about how lonely she must be with no loved ones with her there. I couldn't leave her by herself, that wasn't fair. But there were travel restrictions. It wasn't so hard at that time to leave the US, but it was near impossible to enter the UK. So we waited.

In those trying times, Yomi, my best friend and I banded and grieved together.

She was in another state and I didn't get to see her as much because of the Covid 19 restrictions as well, but we talked often. She had known my sister as well, and had loved her lavishly too.

Yomi was inconsolable about sister Ronke's passing. She would weep and apologize for not playing the role of being my comforter, having reversed roles. We grounded and calmed each other. Her tears actually gave words to mine unwept. It took weeks before I would weep for my sister.

***

Being physically there at Ronke's burial was therapeutic. Before her, I'd never held a deceased person, but seeing her, holding her was refreshing. We had been finally able to get into the UK, just in time for her burial, me, my husband and my daughters.

On April 7, we laid her body to earth. Attendance was limited to family and others joined the service of songs only and that, via Zoom.

There were friends and cousins, all of them had had their lives touched and transformed by sister Ronke. The one face I didn't see on zoom was my friend, Yomi.

It wasn't problematic for me, but it was puzzling. Yomi loved sister Ronke and there was no reason strong enough that would keep her from being in virtual attendance.

***

After my sister's death and burial, I resolved to do things differently, to be more intentional about relationships. I was going to cherish the people in my life the more. I was going to hold on to friendships and nurture them with intentionality.

The first person I sent a text message to when we landed on American soil was Yomi.

"I am no longer going to be a lone ranger. I'm going to spend more time with the people I love, beginning with you. So, prepare for the girls and I. We will be spending July 4 at your place."

She didn't reply.

I called a few times and there was no response.

***

Yomi had gone for a routine check-up with her doctor the same day of sister Ronke's service of songs, intending to join us later in the evening, sometime in the course of the service.

They called her back to the doctor's office before she got back to the car. They weren't going to allow her to go home because they'd found metastasized cancer cells in her body. A large percentage of her body had been invaded by the marauding cells.

There would be no going back permanently to an earthly home.

Like my sister, Yomi had overcome so much in life. Lived longer and better than the average person with sickle cell anemia. Then, she had leukemia and a bone marrow transplant, which had miraculously mitigated the SS genotype. This was a mystery, a testimony we rejoiced for again and again. Crises became a thing of the past.

She was well. She was healthy. There was nothing wrong with her until that routine checkup.

As we had journeyed back from the UK to the US, as I sent her text after text after text, my friend lay in the hospital fighting for her life, unbeknownst to me.

Ninety days after my sister went to be with Jesus, heaven gained another faith giant. My Yomi mi, as she was fondly called by me, Dr. Aunty Yom Yom as she was called by my children, hung up her earthly garment and went home to sing with the angels.

✳✳✳

So we weren't late for the burial, as my befuddled mind led me to believe. We got there in time. But the service was somewhat of a daze, like I was moving underwater and could not see or hear or breathe clearly. To lose two people who I'd willingly give my life for and that within days of each other, pressed my shoulders down into their blades.

After the funeral was over, Yomi's husband, a few other close family members and us, wandered the cemetery where Yomi's earthly body had just been returned to the dust from where it was formed.

"We can't leave her here. It's so cold." I thought in my mind again and again, but I knew we'd have to, the same way we'd left my sister in the ground several weeks before.

That night, I experienced confusional arousal again, waking up in the middle of the night to round up my family with the fear that we were late for our flight. After they calmed me down, I knew something had to give.

The losses piled one on another stacked up too high and I needed time to breathe. It didn't help that we returned to San Antonio to blood draws and specialist visits. My younger daughter was experiencing grief in a way that showed in her physical health, and it would take us many hospital visits before she would be healthy again.

***

It has been more than a loss or two in the two and a half years.

My mom passed away at the end of 2018. Christmas of the same year, we got a call to New York to my mother-in-law's near passing away, unexpectedly. She later passed away in January and we buried both mothers within two weeks of each other.

In August of 2019, light seemed to shine but so briefly. I was pregnant. I wanted more children, and to suddenly have a baby growing within me, to have my body nurture another human being was a blessing. I held the blessing so tenderly and lovingly, until I lost her at 16 weeks. That was the third loss, a hard one to deal with.

I went inside of myself into a deep dark place, and it took the grace of God to warm my heart again. Even then, there remained an ache in my heart to mend.

My sister and best friend who would pass within weeks of each other in 2021 were the final straw. The losses finally caught up to be felt.

There was nowhere else to fall, but into the arms of my Heavenly Father. And He always comes through. He brought comfort from the father-heart of an earthly father that reflects God's. And He brought the "Grief to Grace" family into my life.

CHAPTER 8

From Grief To Grace

would go visit my pastor in May 2021 when the world felt very dark, when I felt like there was a dark cloud following me everywhere I went, perpetually taunting me.

I had returned from the UK after burying my sister only to discover that my best friend was dying. Faith was a hard currency at this time, and I just didn't have enough. I had hung on to hope for so long and now that my sister was gone and my friend was on the brink of death, I lost all hope.

And then Yomi died, and the bottom fell out of my world again.

I so desperately wanted to go to the heaven that my sister and my friend had gone on to. I wondered unceasingly what it would feel like for the rapture to happen now, for Jesus to take me home, flying in the skies to reunite with my sister and my best friend, to put an end to the pain that throbbed in every single one of my veins.

Of course, I'd want my Savior to take not just me away from this fallen world, but my daughters as well, to remove me and those that I loved the most out of this evil world and into His embrace.

It was in this frame of mind, in this battered state, that I went to see Papa in Minnesota. My spiritual seek was simple. "Since heaven is so beautiful and the ultimate attainment for every Christian, why can't I just go there now?"

And this was Papa, who knew my heart, who had felt the same kind of pain I felt when he lost his own father several years ago.

A first son, a pastor, a shepherd of souls, no one would understand the anguish and loneliness such as he may have felt when his father passed on. He was supposed to be strong, as a minister of God. He was supposed to be clear-eyed as he led his siblings through that difficult time of their lives. He was all these things, but his heart ached. How lonely it is at the top.

"It was a test of faith, Folakemi." He said quietly, pausing midway to wipe a stray sweat from his forehead. "But God helped me through as He would help you." "And He has asked me to share a scripture with you."

And I listened.

"' In the year that King Uzziah died, I saw the Lord.' That was what the Holy Spirit asked that I share with you. I know that everything around you is dark at the moment, and I recognize that your feeling of loss is grounded in fact..." He paused yet again and then went on in a voice closer to a whisper, "But the Holy Spirit says to tell you that this is your season to see the Lord. This is your season to see His glory. It was after Uzziah died that Isaiah was launched into his ministry..."

I sat still, and closed my eyes and raised my face upward to heaven, wanting my Father to make it clearer to me, to make me see.

But the understanding came bit by bit by bit. This book is a result of this understanding. The birthing of this book came from being launched into a ministry of hope. Rising from that counseling session and then attending the Grief to Grace workshop, I felt reborn. I felt alive. I felt like I was equipped not only to deal with the back-to-back losses but also equipped to offer hope to those without it. The words in 2 Corinthians 1: 3-4 became very real to me: *"God ...who comforts and encourages us in every trouble so that we will be able to comfort and encourage those who are in any kind of trouble, with the comfort with which we ourselves are comforted by God."*

I experienced a rebirth of my faith, of hope, of my childlike wonder at the goodness of God in every circumstance. And it is my prayer, my most ardent wish, that everyone who reads this book will be comforted, that they will relate, that they will find themselves represented.

We have all been through different kinds of pain, and our experiences will never be the same. But we have the same big God who desires each and every one of us to be comforted. It is my hope that as you read this book, that comfort will find you in the hard places of your life, that you will find peace where there was none before, that you will come to understand – like I have come to – that God remains good all the time.

***

Even as I went through the experience of rebirth and the reestablishment of my hope in the Lord, I knew I needed to do something different. I needed to sit still for the first time in years, to mourn the losses properly, to allow the events of the past two years to flow over me, to experience the healing hugs of Jesus Christ. To feel, deal, and then heal.

After the confusional arousal and the grief that rendered my heart in half again and again when I thought of my sister, Ronke, and my friend, Yomi (which was quite often), I was losing my mind. I felt like I was myself, and yet not myself. A part of me was missing even though I was whole. I was apart from the world even though I lived in it.

I wanted peace. I needed respite.

The thought of returning to work was petrifying. I was a prized employee, loved what I did, couldn't imagine my life without my job. Yet, there was the toxic competition I couldn't handle, along with an ailing child. My heart was fragile, broken, and grief-stricken.

So I called my boss when we returned home from Yomi's burial. She was not just a boss but a dear friend as well, but I didn't have time for niceties. I just felt like curling up and hedgehogging for the rest of my life.

"I took Monday off to attend to pressing matters," I said, "however, I won't be returning to work immediately."

I had never used the Family Medical Leave Act benefit besides the six weeks for each virginal delivery. I always had it together. I had a good husband, good kids, a good life. Or did I? I had never before now endured so much grief in my life.

***

I needed to grieve properly; I needed to allow the intensity of the losses to overtake my human strength so that I could give it all up to God. There was much to grieve and it had accumulated over the years. I was well functional, even well above the average for optimal, but was I in my own destined optimal?

The first trauma retreat I found was for five days, was far away in Tennessee, and would cost $8,500. It fit the bill, but the bill seemed outrageous. And it didn't completely resonate with my heart. The Holy Spirit wasn't leading in that direction. But now I knew such places existed; a place for healing life's wounds.

Then Google turned up New Heart of Texas' "Grief to Grace." It was two and a half hours away by drive, and only a fraction of the cost of the others. I was amazed at the paltry amount being charged, because it included five days at a five-star level of accommodation, several meals a day, and much more. That, in addition to almost around-the-clock spiritual therapy. I needed the therapy. I needed help to make sense of the unraveling spiral of grief that was my then reality.

The next Grief to Grace retreat was scheduled for the end of August. But the website had nothing to do with grief, seemingly paying more attention to abuse - sexual abuse, pastoral abuse, physical abuse.

"Very interesting." I found myself murmuring when I stumbled upon this bit of information. I needed respite from the grief that dodged my heart, and not necessarily a therapist to walk me through the aftermath of abuse. I had dealt with the fallout of my childhood rape issues, hadn't I?

Yet, something (I know now it was the Holy Ghost) prompted me to apply.

"What have I got to lose at this point?" I reasoned.

***

"We are fully booked." Lovely Ms. Tracy was the woman who called to deliver the news, with her soft-spoken voice. "We got your application, but the thing is, we are full for our August session."

She continued. "Our next session is for January. We can slot you in for that session."

I realized that I was shaking my head and that she couldn't see me, "January will not work. I will be back at work and flying high again by then."

"We can put you on the waiting list for this session then. We have interested participants who often decide, at the last minute, that they will not be able to join us. So, please go ahead and submit your long-form application. You wouldn't need to pay until we found space to come..." I imagined her shrugging her shoulders as she completed her sentence, "Who knows? We might just have a slot for you."

And so, I completed the long-form application because I figured it couldn't hurt. The application form was detailed. My life history, my experience, what I wanted to achieve at the retreat.

I poured out my soul, and when I was done with the application, I felt a little better, like a smidgen of the weight I carried had been lifted.

***

Tracy called again, this time with good news. "Do you still want to be a part of the August session?"

"Of course." I exclaimed. Over the past few days, the conviction had grown in my heart that I was supposed to be a part of the August session, that God had something in stock for me there.

"We've had some Covid cancellations. The interesting thing, however, is that while you are number 11 on the waiting list, the Holy Spirit impressed on the leaders, independent of each other, that you should be picked."

Mary Lee, the founder of New Heart of Texas, and Carrie Johnson, the lead therapist, had individually prayed about whom to choose from the waiting list, and the Holy Spirit had impressed on them both to pick me, even though I was down on the list.

I was awestruck by God's intentionality. By the grace that He so generously bestows. He was looking out for me. As I sat back to consider Tracy's words, I was reminded of His word in Isaiah 49:15: *"Can a mother forget the baby at her breast and have no compassion on the child she has borne? Though she may forget, I will not forget you!"*

He was better than an earthly father or mother. He felt my pain. He knew my grief. And He was providing a path through it to the other side. I would never again take His love for granted, for *"Surely He hath borne our griefs, and carried our sorrows: yet we did esteem Him stricken, smitten of God, and afflicted"* (Isaiah 53:4).

***

The safely secluded healing center sat on eight acres.

When I stepped foot on the grounds, I felt the cocoon and warmth of God's love. His presence was here. This was holy ground. The next five days were going to be days of spiritual adventure for me.

"Let me help you with that." The lady that got my luggage was polite and full of warm smiles. She was brisk but not all business. The gentleman was equally pleasant. As he wheeled my luggage to the room assigned to me, he attempted to converse and make me feel at ease.

"You are our special guest. Everything is made ready for you."

"You should get a little rest now. The sessions start soon."

***

The Grief to Grace cohort was a small group of ten guests and half that amount in staff.

There were the regular introductions.

"What good thing has happened to you this week?" Mary Lee started.

I shared the joy of moving my daughter into her college dorm, but even that came with some heartache.

And so we had the first session and the second.

The third session was where the Holy Spirit unraveled me.

"What makes you sad?" it was either Carrie or Mary Lee that asked. Their tone was welcoming, soft, full of all the compassion in the world.

Several participants went before me to contribute.

In the past, I wasn't inclined toward the concept of group therapy. An introspective person by nature who often found my company more pleasurable than that of others, I wasn't the type to tell people what bothered me. And if I was going to speak to someone, it definitely wasn't going to be to strangers. No way, sirs and ma'ams.

"Kemi, what makes you sad?"

I had previously shared how I could cope with almost any situation. How compartmentalization was my secret and highly effective weapon for safety. I didn't call it compartmentalization, but Pastor Blake put the word to it. I knew what it was, but reflected it as creating a new, nice future out of the present pain. One I could make happen with my hard work and emotional grit.

"Kemi, what makes you sad?"

Something tore loose from my insides. The pain I had worked hard to bury washed over me so thoroughly it felt like a physical experience. And I blurted it all out. I didn't even think about what my mouth was saying, as I swam in the kindness and compassion of all.

"I have had seven losses in two and a half years," I heard someone saying, and it took a moment to realize that I was the one talking. "First, it was my mom. She passed away at the end of 2018, and I almost couldn't cope with her death and the relationship that lacked a resolve. But then my mother-in-law too. We buried both of them within two weeks of each other early 2019. We laid my mother-in-law to rest January 14, three days after she died, and then it was straight to the UK to go bury my mom."

By now, tears had coalesced at the corner of my eyes, but I blinked them away. As I went on to the next in the series of the losses I had experienced, my heart almost galloped to a stop. This one smarted and hurt and stung even still.

It was August 2019 that I miscarried at 16 weeks gestation. "I lost my beautiful daughter," I told the room, but I could have very well been in a world of my own.

For several minutes, no one spoke. I swallowed back the tears in my throat and looked up again at the white ceiling. Then I gathered courage around me like a cloak and continued, my voice no longer as tremble-y as it had been a couple of minutes ago.

"After the miscarriage, my husband disclosed some things that shook me to the core, upended everything I knew. It was like hurt had come to roost in my life. And not only did I lose my marriage as I knew it, but I also lost my church family as I knew it. Some of our church members, my pastor included, did not know how to handle my husband and blamed me for his sexual addiction. Even then, I pressed forward. Created new futures to fulfill."

Leading experts on sexual addiction often describe the spouse's betrayal trauma as the equivalent of strolling on a highway and being hit by an 18-wheeler truck. Neuroscientists describe childhood rape also, as a similitude to 4th and sometimes, 5th degree burns.

But what is the prognosis for a 4th or 5th degree burn where the same person gets hit by an 18-wheeler truck? Only God!

I swallowed, "My sister and my friend were my rock in difficult times. Yomi knew everything. And then both of them died, less than three months removed from each other." The tears finally overcame me then. They tore loose from my chest and exploded out of my mouth. I closed my eyes and felt arms around me.

First, one set of arms, then another, and another, and another. I had not been hugged by so many people all at once in a long time, but it felt right. I felt at home, at peace.

"Oh my gosh," Carrie Johnson, the lead therapist, whispered, "That's a whole lot of complex trauma, Kemi. The fact that you are alive, that you are here is a miracle. I mean, people go through just one of those things you've gone through and commit suicide."

As the fellowship of arms around me loosened and people returned to their seats, the sobs subsided, and peace started to still my heart.

***

I realized that I had a whole lot of work to do. The "Grief to Grace" Retreat takes its spiritual foundation from the word of God that says to work out your salvation with fear and trembling.

We began each day at 7 am with family devotion and worked all day and into the nights, closing sometimes as late as 10 pm. We had bathroom breaks and lunch breaks, which meant that we spent between 14 hours and 15 hours each day undergoing intense spiritual and cognitive therapy.

We went through the life of Jesus. We walked with Him through His miracles, stopping every now and then to marvel at the compassion He had for the weights that weighed His people down. We walked with Him as He took our griefs and pain and had them nailed into His palms on the cross. And we triumphed with Him when He said, "It is finished."

We had a symbolic activity on one of the days, burying the body of Jesus (using a symbolic cross). As we stood by the body, each of us, His words, "It is finished," kept ringing in my head.

And then the question came, "So what is left?"

What was left to keep me from my full healing and from maintaining that healing?

Suddenly, it felt like I was standing by my sister's casket again. And then the scenery changed and it wasn't her casket but Yomi's. The scenes receded far back in time, to that place when my sister had been young and healthy, to that place where Yomi and I had been teenage girls who shared their dreams and their hearts. I saw both of these loved ones the way they had been, brilliant, vibrant, suffused with life.

And in that place, standing by that makeshift coffin of Jesus, death lost its ability to torment me. I could finally accept that they had just vacated their earthly bodies and gone on to live in the mansion upstairs with Jesus. They were not really and would never be fully absent from my life.

The peace that had been stealing into my heart in bits and pieces came flooding in, fully. Full, perfect peace.

***

I gave it all up. My anger at death. My fear of death. The betrayal of my church family, their lack of understanding.

In that place, I placed my baby girl into Jesus' arms for safekeeping, inundated with the calming knowledge that I'd cradle her again someday.

In that place, I took strength for my marriage, courage to face the future.

In that place, I surrendered the little girl whose virginity and innocence had been ripped from her.

In that place, I surrendered all of my weaknesses for His strength.

In that place, I released my fight against injustice, into the trustable arms of the God of justice who will repay every single act. He will set it all right.

In that place, I took strength and pulled off the 35,000 pound truck sitting on my back. I crawled out from under the heavy burden; laid down my weight of sorrows, angst, pain, and anguish. I found grace for the grief.

CHAPTER 9

I Wanna Know What Love Is

I would be apart from Akin for the next period of my life while I studied in the US.

I had never been in a romantic relationship before Akin. He was my first romantic relationship. The feelings I felt for the new young man in my life were equally new experiences; there was a desire to be with him, to talk to him, to hear his voice, to learn what made him tick. But I was also petrified. We had every intention of becoming man and wife at the right time, but I didn't know if I knew what all that entailed. To be his wife, to hold a future together in our hands.

Yet, the love in my heart for him throbbed alive each time we spoke.

Love is a beautiful force. It fuels an all-encompassing light that glows from the inside out and makes the world more beautiful to behold. At heart, I was a romantic person and believed in happily ever afters. There were times that doubts assailed me, but deep in my heart, I knew and felt that Akin was my first and my only happily-ever-after. Marriage takes work and dedication, and I had no doubt we were going to both invest our hearts and all to make a beautiful home together.

What gave me this firm conviction? Well, Akin was a child of God, and we both feared God. That, I thought, counted for something. Counted for all.

In the cold winter months of 1999, in a new country all by myself, I didn't feel as alone as I could have. I kept in touch with my family in the UK, friends in Nigeria, and other friends in diaspora around the world. Most of all, the thoughts of Akin and our future together kept me warm.

I called frequently, even though that took a sizable chunk of my funds. At the time, international calls were from one landline to another landline, and were expensive. The advent of Voice Over IP and mobile calling has much simplified that now. But I never missed a call.

"Hi." My voice seemed to go several decibels lighter and higher when I called him. Filled with delight, warmth, and softness, and all the things that made for a woman in love.

"Hi, Love." Akin wasn't the epitome of romance, and didn't always know how to voice what he felt inside, but at that point in our relationship, when the first blush of love was still on us both, he tried.

"How has your week been?" I wanted to know him, wanted to be close to him, wanted our lives to synergize even though we were thousands of miles apart. We had spent years together in the same University, in the same fellowship, nodding at each other in passing, but had not connected romantically. To have known him for three years and only been a couple for two months, a night before I would move to the US for studies, I now wanted to know him as wholly as I could.

"Great." And then he'd launch into what had happened at work, at home, in church.

I'd listen intently and then tell him about my own week. This little ritual kept us connected and shortened the physical distance.

I got to know about his family, about his mom, about those that shaped his life. I had not met his mother yet. She lived in the ancient city of Gbongan, a quiet but strong woman, who had done all to give her son an education. She was uneducated and sold simple wares in the local market, but she did more than that. She had taken on odd jobs, had done all she could physically do to see him through the University of Ibadan. And for that, he loved her. Because he loved her so much, I grew to love her too. I wanted the whole world for her, just like her son did, and sometimes even more.

But first, the plan was to get that son to the US. In the US, he would have a better life. He could parlay his brilliance (because by God, he was brilliant) into better and greater things. In the US, he'd have a chance at a better life, and we could put down roots and begin a family together.

✲✲✲

I thought of him long and hard, and he said he thought of me too. In that first year of long-distance courting, I wanted to see him, to be in the same place as he was, to place my hands in his as we'd done that star-studded night when I told him yes and when we had committed our relationship to the God we both knew to keep it.

***

I had never been so excited to travel back to Nigeria, as I was in December of 1999. It had been 11 months in the US and Christmas would be in Nigeria. I didn't have any immediate family members in the country, but I had Akin. He was my sole reason to visit. Visiting my siblings or Mom in the UK, or Dad in Saudi Arabia, was not an option.

I touched down in Lagos, a city filled with the harmattan haze. The weather was cold and dry, and as the confluence of many native languages washed over me, it felt like home. I was where I wanted to be.

Hugging Akin felt awkward. This was a man whose life I had shared for the past eleven months, but to suddenly be in the same physical space as he was...I didn't know what to do with myself or what to say. But he hugged me, his arms opened, his face alight. I allowed myself to be embraced, but quickly pulled apart from him.

He had organized a taxi to take me to Pastor Oludiran's house because that was where I would stay the whole of my visit. By then, Pastor Oludiran was aware of the relationship between my fiancé and me.

As we sat side by side in the taxi, holding hands, it felt like we fit perfectly together, and all seemed right with the world. My trembling heart quieted, and I regained my familiarity with Akin. God had a hand in this relationship, I was convinced. He loved me and was looking out for me.

***

"What?" I managed to get the question past my throat, with a mixture of confusion and fury bubbling up, heat rising in my face.

We were in Pastor Oludiran's guest room. Akin had asked to talk privately. The Oludirans took me as their daughter, none less; and I had a room upstairs in their beautiful home that bore such a distinct fragrance of God's love. It was easily accessible to others but private enough to talk, to share dreams, to get to know each other's hearts again. However, Akin wanted us in a different room downstairs that afternoon. He wanted us in the privacy of the guest room.

Naively, I had followed him to the guest room. We had started off talking, him on one of the chairs attached to the reading desk, me seated on the edge of the bed. And in the intensity of our talk, I hadn't consciously noted that he had gotten off the chair and was sitting beside me.

I should have guessed that something was off at that point, but I didn't. Today, I realize that being book smart is not the same as being life-smart. In retrospect, I realize I was all kinds of book smart but very lacking in life experiences.

When his hot palm raised my shirt and attempted to creep up my belly, I flipped. It felt like a hot iron had just been applied to my naked skin, like I was going to be burned. Was this for real? Did Akin, my God-fearing fiancé, just try to slip his hand into my bra?!

I froze. I was petrified, but I was more angry than I was scared. What had gotten into him?

He smiled at me. The smile seemed inappropriate and out of place. "It's okay, sweetheart. I wasn't doing anything wrong, you know."

I did a double-take and pushed him away. We were supposed to keep ourselves pure until we got married, weren't we?

"Don't look so crestfallen, Love," he made an attempt to get up and put his arms around me, but I wouldn't have it. He sat back on the bed, but went on, "We are engaged to be married, and yes, I do desire you. You are beautiful, and I'd be crazy not to feel sexually aroused when I am with you. But we are not going to do anything. I am not going to have sex with you or anything like that, until we are married. But there is nothing wrong about caressing each other, giving each other some pleasure that way."

My mouth opened wider, and my jaw almost hit the floor. "Say what?"

He stood again, and when he put his arms around me this time, I didn't push him away. I was just frozen to the spot again. I had been a believer for many years, but this was my first relationship, and while I had read the Bible cover to cover and thought I had a good grasp of what God expected of young people in relationships, I was confounded for a little while and felt the warmth of sexuality.

As I stood there rigidly, he slid his hand under my shirt again. I didn't jump back. It felt good. It took the feel of his hot palm on one of my breasts to get my senses back.

This was my body, not his. I alone decided what could be done to me and what couldn't.

"How dare you?" I exploded, the fury coalescing into that one sentence.

He sat again, and despite myself, I allowed him to pull me into a sitting position as well. He was intent on explaining himself, on making me see reason. "It's not a big deal,

Folakemi. Those young girls in Uyo, those young sisters..."
He had lived in Uyo for a full year during his NYSC year, so
I knew what he was talking about, "those sisters didn't see
anything wrong with it. They allowed me to fondle them all
the time. We didn't sin, because I never had sex with them.
I barely saw their nakedness. It's not a big deal, Love. It
happens all the time. We were just too disconnected from
reality when we were on campus."

My now older self would have stood up right there and then
and walked him out of the house. But I was 24 and very
naïve, despite being well-traveled. I was guilelessly trusting
of this man that I thought I loved and who loved me. I didn't
do what I should have and how truly naïve that was! I mean,
this was a man I was going to marry, and he had the
chutzpah to tell me of his sexual escapades with other girls?
I should have up and left and packed up the relationship. IF
not that, at a minimum, I should have demanded the respect
I deserved. But I didn't.

I would not allow him to fondle me, and he would not see my
nakedness until our wedding night. I set those boundaries
and maintained them religiously. But when I should have
walked, when I should have demanded the honor due me, I
did not.

***

After the Christmas break, I went back to my studies in the
US, with a heart that was rendered in two. One half of my
heart loved Akin, missed him, and longed for him. The other
half, the more logical and critical thinker, picked holes in our
relationship, made me see the reasons why it wouldn't work,
and why I needed to call it quits.

But I hadn't been this way before. I forgave Akin for his errors. There were many. In our two weeks together, all the foibles that could not be witnessed over the phone had been front and center. His awkwardness with the world. His tendency to use language that was not fully wholesome. His preoccupation with what sex would be like when we finally got married. His willingness to go with the flow, whatever the flow was.

But I had seen the other, more likable parts of him as well. His ability to go on the knees and pray. His tenderness for his mom, whom I had finally met in person. His pain in life that I could come to heal. His intelligence and huge plans for the future. And the love he professed for me.

My heart decided I would still marry Akin. Together, we'd have our own picket fence house and raise godly seeds for Jesus. Together, we'd have our own piece of nirvana.

***

I graduated from school and returned to Nigeria in the Fall, for the fancy and exuberant wedding ceremony that many called the year's essence of a "Celebration of Love." After we were pronounced man and wife and kissed, the lines for our future seemed to shift a little closer into place.

The honeymoon was at a beautiful location in Jos Wildlife Reserves, one of the largest manmade wildlife sanctuaries in Nigeria. Located in the Rantya area of Jos, Plateau state, and extending into the pine forest and into Vongnifwel Hill, our nighttime visitors included its variety of exotic birds, monkeys, lions, and elephants. We were in our own little slice of heaven, exploring all that a bride and groom did.

And then it was over and I was back to the US after the brief marital haven.

Before and after our marriage, Akin had severally applied for a US student visa, having gained admission to a handful of schools to pursue his graduate degree in Computer Science. But he had been denied repeatedly. Nothing seemed to work again and again. It only worsened after we married.

So, I went back to the US, to work, to heartache. I wanted Akin with me with an intensity that took me by surprise.

Several months after returning to the US, I was back to Nigeria for a third time. This time, intending to complete the process of getting Akin to the US with me.

My original nonimmigrant student status had been approved for conversion to a nonimmigrant visa classification that applied to services of exceptional merit and ability and specialty occupations. With a Master's Degree under my belt, and employment with a local telecommunication company, I was approved for the working visa. I could stay put with that approval until I needed to travel out for whatever reason. I could also elect to visit nearby embassy stations for a visa stamp of this H1B visa. A large percentage of peers visited the closest visa port in Mexico. H1-B visas were much less guaranteed in places like Nigeria. However, for me, returning to Nigeria for a visa stamp would serve a more important purpose. I would get an opportunity to support Akin in his quest to relocate to the US, which at that point in time, was in jeopardy. I elected to put my own US stay at risk, in faith that I could bail us both.

Akin had applied for a student visa so many times and had been refused for so long that we couldn't go that route again, at least not for another two years. Now that we were married, he could get a H4 visa, as the spouse of a specialty knowledge worker. The H4 visa was the only hope. And even then, not a guaranteed hope. For one, the decision was not in our hands, but in the hands of whatever consul we got at the American Embassy. Secondly and worse, Akin's most recent denial came with a moratorium. He could not apply again for any visas in a 12-month period. My strategy and hope was to somehow onboard him real-time on my own eligible application, as of the point of interview. It could in no way be done prior.

✳✳✳

The adjudicating consular officer at the US Embassy in Lagos had a stern face that seemed to be made for frowns. Not uncommon for them to, since they are inundated with trickster applicants. But that was just my initial impression of him. He turned out to have a great smile when he finally allowed himself to, his stern features relaxing into a more approachable one.

"Sir, the only reason I came back to Lagos is because of my husband..." Still felt strange to be calling Akin my husband. I went on, "The only reason I came back is so he can get his H4 as he could not apply independently due to an embargo after his last denial of many denials."

God was gracious. God was kind. God came through. Because the interviewer smiled another of his rare smiles and asked one of the office assistants to go get Akin from the embassy gate entrance where he had to be standing.

"I will give you guys your visa, but first, I will need to confirm with your employer," he pointed at me, "that you are still with them. That's the only way this is going to happen."

That was good news, but it came with a wrinkle. In faith, I had purchased tickets to leave Nigeria two days from that interview date, on the night flight out. Confirmation from my employer would take between 24 and 48 hours and our passports would be held at the US embassy until visas were issued. Since our tickets included a layover in London, UK, Akin would need a UK transit visa. I had thought we would do all that in the in-between day from interview to departure. Taking so many risks in faith, we did not have the luxury of time.

It suddenly looked like a complicated mess, and I took the time to explain this to the nice interviewer.

"Why have you made things so complex for yourself? Why the rush?"

I sighed, "You know, I have to be back at work ASAP."

That response, although true, underbellied the complete reality. I was eager, could barely wait, to fulfil Akin's dreams of setting foot on US soil, hence with several days of water-only fasting under my belt (also known as *biribiri* by Nigerians), and with a lot of faith in my heart, I knew somehow that mountains would move and the dates I purchased for departure would work.

The consul shrugged, "There is nothing the American embassy can do about that. It is standard regulation to contact your employer. And once we have the response and approve your visa, then you can visit the UK embassy to get this guy..." he pointed at Akin, who seemed bewildered by all that was happening, "...his UK visa. I have helped as much as I can; there is nothing more than I can do."

And that was the truth. He had done his best, had gone out of his way to be gracious and accommodating, and I had so much gratitude in my heart for this stranger whom God was using to open an iron brass door to the fulfillment of our dreams.

And my creative brain was in action. With no sugar in the digestive tracts, all of my energy, I admit, proved very effective for brain work!

We raced to the UK embassy. At that point, we did not have passports on us, having left them for the US Visa. But God came through again, this time in the form of a blast from the past. Someone with whom I had a not-so-pleasant encounter in 1996. This man, a UK embassy employee, had requested surrendering my Christian values by exchanging sexual favors for a UK visiting visa for which I had applied. I politely declined and left dejected. When I shared the saga with my one and only beloved sister, Ronke, she challenged my faith.

"Did you not tell me that you sensed the Holy Spirit's assurance that you will get this particular UK visit in before you graduated?" I did indeed. "So why would you listen to human threats and withdraw your application for fear of a denial when you were being God-honoring?"

Empowered by this challenge, I returned to the UK embassy, resubmitted an application, and took the risk of a denial that could equal a long-term blacklisting. I got the visa. A letter from Dad in Saudi that described his hopes for me to vacation, return to Nigeria, and graduate with top honors did the trick. It came up randomly, and the consul asked to read it if I had it on me. I did.

On meeting again with this man four years after that first encounter, he was gracious. He remembered me as a god-fearing girl and said so much to that effect. He told Akin that he was a lucky man to be married to me. Said he found the true virtue definition of a Christian in our interaction. He went all out to help.

"You say you have a current 5-year multiple visa into the UK and Akin has never travelled abroad and needs a visa but your passports are not here? We'll find a way around it, no worries." He went in to speak with someone, and they agreed to look me up in the system to prove the assertion.

"We've confirmed this," they came back to us about one hour later, "Now, the only way to get Akin a visa is for you to apply for a longer term visa, let's say ten years, even though your current visa has not expired yet. You guys need to do a spousal application for a longer period, and we'll approve that."

I opened my eyes in amazement. This wasn't supposed to be happening. This was miracle after miracle, on top of miracles, and I knew that God was front and center of the whole thing.

We applied and received approvals for UK visas without passports, with the promise to bring our passports once we received US visas. The British consul jokingly told Akin:

"So those Americans refused you visa time and again because your wife was there? Let's teach them a lesson. How about your first visa to the real Queen's land, be a multiple entry 10-year."

Just another miracle in a long line of miracles.

We travelled to Gbongan on Day 2 to bid farewell with the assurance of visas. We did a same day return, delighted to have seen Akin's mom dance around the public market place in gratitude for getting her son a chance to travel to the US.

The US embassy received employer confirmation late Day 2, and granted our visas on Day 3. With passports in hand, we returned to the UK embassy, where by now, always clothed in our romantic newlywed matching branded T-shirts, we had become a known and admired staple.

It had been quite the whirlwind three-day period. With just enough time to bid farewells, we treated Akin's office colleagues to a sumptuous celebratory late lunch. That same night, we were on a flight to the UK. Two days after that, we would be on a flight to the US.

I was a married woman, on the way to the land of dreams with my husband. Our lives seemed like heaven on earth stretched out in front of us.

I couldn't be happier. So I thought...

But I could not have predicted the heartache ahead.

CHAPTER 10

The Cake Is Crumbling

He was the perfect spouse, at least at the beginning. Sometimes, I wondered if he was too perfect, if he was masking a lot of nastiness under a perfectly shined exterior. He was quiet, extremely so, and he never really took control of conversations when we were with others. He didn't even contribute to discussions that much. At first, I loved this quiet side of him, this introspective, gentle spirit. He didn't come across as brash or boastful or full of himself, and I took his quietness as humility.

When we landed in the US, it was straight home to Uncle Lance's and his wife, Sister Temmy's. Uncle Lance was not technically my uncle; he was my dad's first cousin. But I had and have never considered him anything less than an uncle because he always had a positive presence in my life. A physical therapist, he had been in the US for as long as I can remember, and even though I had never met him before I came into the US for studies, we spoke on the phone from time to time, and he felt familiar, like family should.

I had stayed with his family when I first got into the US to study at UTA. They had been nice and welcoming and treated me like a daughter, a favorite daughter, I must add.

While in school, Uncle Lance never failed to call me every weekend, "Hey, do you want to come home?" He'd ask.

I only had to say yes, and he'd drive the one-hour distance to bring me home. And their home did feel like mine. I felt a part of the family. Over home-cooked meals lovingly made by sister Temmy, I felt cherished. Loved, wanted.

Two years after UTA, now married to Akin, this was the place we would also first call our home together in the US.

We had a little room to ourselves toward the back of the house, so we had some privacy that allowed us to explore our marriage. It was in that little room that Akin was entirely himself, and then perhaps, not so fully himself. But at least he opened up more there than he did in other places.

Seated in the living room, where there was the boisterousness and noise of everyday life, Akin seemed to recede into himself.

That worried me a bit, but perhaps not as much as his initial laid-back attitude to life. I was a dreamer, but I was a fighter as well, a go-getter who went full blast after dreams. While we had been separated by distance, he had seemed, sounded every bit as fired up as me, like he couldn't wait to take on the world, like he was practically straining at the bits to get to the US to begin his life.

In retrospect, I now realize that his US dreams had driven him exponentially that period in his life, and now that he had the dream in his hands, now that he had both feet on US soil, he didn't at first know what to do with himself, or how to fit in. In later months, as he got more and more familiar with his new world, he'd take on a more dominant role, a go-getting role.

At the moment, though, weeks and months after we got to Uncle Lance and Sister Temmy's home, he seemed a hollow shell of himself.

***

Akin was petrified of the English language as a subject. As brilliant as he was, this was a weak spot. Coming from an impoverished background, he had not had access to the best elementary schools and had had to make do with poorly funded public elementary schools where teachers were underpaid, overworked, and just didn't care.

His brilliance shone through his science subjects, mathematics, and every subject that required logic. He just did not have the same love for the English language. By the time he would enter the university, he had a good enough grasp of the language, could hold conversations in good English, could hold his own in an informal debate. What he didn't do well was to pass English language tests.

It was obvious that Akin needed to go back to school the same way I had done. It was the only way to a good-paying job because even though he had graduated with a first-class at the University of Ibadan, it didn't count for much in our new country.

We prayed and fasted about him getting into a graduate assistantship program rather than having to do a master's because there were only scholarships available at the PhD and graduate assistantship levels. We couldn't, I couldn't afford to pay the full tuition for a master's degree; out-of-state tuition for him was prohibitive, and a graduate assistantship would ensure that we could pay the in-state fees instead. This, I could afford.

The only problem was that he didn't do well in the reading and writing portion of the GRE. This wasn't unexpected, but it was a blow nonetheless. I had such high hopes for this man, and I knew without a doubt that we were on the right course.

The night the results came, Akin almost couldn't get out of bed for the grief that crippled him. My heart went out to him.

"English is not that big of a deal," I said, trying to console him. He was curled in the fetal position, and his eyes were closed, but I knew he wasn't sleeping.

An idea lit up in my brain, "We should write all your professors, tell them you can speak English quite well, fluently even."

He opened his eyes then, looked at me briefly, and then closed them right back.

I went on. "You didn't do so well in reading, no problem. But what if we can convince the professors that you speak great English, which you do by the way."

He unfurled himself and sat up slowly in bed, "And how do we do that?"

"We try. No harm in trying, right?"

And so we did.

I wrote so many letters that I eventually lost count, but I was fired up, couldn't wait to get my husband into the program he needed to be in, couldn't wait for him to start succeeding.

And then we got a letter of admission from the school that mistakenly omitted the conditions of admission upon a new GRE score in reading.

He was called into the office of the dean of the engineering school one sunny afternoon. The dean gave no indication of what he wanted to speak to Akin about, and I remember the trepidation and anxiety that filled the air. But the dean had good news, rather than bad.

"If you can get a professor to take you on as their research study, I'll waive the mistakenly omitted GRE as a need for a PhD." The dean was a tall, wiry man, and the chair he sat in seemed too small for him. "If you do find someone to take you on that way, it's fine by me. You can convert automatically from masters to PhD rather than having to redo the GRE. Otherwise, we would have to reprint your letter."

We floated out of the dean's office on cloud nine. Akin's spirit seemed to come up a little bit after that, and he got more into the spirit of things.

Our letter-writing adventures continued, this time with the intention of having one of the professors agree to take Akin on as a graduate assistant.

Eventually, one professor, a woman whose name I have now forgotten, wrote back, accepting to take on Akin, which itself was a miracle, something I had never heard of happening in that university before then. It was astounding, mind-blowing.

***

It was supposed to be a romantic getaway, a sort of celebration. But it was a disaster.

It was still within a year of Akin's arrival in the US, and we had not really had a cause to celebrate since he got there. We still lived with my uncle's family, and even though we had our own room, we were constrained. We were both private people and did not engage in PDA, so we had to limit any show of affection to the room that was ours.

To give ourselves the luxury of freedom and to celebrate Akin's acceptance into the graduate assistantship program, we took ourselves to a hotel for a romantic weekend. At least, it was supposed to be a romantic weekend.

It wasn't a luxury hotel, but it was close. Our first contact was friendly, and the food and drink were excellent. The room was beautiful, had a high-quality bath and gold plated door handles. And the bed was incredibly soft, seemed to contour our bodies and make us feel positively luxurious.

I was in bed the following day, waking up to a glorious sun that streamed in from the window blinds that Akin had drawn. I had lived in the US long enough that I no longer drew the blinds as soon as I woke in the mornings. But Akin still had this Nigerian characteristic about him, and it was one of the things about him that I enjoyed. I had almost forgotten what it meant to wake up to brilliant sun rays, and he was teaching me that all over again.

But this morning, I woke up to much more than the glorious sun. I also woke to Akin sitting in one of the plush armchairs closer to the bed, a knowing smile on his face. He had on a bathrobe, but I knew he was naked beneath it because he had a thing for going to bed fully unclothed. He had rearranged the TV station, brought it closer so that it was now only inches away from the bed. He had obviously been watching something, which was now paused.

"Hi, Sweetheart." He greeted, even as I propped myself up on my elbows and attempted to lift myself off the bed, "I thought I'd give us a little treat this morning, something to help us spice up our sex life."

I released my elbows and fell back into bed. Akin had a preoccupation with sex that unnerved me, but I had grown accustomed to making excuses for him. I had never been in a romantic relationship before him, and perhaps just didn't know better, didn't know how sexually driven men were. Perhaps this preoccupation with breasts and other sexual body parts was perfectly normal.

We had had sex the night before, and I didn't expect to wake up this morning to another session. I wanted to get back under the covers, go back to sleep.

Akin proceeded to press the play button for the paused DVD to continue to play.

The man and woman on the screen were fully unclothed, in the middle of a sexual act I had never seen before.

I immediately looked away from the unfolding scene, unintentionally embarrassed for the actors, until I realized this was a job to them; this was what they did for a living. By God, we were watching porn. Akin was making me watch porn!

I looked at my husband, and he had this look about him, sheepishness, an uncharacteristic smugness.

"Why are we doing this?" I asked, because I didn't know just what else to do. Akin was a sequence of surprises, and not all of them were good.

This was depravity being displayed in front of me, and I would not be a part of it. I had suspected for a while that he watched porn, that he was not the straight and narrow guy he professed to be. For weeks, I had observed him asking different things of me in bed than when we had just gotten married. At first, I chalked it up to him becoming more relaxed and permitting himself to be free with me.

And then, I found that he was also more critical. He wanted me in certain positions that by God didn't feel or look comfortable. He wanted me to do things I'd never even thought was possible for the human body to do. And each time I objected, he withdrew into himself, fell into a silence so deep the room we shared seemed to reverberate with it.

The porn he had put on for us to watch that Saturday morning at the hotel getaway shifted everything into perspective.

I had a husband who watched porn.

The dizziness took me as I sat up. I curled my feet under me, scrutinizing this man who was my husband, looking for traces of the firebrand spiritual husband I had married.

The smile had frozen on his face, and its place was now a smirk. The smirk was familiar; it was what replaced the nonchalance on his face anytime he felt that I was being too holy.

"We shouldn't be doing this. You shouldn't be doing this." I said in a small voice after the dizziness had passed.

"Says Folakemi, the Miss Goody-Two-Shoes." The smirk on his face was full-blown now, "For the umpteenth time, we are married. We can do with ourselves as we please. Porn, as you call it..." he made a quotation sign in the air to show that I was the one who called what he was doing pornography and not him, "is not wrong for us. Because we are married.

Get it! We are married and have the freedom to explore each other's body the way we like."

The air conditioner in the room was on, so it was by no means warm. I broke into a sweat nevertheless because I didn't recognize the man I was married to.

Was he mad? Had the whole world gone mad?

"You do realize that what's going on on that screen…" I still wouldn't look at it, even though the sounds of the screen filled the room, "…you do realize that's a sin, right?"

He smirked harder. "Are you saying sex is a sin?"

I whirled. My head was heavy. "Sex is not a sin. Watching two people grunting and humping each other on screen is a sin, Akin."

"Show me that from the Bible, seeing that you are the most spiritual person alive." He spat out.

He stood up then, walked to the TV screen, and clicked off the DVD player. His face was livid, his body physically shaking. I knew I was about to be treated to another of his long, silent treatments. But at that moment, I didn't care. I had married a stranger, it seemed, and I didn't know what to do with him, what to do with myself, what to do with us.

***

We left the hotel that day, a day earlier than we had planned to, but I just couldn't bear to be in the same physical space as Akin. He was furious, and I was also seething with a low burning anger. Besides my anger, I felt humiliated and kept on wondering how I had married a stranger. Because he was at that point nothing but a stranger.

***

He never brought porn front and center of our relationship again, but I knew it was there in our lives. He was secretive, even more secretive than he had always been. And now that he was out of the house more for school, he seemed to have a whole new life of his own.

His foibles became more glaring. I noticed that he was dismissive of ideas that weren't his. I noticed that he was short with me and lapsed into silence again and again as a punishment.

They say the first year of marriage is the hardest, so I chalked up our difficulties to that. Plus, our first year of marriage was anything but typical. We were not living in a home of our own. He had just transited from a country he had lived in all his life to a new one and was finding adjusting a little difficult.

That first year of marriage, I would remember again and again all the signs I should have been wary of when we were courting, but that I had excused. Was I making excuses for him now in the marriage as I had done then? Was I going to regret this later?

I knew he kept watching porn because he spent an excessive number of hours on his laptop when he was home, and his criticism of my sexual abilities never relented. I didn't know who to turn to, who to ask if what was happening in our marriage was perfectly normal. But somehow, intuitively, I knew it wasn't.

***

My friends assumed everything was perfect. What could ever go wrong in a marriage built on a perfect celebration of love where the lady was the giver? To their credit, they knew no different and I was lip-sealed.

Sade, my friend from the University, who had known Akin as well as I did when we were all members of the same fellowship, was the first to voice her concern and ask questions. "How are you making your lifestyles fit each other, Folakemi?"

She was one of the first people I told when Akin started to ask me for a relationship, long before I would say yes. She would only then be told of the victories and joys, and never of the challenges and surprises. After all, doesn't a wise woman build her home and not tattletale? Until too late.

Kate, a dear friend of mine, who has now passed on to glory, seemed to be more intuitive than others. We spoke on the phone every now and then, and I'd often respond "great" whenever she asked how Akin and I were faring as a new couple.

One day, she decided to scratch beneath the surface. "Hmmm," She sighed, "That man is not as innocent as you think, dear friend."

I remember my fingers curling tightly against the receiver at her words.

She went on, "He knows way more than you think he does, Folakemi; He is worldlier than you think. And I don't say this lightly. All these men who want to prove by all means that they are holier than thou, check their wardrobes. I bet they all have a thousand skeletons in there."

I felt compelled to jump to Akin's defense, because that was what wives did, that was what I was supposed to do for a man I loved, "Don't go there, Kate. I know this man, I know his heart. He loves God wholeheartedly, and he loves me as well."

Kate fell silent for a while, and then she came back. "I just want to be sure that you are safe. From experience, these kinds of men..."

I jumped in again, "Which kinds of men? First, Akin is not like other men. And who told you that men who love God must always have something to hide? That is not the case, especially with Akin. He is a good man, makes a great husband."

I imagined her shrugging at the other end of the line, but she came back with a quiet answer, "Check your heart, sweetheart. I know you are in this for the right reasons, but please make sure he is who he says he is."

I left that conversation feeling like the earth had been rolled up under me, like I was standing, suspended in the air, held up by nothing more than hope and faith.

I did ask myself some serious questions after that. Did Akin and I really love each other? Was he in this marriage for the right reasons? He had told me that God led him to me; had he been truthful, or had he beaten a path to me all by himself because of the better life I could offer him?

And his sexual depravity and lapsed silences? Were these things I could deal with, live with? Now that we had been married for months and were continually in the same space, did I still see the spirituality in him that had been the initial magnet? Was he still the same godly man I thought I had married?

I didn't have the answers.

CHAPTER 11

Sweetness Of Love In Procreation

We stumbled along in a marriage that shouldn't have been or shouldn't have been hurried.

We had barely lived together one year as husband and wife when we started to struggle with compatibility, and intents were becoming clearer. Marriage requires two committed individuals that love each other, not for what they can use the other to achieve, but for a purposeful partnership of love. And even then, it takes hard work. I tried to make it work because marriages were supposed to be forever. We were Christians; I was a Christian, and prayer solved everything, didn't it?

Outwardly, we were everyone's idea of a great couple. We looked the part. We talked the part. The whole world seemed to be stretched out ahead of us. But the ground underneath me felt like quicksand.

When he wasn't happy with me, which was often, he resorted to either of two responses. The first was to accuse me of wanting to lord it over him and not be a submissive wife.

These allegations hurt, almost always going straight to my heart where they would lodge and throb for days. Or he would lapse into silence. I witnessed the use of silence as a weapon. It was a weapon of dismissiveness and control, meant to belittle and demean and put you underneath the other person's feet.

I prayed, but Akin didn't seem to care as much as I did. An expert in dry fasting by this time, I seemed to be perpetually in fasting, food seeming to lose its appeal. And on a broken wing and hope, we limped along. Yet, these issues, as well as his ongoing addiction to porn bothered me no end. Sometimes I could forget it and put it behind me, but sometimes, it felt like the performers were in bed with us.

***

I wasn't the perfect wife, but I threw myself in, spirit, soul and body. Even though I didn't like how Akin acted and his nonchalance to a committed marriage, I still loved him. When he smiled his lopsided smile and made an effort, my heart still lurched inside of me.

And he wasn't all bad. There were flashes of brilliance and affection every now and then; when he cupped my chin in his hands and looked at me the way he had looked at me that star-filled night when he asked me to marry him, and I said yes, when he put his arms around my shoulders and crushed my weight against his. Despite being a very tall woman, Akin was even taller than me, although barely by an inch, and he made me feel safe when he had the mind to.

We took a trip to Austin to celebrate our second wedding anniversary. The night of the anniversary itself, we had dinner in bed, something that I enjoyed immensely. The salmon was tender and delicious, and the wine, even though nonalcoholic, tasted crisp and refreshing. Akin looked like his younger self. He also acted like his younger self; courteous, agreeable, like a young man in love.

During that trip, seeking God for the future, the Holy Spirit spoke to me. I heard Him clearly, felt the peace course through my heart as He spoke.

Returning home, one morning I curled up against my husband as we continued in love like we hadn't been in a long time before our trip. I rearranged myself on the bed so that I was no longer curled up against Akin but facing him because this needed to be said face to face.

"Guess what?"

"What?" He murmured sleepily.

"The Holy Spirit spoke to me during our Austin trip last week. We are going to be pregnant pretty soon and have a child before our next anniversary."

At my sentence, Akin's eyes popped wide open, the sleep instantly fleeing. I knew his stand on babies. He wanted them down the line, but not anytime soon. Time and time again, he'd say that he didn't want to be a student, husband and father all at once, not in a new country he was just getting to know, and not before he completed his degree, the most important thing to him.

"The Holy Spirit has not consulted me on that one." He murmured. It was halfway between a joke and not a joke.

"Want to talk about it?"

"Nah." He waved a dismissive hand and closed his eyes. Minutes later, he was asleep again.

In the quietness of the room, I weighed what I had heard. It wasn't the first time I would hear the Holy Spirit speak to me, so there was no mistaking His voice. But I wondered at the miracle of a baby.

***

A couple months later, in the midst of everyday life, I took a pregnancy test, confirming what I had felt for weeks. I was pregnant. I had missed my period, and my breasts were tender and swollen. Even without the physical evidence, I knew, just knew it in my heart.

I vacillated between exhilaration and worry. I knew I was going to be a good mom. I knew what to do and what not to. I knew I would love this child, gladly give my life up for him or her. I knew there wasn't an ocean I wouldn't cross for them. I knew all this, yet I worried about the concerns of everyday life.

Would I be able to differentiate between the cries of hunger and discomfort and pain? Would I be enough? Would I be able to hold on to patience while rocking a baby who perhaps had not slept for hours? Would Akin be the great dad he always promised he will be? Would he manage to sustain the newfound alignment and be supportive of my motherhood?

Akin was not exactly displeased at the news, but he wasn't hopping happy about it either. This wasn't his dream, and yet he had to live it.

Standing by the bathroom door as I dipped all five PT strips into the little cup, Akin seemed to want to be everywhere but there. And when all five strips came up with the same result – positive, my face ripened into a smile. Akin smiled a little bit, just for the flash of a second, and then his face rearranged itself into a stoic mask.

I called my sister in faraway London first. Her squeal of delight, the way she asked if I was okay, if I needed anything, brought peace and contentment flooding into my soul.

And then I called Yomi and got the same ecstatic response. I knew that it took a village to raise children and knew that I had my village. This baby and every other child that followed would be loved, cared for, and held in the palms of our hands as the most precious gifts ever.

The pregnancy seemed to change the dynamic of our relationship. Despite himself, Akin appeared to soften a little bit. He was helpful, took up quite a bit of the housework. He was attentive and made sure that I wasn't home alone at night. But even in this, he seemed distant, like he was not fully a part of the experience.

On a cold morning, I felt the first butterfly movement of the baby within me. That soft initial movement felt like a whisper travelling over my belly, and it brought me peace.

My pregnancy with Joy was easy, and she brought me more than peace.

I had missed out on a British citizenship when my parents returned to Nigeria for a little while (which turned out to be a long while). I had also missed out on US citizenship by the space of a few months, turning 21 just a few months after my father won the Green Card lottery that should have automatically conferred permanent residency, and later US citizenship on me and my younger brother, Sean.

A few months before I conceived Joy, I decided to give it a try again. I was in the US already and there was no legal process for someone who was already in the US on another kind of visa to apply for the Green Card lottery, at least not at that time. But I decided there was no harm trying. So I applied.

I was pregnant with Joy when I got the call. I was approved for the lottery, but there was the snag of me already being in the country. Could I go out of the country for one month, come back, and then claim the lottery? It sounded preposterous to me. Yes, the only approach to processing the lottery was to use the US embassy in my home country.

"Look at me. I am pregnant; I can't go out of the country, not even for a week. There has to be a way around this."

I was legal and had a migrant workers H1-B visa.

I began writing to the immigration service. I wrote the first, second, third and fourth letters. I am sure the case worker must have felt overwhelmed by the number of letters she got from me.

I kept on reiterating that I had a baby coming in June, that I couldn't go back to Nigeria and would take whatever help I could get. I ended every letter loading God's blessings on America, referring to it as "our" beloved home, creating a joint alliance with whoever read my letter.

I got home from work one day to a voice message on the landline. The case worker had finally responded. I can remember the message almost verbatim.

"Mrs. and Mr. Oladimeji. I've received all your letters and I just have a burden to help you. So, here's what we're going to have to do. No, you won't have to go back to Nigeria. Once your lottery number comes close to processing, we'll find a way around it. If need be, we'll find a tunnel through it."

It was a numbers game, as winning the lottery did not guarantee you got the visa. You had to wait for your assigned number to come up as they did in batches, and you only got a visa if there were still available visas at that time.

Here is how it worked: the US State Department allocated about 55,000 visas for the lottery yearly and drew a lottery from applicants. 55,000 winners are informed they won the lottery. However, one person who won the lottery became entitled to a visa not only for themselves but also for every member of their family they chose to put forward and who qualified. The visas still remained 55,000 to allocate out. This is where winners prayed to have an early lottery number, because the earlier your batch was processed, the greater the chances are that there were still visas available at your turn.

Me? I happened to have a late number. And we had to wait, because there was nothing else we could do. Or so I thought.

"It's tricky," the caseworker explained when I returned her call, "your number is probably going to come up around August, so we are going to wait until then. But in the meantime, here is what I'm going to do. I'm going to use the expatriate background check process to get you going, because otherwise, you have to go back to Nigeria for a medical background check."

She wasn't done, and every word she spoke seemed to lift the air out of my lungs. She said, "I will treat your application as an expatriate from Nigeria to the US. I will designate you as a diplomat! A diplomat-expatriate; this way, you can do all that needs to be done here."

I expressed a heartfelt message of gratitude and several minutes after the conversation, I remained rooted to the spot, in awe. I temporarily lost my voice. I went into the kitchen for a cup of water, and felt calmer.

***

Joy came into the world on a bright June morning, not too far from my estimated due date. Before she would make her grand entrance, I had been filled with the need to see this precious child, this special gift that the Holy Spirit had told me about beforehand.

My child came into the world close to thirty hours after my mother had first noticed the meconium on my clothing.

When they placed her into my arms, the whole world fell away. This was the only thing that mattered. The whole world and the galaxies and everything else in between did not matter in that moment. I felt love; unrivalled, undiluted, luxurious, lavish love filled my heart for this little baby that was all mine.

I would experience this kind of all-encompassing love ten years later when I had my second child, but for a first-time mom, the love I felt for that small child at that point was wholesome and overwhelming at the same time. I would lay down my life for her, but I would also kill for her, damn all the consequences. I would take a bullet for her, and I would also take up arms for her.

***

End of July or early August, the case worker called again and said, "Hey, your batch is up. Come over to my office."

I had a one month old baby who stubbornly refused to take formula. I breastfed her every couple of hours and had my sweet mom with me, but no babysitter. I took all of us to the case worker's office with me.

By the time she reached the one month mark, Joy had gained a full head of hair even though she hadn't been born with one. She had lost her newborn look, had started to gain the baby fat that made people ooh and ahh. She had perfectly round dimples that were made for kisses. She was adorable.

The case worker thought so as well.

"Beautiful baby. She is absolutely gorgeous."

My heart swelled. Every compliment that Joy got was mine as well and I loved it that people loved her.

The beautiful, absolutely gorgeous baby took that moment to begin crying. She squeezed her face together, lost that beautiful dimple and let out a startling yell. I had only fed her an hour ago, but this baby loved to eat.

"Do you mind, please? I have to breastfeed her. I can go out of the office, come back in when we are done." I didn't want to waste this woman's time but I also needed to feed my baby.

She waved a dismissive hand. "Go ahead. Feed her right here."

As I breastfed Joy, covering our actions and maintaining discretion with a large, breathable feeding shawl, the case worker was all business.

She slid some forms across to me. "Where is your husband, by the way? He should be here as well, signing his papers just like you are about to."

My heart sank to the bottom of my shoes. Akin had taken up an internship with IBM in another state and just couldn't attend the interview with us. Doing so would mean risking his internship, which was a big deal to him.

Snuggling Joy closer under the shawl as she began to nod off to sleep, I explained as best as I could that my husband couldn't make the interview.

"I don't know why, but I've just felt this irresistible urge to help you since I came across your file. Don't know why..." The woman, who had striking gray flecks in her eyes, shrugged, "but I'm gonna do my best to ensure that your family has a smooth ride getting your visas. That said, you sign your form. Then go ahead and sign your husband's..." she chuckled, "Today, you'll really be living the Bible, just go ahead and sign for him. What God has joined together, let no 'America' separate."

In absolute awe of a God who was an expert in doing the impossible, I signed both papers. I signed Akin's application forms for his green card approval, without the risk of being accused of impersonating. At least not by the US government!

And that was how we got our green cards, how we got our official immigration status in the United States. Down the line, we would use these to naturalize ourselves as US citizens.

CHAPTER 12

Marital Miracles

After Joy was born and we got our permanent residency miracle green cards, things seemed to change a little, at least for a little while. We seemed to smile a little more at each other. We went with Joy to the park some weekends. We had joined a church, and he went with us whenever he was in town, which was not as often as I'd like.

Sadly, it didn't take long for the conflicts to begin again, and this time, they continued unabated. Apart from his silence, the only way I'd know I erred was from being broadcasted outside to others. My confusion continued too. Weren't we both strong believers in Jesus Christ, both invested in the marriage till death did us part? Shouldn't we both be absolutely totally open and honest with each other and build a friendship that no outsider could crack? Even when we err, isn't forgiving what God expected?

It had been four years of dreams held together by a string of prayers, only that the lines were now frayed and couldn't hold things up anymore. The occasional flashes of love I felt for Akin were no longer there. They had been sufficiently eroded by the ceaseless lack of equal returns - what I now know to be emotional abusiveness – and had been replaced by a deep, deep resentment.

Akin was busy introducing himself to the US, getting familiar with towns and cities I had never even been to. He feigned a loss of his Nigerian accent when he was with the right people – those he wanted to impress - and I was often startled to hear my SU (spiritually legalistic) husband speak in the forcedly perfect (but highly imperfect) American English. His dress sense had also come a long way from the time we were students, when he only had one suit to speak of. He favored the colors blue and white and often looked dashing with either a white shirt or a blue one, worn under a crisp blazer.

He also seemed to have grown in heartlessness and cruelty.

We fought quite a bit. I wanted to make my marriage work, but I was not subservient the way that he expected me to be. I had a mind of my own and spoke it. Yes, my opinions were tempered with love and respect because I wanted our marriage to work. I wanted to hold onto Akin, to our little family, but some things don't just happen the way we want them to.

One morning, after an argument the night before, I woke up to closed windows and the choking smell of frying palm oil.

I couldn't draw a breath, no matter how much or how hard I tried. This pain in my chest had gone beyond tightness. I felt like there was a grappling hook tethered to my chest and being pulled for all that it was worth. I placed a hand on my chest to prove to myself that there wasn't a physical weight there. I couldn't breathe, and as I struggled to lift myself off the bed, the wheezing and the coughing took me.

They rocked me for several minutes. I sat there, coughing and spluttering, frantically searching for my inhaler, which was supposed to be on the bed stand, only that it wasn't. Two minutes later, now on my knees and hands, I found the inhaler on the floor, where it must have dropped in my agitated search.

It helped, but just a bit. The pain in my chest was still tight, and the wheezing wouldn't stop. Blindly, still spluttering, I found my way outside the bedroom, first into a cloudy hallway and then to the doorway.

It wasn't until I was out of the house and into the open air that the cough abated, that the world shifted back into place.

Turned out that Akin had decided to punish me by heating red oil in a house that he had deliberately chosen not to open the windows that way he usually did.

Palm oil is a lot different than other cooking oils, red instead of the more common light yellow color. In Nigeria, it is used to cook stews and soups and beans. To give it a lighter taste in stews, it is sometimes heated past its smoke point until it is pale and bleached. In the past, this was done for a commonly desirable taste. However, the process of bleaching also created a dense, smoky atmosphere that for an asthmatic, can be their worst nightmare. Even perfectly healthy people avoid the choking smell of palm oil bleaching.

To punish me for the argument of the previous night, Akin had decided to bleach oil in a closed-looped air system while I slept.

He was not remorseful, insisting that he hadn't done it intentionally, that he had simply been trying to get himself some food.

***

It wasn't the last time that would happen. Managing asthma with steroids from my doctor became routine, as did their associated weight gain.

I became dead-scared whenever we had a conflict and often did not sleep well. Sometimes awakened with the feeling of falling off the edge of a cliff and engulfed in panic. Lightning would lance across my heart until I realized that the air was clean, that I was not suffocating.

I knew Akin had no intention of killing me, but I also knew that asthma had killed many a careless soul, and living life on steroids was not my ideal. Making a choice to live in fear was not my purpose on earth either.

At another doctor's appointment, the remedy needed this time did not just include a prescription for steroids, but an emergency injection of Dexamethasone, followed by a breathing treatment in office, along with my lovely caring Dr. Clark's stern counsel to hereby desist from doing whatever it is that kept bringing me there.

At that point, I knew I had to take action. The house we lived in was mine and paid from my funds, but I didn't want to become a statistic of domestic abuse. I could not continue in the same space with my husband. I left the house with my child and got a hotel space for safety – mental, emotional and physical.

The next day, realizing that I left some important work documents behind, I went back home to retrieve them, only to find the locks changed, every single one of them.

"You don't have a right to come back, Folakemi. You left, so please stay gone." His voice was deep and gruff over the phone and chilled me to the bones.

"I... I..." I was uncharacteristically short of words. I just didn't know what to say or how to frame my words.

This is the same person who made me pay handymen for the simplest tasks, at the pretense that he was not "handy." Same person who took three weeks to change the house key when we suspected exposure by a contractor. And this same person had now changed the locks and keys within 24 hours?!

"You can't go and come as you please. Yes, this is America. I realize that, but you need to start acting like a respectable married woman. When you move out of my house, you move, never to return."

I swallowed back all the words I wanted to say and called his brother, who was in another country, pastoring. We were not the closest in-laws, but I liked him quite a bit because he had a level head on his shoulders and wasn't afraid to call out his brother when needed. He had also warned me about the spiritual voodoo in their household and shared at length what he personally experienced. He was quite shocked at what I narrated to him and promised to address it.

I don't know how the conversation between them went, but Akin called and gave me a copy of the new keys to the house.

I moved back home, Joy in tow. Joy went with me wherever I did. She was the one thing that I would never leave behind.

***

Fighting tires the soul out; I was fatigued. I sadly saw us becoming one of those pairs of parents who seemed to go at each other incessantly in front of their children. I bit my tongue when I could hold back. But Akin was often tight faced, and that could not be hidden from young eyes.

Marital problems can leave you shaken; make you feel alone, play mind games with one's sanity. Most of the time, I kept our problems to myself. But there were times I felt overwhelmed, felt like a truck sat on my chest, and I confided in a select few.

Yomi was one of such people. My sister was another. Sade, my university friend, was yet another.

After a particularly nasty quarrel, Sade's husband made plans to visit all the way from Nigeria to mediate, to sit us both down and shine the light on the love we both professed to have shared. He would have made it, but for a failed visa application.

Sade's mom would make several mediation calls. Akin was always calculated and rude, pretensed in engagement.

It didn't matter who was trying to meditate. Akin remained Akin and always did just what his stony heart told him to do.

***

Then I got a call from a dear friend in October 2005.

This was a friend I had had since my university days. Both she and her husband attended the University of Ibadan with Akin and me, and we kept in touch with this couple as we did many others. We were always delighted at the progress each were all making in our lives. Most of us were married, had kids, and were making giant strides professionally.

"Folakemi, I share one email address with my husband, and we received something that has made me very troubled. What I'm going to do is to give you the password to the account..." She hesitated and then went on, the line less staticky than it had been a few seconds ago, "I can't even begin to tell you the content of the email. I can't forward it to you. I just can't..."

She was referring to an email that Akin had sent to her and her husband, and many other acquaintances and friends we knew.

"Just tell me, please." I pleaded. It sounded very troubling. I wanted to know. "Read it to me." I tried to convince her, as my legs buckled under me.

"I can't..." She exhaled, "just read it yourself."

I took the details of the email account from her and logged in as quickly as I could. The email was a litany of how wrong I was as a wife, how terrible of a human being I was, and how promiscuous I had been.

I was described as a slut, a waster, a bad mother. Akin wrote that I slept around and had probably slept my way up the ladder at work, because no way was I intelligent enough to have advanced in such leaps and bounds over the years in a foreign land. He described how I wasted his hard-earned money on frivolous things. He asked if his readers could imagine that I was saving for Joy's college fund even though she was not even yet two years old, intending for her to attend a top school like MIT or Yale? He expected their shock at such wastefulness when local schools in the US were already better than in Nigeria. He lamented at how my dad had spoiled me and how intent I was on equally spoiling my children instead of letting him be their dad and treating them as his own parents had treated him. No one had sent him to a top school, and he had made it, was making it in life?

He described his terrible human being of a wife. One who nagged him constantly for no reason. One who didn't allow him to live his life. One who didn't support his PhD completion in a timely manner by taking all the load off him completely. One who wanted to be in control. Not respectful.

It had been a mistake to marry me!!! Each sentence of this email barbed my heart afresh.

I wasn't halfway through the email when I began to cry. A tremor came from my belly, cascading in both directions, until I was shaky in both my feet and in my hands. I abandoned the mail and went into the bathroom to be by myself. I wept silently, holding on to the wash hand basin for support. I got in the shower, the water washing over me as I shook violently.

I hurt. I felt humiliated. I felt at a loss for what to do. It seemed I had married a mirage. Akin was none of those things he had appeared to be in the past. Underneath the man I married was a thick layer of cruelty, lathered by a tyrant's tendency to betray a close relationship with no regrets.

I must have sat in that bathroom for upwards of an hour, trying to regain composure. I would dab my eyes dry and talk myself into no longer crying, and just as I would be about to open the door, the sobs would take me again.

My heart was broken, crushed, and then crushed again. There was a twist in the pits of my stomach that refused to unravel. I writhed in pain.

I did not want my daughter to see me so disheveled and found the will to stop crying. I reached deep down into my soul to dry my tears.

***

After then, I called Akin. His voice was gravelly and confrontational, like he already knew that this would not be a pleasant conversation.

"Why would you do this, Akin? Why?"

"Why would I do what?"

I was determined not to cry, and the anger that had overtaken me was now far more potent than the sadness that I felt.

"The email you sent....to everyone?" I spat out.

He hissed. "I wasn't lying. I meant every single word."

I hadn't expected him to deny it but was shocked that he would say to my face that he was not lying. Truly, I was married to a stranger. Who was this man I thought I knew?!

I choked back on a cry that was part rage, part animal instinct. "This is not a marriage, Akin. This is not how marriages work."

"We can't continue like this. I won't live with a man who treats me like this. I am done with this marriage. I won't live like this."

"File for a divorce then, if you won't live like this. If you must know, I am also done living with you. Done with all your rubbish."

I swallowed back my tears and fell onto the bed. Even with all the heartache that living with and being married to Akin entailed, I didn't want to get a divorce. Good girls didn't get divorced. I was a good Christian girl, from a good Christian home. None of my elder siblings had gone through a divorce. Even my parents were still together, still writing their love stories. How on earth would I begin to approach divorce?

"Are you serious, Akin? Are you for real?!" I said quietly, my hand holding the cell phone a little too tightly.

"As serious as a heart attack, Folakemi. Go ahead and file." By now, I didn't expect any romantic begging, yet, the disposability of my love was like a dagger, deeply stabbed.

***

I filed for divorce in November 2005.

The divorce papers in my hands felt like a white surrender flag. Like maybe there was just one more thing I could've done to save us. Some magic thing I'd missed.

I was also relieved, but relief was just the beginning of it. There was this juxtaposition of emotions. One minute the guilt would hit me. Who was I to separate Joy from her father? What right had I to offer her a fractured family instead of a full one?

I felt conflicted, heartbroken, and bitter. But I stuffed my feelings deep down into my chest and signed the divorce papers.

My hope, the hope that burned deep inside of me but that I wouldn't disclose to anyone, was that the divorce papers in Akin's hands would shock him back to life, would open his eyes to the fact that we could work, that our marriage would make it only if he put in the effort, if only he were willing to meet me halfway.

When the divorce papers got into Akin's hands, he simply up and left. He abandoned the house for me without as much as a backward glance.

And then, perhaps to prove he was boss, he counter filed against me for a divorce in another county.

Still, I held on to hope. These were our hard times. We were going to get through it; we were going to come out on the other end stronger and more tolerant of each other.

Then we got a court date and the day before we were to meet in court, I sensed God impressing on my heart to withdraw the divorce proceedings. I mentioned this to my lawyer, a loud and boisterous Nigerian-American who wouldn't have any of it.

"You'd be pure crazy to withdraw the petition. Your husband is a leech, an arrogant one at that. You don't want to continue living with him, kowtowing to him. He enjoys making your life a living hell, can't you see? How could you want to continue being his ATM for how horrible he treats you?"

I smiled a little smile. The lawyer was a classic case of someone taking up your fight and fighting even harder than you personally would.

The following day in court, I watched as Akin sauntered down the aisle. I hadn't seen him in weeks, and he looked a little different than he had when I saw him last. His confidence was brimming, his eyes casting baleful glances at me.

Still, I had to approach him, talk to him. Perhaps we could stop this train before it wrecked us both.

"Can I talk to you briefly, please?"

He looked me up and down, like he'd rather be doing anything than talk to me. He looked about to sweep by me and walk away when his lawyer loped a hand through his and stopped him midstride.

"Go talk to her already, Akin. Remember what I told you?"

Akin cut eyes at his lawyer who just spoke, but he stopped walking.

I didn't go into preambles and went right into the heart of the matter. "I want to withdraw the divorce. I don't want to go through with it. I believe this is what the Holy Spirit is asking me to do. To withdraw it."

The smirk that birthed on my husband's face was huge and fixated on me. He looked from me to his lawyer and then to my lawyer, who had come to stand by me.

"You want to do what?" He finally asked, his eyebrows almost forming a perfect convex.

I swallowed the huge lump in my throat. "I feel the Holy Spirit asking me to." At my words, my lawyer frowned; he didn't want me doing this. He was silently seething.

Akin's lawyer, on the other hand, suddenly birthed a huge smile. He nudged his client. "I told you. I told you I sensed your wife was a godly person. I told you I had a strong feeling that the devil was using you to destroy your marriage...Akin, you need to go back to her, find yourself a godly therapist that can kick your bottom and teach you godly husbanding."

Akin was belligerent and was having none of it. "She served me divorce papers!!! And so, I will give her the divorce she wants."

It was my lawyer's turn to nudge me. "This is crazy. You want to stay married to this man? This man?"

I stood there speechless. I don't want to in his current state, but I could do all things through God. I could trust God to fix this situation, although I knew not how.

Akin's lawyer flashed me a smile and held me by the arm. "He'll...we'll do as you say. Please go ahead and withdraw the divorce petition and we will withdraw ours too. I am most happy to let you know that my client has no problem with it.

CHAPTER 13

When Life Must Come From Death

December 2005 was the lowest and darkest point in my life. I felt a sense of possible solace in the unimaginable and imagined the peace and calm a life beyond could offer. It was for the briefest breath of time, but the prospect of leaving it all, ending it all, offered warmth and welcome. The thoughts formed rather quickly; I would take myself and Joy and drive both of us directly into the path of an oncoming truck. But God!

Even though both Akin and I had mutually withdrawn the divorce petitions against each other, he did not move back home. Neither did I want him with us. I was yielding to the Holy Spirit to give my marriage another go, but I didn't know where that would begin or how. There was too much hurt and heartache. Too much heart piercing to reconcile to healing. And all that with an unrelenting unrepentant collaborator in the matter. I was an outlier in my social circles. I did not have any other acquaintances that had been through a divorce, none even separated. I had to navigate this whole new chapter of life by myself, with no one, no precedents after whom to fashion my footsteps. I was in a foreign and uncharted territory.

But God brought support, although not from where I expected it. The support I wanted most at that point would have come from my parents and siblings. I wanted them to gather around me, to cocoon Joy and I with love, to assure us that we were loved, that it was all going to be okay, to encourage us and place no blame on me. But God had a different path. Family members did encourage us, but in their own imperfect humanity. I didn't get what I wanted. In retrospect, I realize I was asking a lot of them. Not unduly so, not unheard of, but a lot nonetheless because they themselves had struggled with the divorce. Just like me, my family had never known someone who was divorced. Just like me, they didn't know how to handle my situation. Just like me, they didn't know what to say or do to make it better.

So, they tried what was their best. What I knew unfailingly was that family prayed for us all the time. Sometimes, they said nothing. Sometimes they expressed their sadness. Sometimes they prayed with us. Sean called often and stuck with us as he could, his words often filled with grace and hope. So did my sister and brothers to their best ability. Yet, sometimes they heard things and wanted to validate them from me. Sometimes they said they wanted to stay neutral. That was painful. But they hoped for a marriage restored, hence neutrality made sense to them.

But not to me. I was flesh and blood. I deserved to be believed, even at the risk of them learning I was the liar. But I didn't get that. Sometimes, they did nothing. And sometimes, they flew all the way from the UK to Dallas to be with us and pray with us. Those times, those lonely times, every minutiae effort of their care meant a lot to us. It meant we were not alone in that dark, dark night of life. But their doubts and neutrality no doubt made it that much more the loneliest and darkest spot of my life.

We all know better now. And everyone has expressed their sincerest regrets and made up for that time in many ways. What's more important, they played their part, the part scripted from the foundations of the world, the parts that would let God do His perfecting of this saint. It was not the brothers of Joseph that sold him; it was purpose, God's purpose for his life. For his calling as deliverer.

I would come to realize that this was the same for my life.

***

We had experienced the first snowfall only the previous week, and by Christmas morning, the street was blanketed by a fluffy pillow of white snow. At two, Joy was growing up to understand that Christmas mornings were made for gifts. She'd been too little to understand it all the previous year, but this year, she'd picked up the Jingle Bells song that seemed to throb from every TV and radio station. She was excited about Christmas.

I wasn't.

It was the first Christmas I would spend alone, without a husband.

I was still in bed when Joy toddled into my room on Christmas morning. It was already 8 am, and dawn had since broken, but I had no energy to get out of bed. I was physically, mentally, emotionally drained.

"Christmas, Mommy?" Joy cooed to me, her voice still thick with sleep.

We lay together in bed for half an hour or more, mother and daughter. I listened to my daughter's soft snores as she fell asleep again. And then I tiptoed to the window. I stopped myself just in time from throwing back the curtains the way that Akin did, and peered into a white world through a half-drawn curtain instead.

I knew Joy would be excited to see the snow. That she would be excited at the parcels waiting for her under the Christmas tree.

I also knew she was going to ask after her dad.

***

We ate at a diner because I didn't feel like cooking. The restaurant was more deserted than usual because hey, it was Christmas and people were celebrating in their homes.

It was about two o'clock in the afternoon. I felt alone and lonely. An irrational part of me wanted my old life back even though that life had hardly been idyllic. But it was the familiar. It was unhealthy, but by God, it was familiar.

As I drove us home with the tires wet and slick and the car fishtailing every now and then. The tears took me over.

That's when the envy took me over. An envy for the dead relieved of such pain as I suffered. And then, it occurred to me that I had the choice to be them. It would be calm, it would be peaceful, what a joy to never feel this pain again. Just to be gone. To be dead.

At the intersection to the freeway, an 18-Wheeler rumbled by us, sending a blast of icy cold air our way. I wondered what it felt like when drivers collided with the heavy truck.

Would it crush us instantly? Would life on the other side be easier than this one?

Five minutes later, I was shaking so badly that I had to stop the car on the shoulder of the road to catch my breath. Of course, I didn't want to die. I couldn't deliberately take my daughter's life. And I couldn't take myself out of this world because I needed to raise her. I needed to fill her up, all the way to the brim, with all the love that God had placed in my heart for her.

Life was hard, yes. It was tough, crippling, and there seemed no way forward. But it was still life. It was to be lived, not thrown away. Its battles were to be fought and won with hope, not hopelessness.

As I shook, as the tears coalesced on my frozen face, I held on to the hem of Jesus' garment for the first time that day, that month perhaps.

"Help me through this, Jesus." I cried. "Help me through this because I can't do it on my own."

That holiday period was a long one, but we survived it.

Jesus sent help. It was in the person of my brother-in-law, Dr. Kayode. The same one used originally to guarantee the financial support that I needed to obtain a US student's visa.

My sister had called him, her brother-in-law, in helplessness when she knew about the thoughts of hopelessness that had overshadowed me. And he called me. It was on a Sunday. All he said was "*jo, aburo, mo fi Olorun oba be e, jo tori Olorun, maje ka foju sunkun e*" and over and over again, he repeated "*jo, mo bee, ma je ka sunkun e,*" meaning, "I beg you in God's name, please don't place us in grief of you."

Somehow his words penetrated the heavy shadows of this present darkness.

***

A year later, petition withdrawn, still married to me but living separately while trying to figure things out, Akin traveled to Nigeria and remarried.

Yes, this was polygamy, and he knew this was prosecutable under US law, but he did it anyway.

I learned about his remarriage from one of his brothers, who felt compelled to tell me. I was at work when the news came to me, and the same way I'd felt when I learned of the evil letter Akin had circulated about me, my legs started to shake.

I'd known for a while now that there would be no future with Akin, that our paths had crossed solely for me to birth Joy. Yet, it hurt. The dissolution of a marriage, no matter how brief the marriage was, is never pleasant.

"What do you want me to do with this news?" I asked shakily.

His brother paused. I knew he was hurt by his brother's actions. I was also aware that this was still his brother and that he loved him nevertheless. He sighed. "I don't know, Folakemi. I can't tell you what to do. I only felt it was right to tell you, to not have you find out from elsewhere."

***

It was a Friday evening in March, and winter was gradually giving way to spring. As I made my way down the sidewalk, I saw the first splash of color after a grey winter. The milder weather had brought out a host of golden daffodils, and they were fluttering and dancing in the evening breeze.

Despite the allergens it brought with it, I had grown to love spring. I loved that everything was new again. I loved the freshness in the air and the fact that the long winter had passed. The butterflies would soon be here, and I loved butterflies as well.

As winter rolled up its carpet and spring unfurled its, my heart lightened. Easter was also around the corner, and I loved the newness that Easter also signified. Dead and resurrected with Jesus. The impossible becoming possible. Life anew.

It felt like a new chapter for us, for Joy and me. Life started to become rote. I could do this. I could make this work. God had us.

Then came summer, fall, winter, spring, and repeat. We had it all down and were living. We were functional. Perhaps not thriving as best as we could, but functional nonetheless.

I had gone to the corner store to pick up a gallon of milk, a quick trip and a great excuse to be out in the mild weather.

I was rounding the corner to the house when I saw the gentleman waiting on the porch. He was not in uniform, and there was nothing the least officious about him, but somehow I knew.

Somehow, I knew. And I was right.

Akin had filed for divorce, and this was the bearer of the news. Crippling news, but yet, this was indeed the deliverer. I managed a smile as I signed the document he had for me to show that I had received the petition. His returned smile was small and sickly. Even he apparently did not relish this job.

In the foyer, I ripped apart the envelope and read the grounds on which Akin wanted a divorce. There were accusations and allegations. There were all sorts of things, but the only thing that was missing was the fact that he had gone ahead to remarry even before filing.

***

We began a mediation process. I was too tired, too emotionally drained to go to court to battle. And I didn't want that experience for Joy. By this time, I wanted the marriage gone and done, but I wanted to ensure that I got custody of Joy. I would lay down my life for my child, and I wasn't about to let him have her. Not after her returns from weekend trips oftentimes unkempt and uncared for, sharing his hostel-home with other men unknown. Not after she reported their hotel trips with an "aunty" unknown, with whom "Daddy slept in a room and I slept alone in another."

The easiest way perhaps to ensure that I had primary custody would be to disclose his new marital status, to let them know that he had gone ahead to get himself hitched while still married to me. That could be a sure way for him to lose custody. But what all else would be lost…what about his citizenship? What about jail time?

As much as I disliked Akin by that point, I loved my daughter even more. I wanted her to have her father there in the US. For her sake, I didn't want him going to jail. I didn't want to be married to Akin anymore, but I didn't want to take his daughter completely away from him. I would have primary custody of her, but that didn't mean she didn't need her father.

So I kept quiet about his new marital status. I had to bite my tongue many times when I so desperately wanted to hold the trump card. But bite my tongue I did, for the love of Joy.

Akin wanted half of my assets. Half of the house, half of my retirement funds, of my savings. He wanted it all. And the truth is, he had a right to all these things, even if only by law. Morally unjust. I knew that, but the knowledge didn't make it hurt any less. This was a man I'd single-handedly brought to the US, a man whose poverty I had worked to help get rid of, a man who owed me his green card, and he was going after my assets. Not shared assets, but those assets for which I alone sweated while he parasited on me.

***

A miracle happened along the way. One that would come in useful at the mediation session.

"Your retirement fund." I heard that quiet, still voice, and I just knew.

While attending the annual event of a large church in the area that I often visited, they had asked for donations to build a new campsite, and I had felt the strong urge, that pull to be part of that work. But I had shrugged off that urge, had chalked it up to the pastor's persuasiveness and charm.

That same urge came over me now, only that it was now expressly linked to my retirement fund. It suddenly occurred to me. I couldn't hide assets from Akin, but no one said I couldn't gift some of those assets before we got to the mediation table.

I got the process started. And a couple of days later, I wrote a check for $20,000, every single penny of that retirement fund.

Funny enough, my retirement fund was one of the assets Akin was staking a claim to. Only that it was now no longer mine. I didn't have it and couldn't share it. When he presented the claim at mediation, I felt victorious with a chuckle. No hesitation, this $20,000 was one of the most satisfying donations I ever made. Even the mediator, a tall lanky gentle man, had a chuckle escaping his lips. He was unbiased in all matters but was not fooled. At one point he asked Akin mildly, what he expected to leave for me for all my own sweat, if anything.

And even more miraculous, what a wondrous God we serve. Years later, I would get a call from my ex-employer, the one that had funded that 401k account. That organization had gone through many changes, and restructuring. As they reviewed records, they were reaching out to pay off creditors and go after debtors.

And there was my name in their books as a creditor. One owed an original 401(k) amount of $20,000, which according to them, had about doubled itself in the interim. Unclaimed and unpaid. I was in disbelief.

I sent in paperwork to show that I had cashed in my money, but the woman I spoke to, the one who received my documents, insisted that I was still owed what was now around $40,000 due to investments' yield. No explanation would persuade her otherwise. The only alternative was to yield the money to the government or to take it in my name and assign it to another retirement purse.

Gladly, the latter I did.

***

Akin was so focused on what he could grab from the mediation table that he neglected what truly mattered; Joy. He did not pay attention, or perhaps it was intentional. Whatever the case was, he didn't quite realize where we were going to land with Joy until everything was done.

And so I had what I wanted. I had custody of Joy. She would live with me. I would have responsibility for her. I would make the major decisions about her upbringing, her education, her health. The future looked hopeful. We would take on the world, the two of us.

***

And so, the divorce was finalized. Divorce was something I never imagined would be in my history. But looking back now, I can say that divorce softened me, tore off my hard edges, and gave me compassion instead of scorn for others. The fires of my own divorce forged the empathy in me that I would need to fulfill my life's purpose.

Before Akin, before my world crashed, I carried a holier-than-thou attitude. I had been raised by Christians, had gone to church all my life, and had had a personal encounter with the Lord Jesus Christ. I had a clean life that by superficial accounts, had none of the sticky residue of sin.

Before the divorce, I tended to look down at people who were "sinful," those single moms and single dads should have done better and saved their marriage. I unwittingly judged every person whose life did not follow the straight trajectory I thought holiness brought. I did not mean to be mean nor unkind. I never talked down to others. I didn't thumb my nose at them. But at the back of my mind was always this feeling that these people were not living their best lives; they were not living life the way that God intended and it had to be their fault.

Divorce created space in my heart that recognized fallibility like never before. That a human can do all things at their best yet come out with seemingly failed outcomes. One could line up life according to God's precepts, do all you could to please Him, and still have your life fall apart.

Divorce taught me empathy and birthed in me compassion.

***

Dallas held too many haunting memories, and my heart seemed to seize in my chest when I passed landmarks that held some sort of meaning for my life with Akin. I wanted to leave. I prayed to God for a sign, for a prompt. And I got it.

I got a new job in Minneapolis. And it was as far from Dallas as anywhere else in the world at that point. It would be a new start, a clean slate, a chance to begin again.

Because it was never my intention to keep Joy away from her dad, I had carried Akin along throughout the interview process. I wanted him to know that there was the possibility of us moving away, and I didn't want the news to come as a shock to him.

The night before we would fly to Minneapolis, Akin came visiting with one of the agreements we had signed at the mediation table. He was all nice and everything, but when he handed over the agreement, I just knew that something was wrong.

There, in plain English, were words that had not been in the original agreement. Words added by him retroactively. He wrote in there that I had agreed not to leave the state of Texas while Joy was a minor.

The floor reeled underneath me. The one thing I had gone to bat for during the divorce proceedings was Joy. How on earth would I have signed an agreement that would not allow me to take her wherever I would relocate to?

Akin, who had been taking our mediation agreements to court to get them finalized, had apparently forged this new clause and carefully inserted it into the agreement and got it signed as final by the judge.

I lost my voice for a second, but I found it soon enough, only that it was hoarse and broken, "Oh, my God, the judge has signed it. This is not what we agreed to. This is forgery."

And my ex-husband just shrugged, left the agreement with me, and walked away.

CHAPTER 14

The Flames Shall
Not Consume You

For several minutes, I couldn't stop shaking. The tremors took me, beginning from the inside out, so violently my teeth started chattering. Joy was asleep on the sofa, her little body curled in the fetal position. Her hands were pillowed underneath her head, her hair tousled this way and that. She looked so innocent, so beautiful. She didn't deserve the trauma that a broken family would lay out for her. I prayed, and hoped that I would be God-equipped to help mitigate the effect of a bitter divorce on her.

I sat at the dining chair, still shaking, unsure of what to do. Gradually, my shaking subsided, and sanity began to return.

I called my prayer partner. "I don't know what to do. Akin just brought me an agreement I never signed, that I would never leave Texas. I never signed such a thing...that was never included in what we discussed and signed...He is very much aware of my imminent move to Minnesota. I didn't hide it from him..." The tremors had returned. It seemed the phone would slide out of my hands, but I managed to hold on to it.

"Shh, calm down, Folakemi, calm down." She shushed me.

I started to talk again, but she reminded me to keep calm, to take a deep breath. I took that deep breath, and the tremors subsided again.

"Tomorrow morning, go to court."

"Court?"

"Obviously, you can't fly out to Minneapolis without resolving this issue. You know you can't. What the Holy Spirit is telling me is that you go to court tomorrow morning. Tell them what has happened."

That night, I could only fall asleep to soft Christian music because I was otherwise too agitated to sleep on my own. Even then, I woke several times before dawn broke, my heart pit a pattering. Each time I awoke, I'd check in on Joy. Her sleeping form comforted me, grounded me.

***

It would be my first of such an encounter with the legal system in the US. As we raced towards divorce, all court proceedings had been handled by Akin. It was he who filed for the divorce, and because I still trusted him at that point to at least do what was right for his daughter, I had allowed him to handle things. Obviously, he had used the system fraudulently to his advantage.

I repeated myself to the law clerk because he had asked me to repeat what I said, "I never signed this…" I placed the agreement in question on his table. My mouth was dry.

He seemed very distracted because he asked me to repeat myself, and I went through the whole story again. He seemed to get it then and picked up the agreement, going over it line by line. "There is no problem, ma'am. All you have to do is recall this agreement. There is a process for the recall, and I will take you through it."

For the first time in twelve hours, I sighed in relief. I didn't know there was a process to recall such agreements, and the fact that I didn't have to be, wouldn't be stuck in Dallas against my will, was a huge weight lifted off my shoulders.

***

We went to Minneapolis as planned. God had shown up on time, and the court had scheduled a hearing to rectify the agreement. I would have to come back to Dallas on the day of the hearing, but this was a price I was more than willing to pay.

When the day of the hearing came around, I was in court, but Akin wasn't. Obviously, he knew he had falsified my agreement and that there would be repercussions to admitting to that in court. So, he never did show up, and the agreement was torn up.

I was free to take Joy every and anywhere I moved. I had primary custody.

On the plane back to Minneapolis, which was now home, I couldn't help but sing songs of praises underneath my breath. He was God, and there was nothing impossible for Him to do. He was my God, and He was Joy's as well. He would move mountains to keep us in His will.

***

That was just one of many victories won in battles fought.

My new company had contracted a professional moving company for the move. They would pack up the house in Dallas and handle everything for our personal effects to arrive safely in the Minneapolis suburb choice of home.

My parents still didn't understand what it felt like to be me, to be in my circumstances, but they were making an effort. They had come up from Manchester, UK, to help us with the move. It was an emotionally taxing period indeed.

So I was there along with my parents with the movers in the midst of their packing the entire house. It was emotionally wrenching each time a memento was packed up and placed into a Styrofoam-filled moving box. I had to step out several times to catch wind.

Finally, we left the packers to their job and took refuge in a hotel. My mom had been quiet throughout the whole process; Dad too. But it was a comforting kind of quiet. Their presence steadied me, grounded me, made me less jittery than I would have been.

Yes, they still didn't get how this all felt for me. Yes, they were focused on the shame it brought on them. But there was a comfort they brought with them that felt lost as they returned to Manchester just the day before the rest of us would leave for Minnesota.

We went back to the hotel: I, Joy, and an aunt who had also come along.

It was around 2 am, and my parents were still in transit to Manchester when we arrived at the hotel. I was exhausted in every way.

"Can we sleep in the same room? It's going to be morning before we know it. And we'll be catching a flight early morning, so we are basically just napping, right?"

And so all three of us slept in the same hotel room.

**

Around 4 am that morning, the strangest thing happened. Joy got up to go to the bathroom. I was in a groggy state between sleep and wakefulness. I was aware, yet unaware, awake yet unawake. The bathroom was en suite, directly opposite the king-sized bed, and I kept waiting for Joy to return to bed, to curl her body into mine the way she did when we slept in the same bed.

I fell asleep.

And awoke to a knock on the hotel room.

My heart bunched crazily in my chest for an unexplainable reason. It was 4 am for heaven's sake. And no one knocked on hotel doors randomly. I tumbled out of bed, and instead of heading to the door, I ran to the bathroom to check on Joy.

She wasn't there.

Panic set in, and for a wild moment, my vision blurred, and I couldn't see anything.

"Mom...Mommee...Open the door." It was Joy's voice, and she was the one knocking on the other side of the door.

My vision cleared, and I ran to the door. It was exactly the way it had been when we got into bed. Dead bolted and reinforced with a steel bar. There was no way on earth Joy was able to open that. And there was definitely no explanation for how she was on the other side of the door that was still bolted and reinforced. How did she disappear from the room?

My palms and hands were sweaty as I threw the door open, my breath coming in heaves, my chest rising and falling with the exertion.

But there she was. My Joy was outside of the door, still clad in her pajamas, still tousle-headed from sleep.

My senses left me, "How on earth? Where did you go? What happened? How did this happen? The door is still locked."

She didn't understand me and just stared at me with her big brown eyes.

"Aunty...Aunty!!!" I shook my aunty awake.

After I had told her what had happened, we sat in bewildered silence for the longest time. And then I stood and made a mug of hot cocoa for Joy. In a small but confident voice, she started to talk.

She had gone to the bathroom, and the next thing was that she found herself in the parking lot. Everywhere she looked, there were cars but no people. Scared, she'd started to walk in the direction of the hotel lobby. And then two people came to her wearing white and carrying with them a cordless phone.

She said that somehow, she had not been afraid of them and had felt comforted by their presence.

"Here," one of them had said, handing her the cordless phone, "Dial room 419. We'll take care of you, you're safe." We were lodged in room 419, and she'd taken the phone and dialed our room number. And she was transported yet again, this time not into the bathroom, but right outside our room door. That was when she knocked.

I was flabbergasted and thought I was going mad. But I couldn't be. All three of us couldn't be hallucinating simultaneously. If I was crazy, was Joy crazy too? And my aunt too?

I called my pastor and retold the unbelievable story. He was as flabbergasted as we were, but he assured me that I wasn't crazy. "God did a miracle here, Folakemi. God did something here."

I called my parents after that. They were still en route, perhaps still mid-flight, so I dropped them a message. "When you get home, you better be praising God that you didn't get home to evil news. Just call me."

So, we didn't sleep again. For the rest of the morning, we heard knocks at the door. The first time I went to check, there was no one there. The second time, I sent my aunt to check, and still, there was no one there.

At five am, my parents called. They had gotten in and gone straight for messages. Mom couldn't believe her ears.

"That's not possible, Folakemi..." She was still in the middle of that sentence when another knock went off at the door, this time louder and more insistent than the ones before. The sound carried loud and clear, and Mom could hear it on the other side of the world.

"Did you hear that?" I asked her, my voice an octave lower.

When Mom's voice came to me, it was low and quivery. "Jesus!" She exclaimed. "Go check the door. Don't go alone. Go with Ope." Ope was my aunt's name.

"We've checked several times already, Mom." But I obliged her, and we went to the door, my aunt and I, opened it, looked up and down both ways of the long hotel hallway. Like the other times, no one was there.

We had to let Mom get off the line because her eyes were practically closing with fatigue. She didn't want to go to bed, afraid that something would happen to me, to us. But she was so incoherent with sleep that she finally succumbed to the pressure to go to bed.

"Only for an hour or two." She finally agreed.

Ope and I continued our vigil. Joy went back to bed and was asleep not quite long after.

***

Later, The Holy Spirit would reveal more.

I learned about one of Akin's girlfriends who had a double-syllabic name. He'd met her in a church program and had begun an affair with her while we were married. I wasn't supposed to know about her, but the church she attended happened to be the same one a close friend also attended.

This double-syllabic-named girl had run her mouth about me, how controlling I was and how she would take my husband off my hands. You know what the Bible says about evildoers even in His house. This was a worker, an usher for that matter, and she was talking about taking my husband off of my hands.

By the time I heard of it, the marriage to Akin was already damaged. But I filed the information under a mental information file.

As the divorce was culminating and I was preparing for a new life in Minnesota, I'd also been told of another comment the double-syllabic named woman made.

"They said Folakemi is leaving town. But you see, she's not going anywhere. You'll see."

So that strange morning when my child was spiritually kidnapped, I knew the devil and his cohorts were doing all they could to cause an interrupt.

"But the Lord has seen to it that you will get to Minneapolis. And that you will be happy there." Thank you, sweet Holy Spirit.

***

Indeed, we were happy in Minneapolis, just as the Holy Spirit had foretold. We had breakfast together in the mornings, and dinner together at night. I worked when Joy was at school, and even though I sometimes had to work at home in the evenings, Joy was my priority.

She loved drawing, not the squiggly wiggly kind of drawing other first graders did. Instead, she favored straight, mechanical drawings. She drew engines and computer parts and robots. And boy, did she do a good job. She also had a profoundly analytical mind, and we often laid together, side by side, discussing things that would normally seem too complex for a child so young to grasp. But she caught and held them.

We talked about her fast-tracked education. We spoke about my work. We spoke about life lessons, about mistakes and love and redemption and hope and all the things that made humans, humans.

And I got to rediscover myself. I had gotten married a little younger than most of my mates, and for the longest time, I had been nothing but one half of a couple. I didn't know my own tastes because I had automatically gravitated towards liking whatever it was that Akin liked.

I suddenly realized that I wasn't really a fan of dark-colored blazers and had only worn them because Akin said they made me look good. I realized that I didn't really like chocolates and preferred peanuts. I realized that I was more of an early sleeper and that watching late-night movies wasn't really my thing.

I got to like and then love the new me I was meeting. Once again, I enjoyed my own company, often retiring to softly playing Christian music as I fell asleep.

✸✸✸

Akin was supposed to have Joy once a month, but he never came or sent for her. All he had to do was pay a paltry $150 ticket to have Joy put on the plane to him, but he never seemed to be able to come up with the money. The funny thing was that he was earning six figures by then and could easily afford a ticket worth 10 times more. I guess he didn't see this as a priority.

He wrote to Joy when she was six, and although I knew she received a letter, I was unaware that such a letter lit a fire, until she started to act it out. She was silent and sullen, which she usually wasn't. She slammed doors. And she crossed her arms in front of her chest at every turn.

"Sit beside me, will you." I finally asked her.

And her tears started to flow. "Why do you want to send me to Dallas to spend two months with Akin? Two whole months, Mom?" She often called him Akin instead of Dad.

I didn't know what on earth she was talking about and had to tell her to slow down. "Calm down and start all over, please."

She stood and went to retrieve the letter she'd picked from the mailbox. It was from her dad, and he'd said that I had agreed with him to send Joy to him for the summer.

"You could have told me, Mom." Now, she was crying with the whole of herself. As I stroked her head while she tried to regain her calm, I pondered this. I had never discussed such a thing with Akin. This was a child he hadn't been to Minnesota to see once or allowed to come to him the way she was supposed to, and now he wanted her for the whole summer. He had an entitlement to have her visit one weekend every month and the summer. And he picked the summer more than a year after last seeing her?

What's more, we had never had the discussion that he claimed we had.

I went to the Minnesota courts. He was subpoenaed and had to fly in for our court appearance. I hated this court back and forth, but I would fight for Joy's safety with my last breath. This man was a risk.

***

"She stole my child away." His voice was loud and insistent in court. "And she should be sending her to me every month, but she is so cheap she doesn't want to pay. She is a terrible person, a shitty mother. Your honor, she is doing all she can to keep my child away from me."

The judge was a lovely, bespectacled mature Caucasian woman. She had a kind and placid face, but her eyebrows rose at Akin's words. When she came back, it was with a quiet question. "How many times have you seen your child in the last few years?"

The cat got Akin's tongue, and he couldn't speak.

The judge shook her head in what seemed like contempt. "Okay, I will believe everything you've said about Folakemi. She's an evil woman. She's the worst human being. She stole the child away. But you have a legal paper that says you're entitled to get this child once a month, and you decided that it was too expensive to fly down. I totally get it."

She continued, "You are perfectly right and are entitled to your opinion about your ex-wife. But based on the fact that you've not seen that child in years, my ruling is that you're not allowed to have any interaction with her until you undergo reunification therapy. Meaning you both go to a counselor. You'll meet together with the counselor, do whatever the counselor tells you. And over time, when the counselor says that your child is safe alone with you, you'll get back your visitation rights. Until then, such rights remain suspended."

✱✱✱

He attended the reunification therapy with Joy just twice, and then he stopped coming.

"I am so busy," He'd say, " It's been a crazy couple of weeks at the PhD lab."

Three months later, I got an email from the counselor that said, "Do you know where Akin is? I'm not hearing from him; I mean, he's not responding."

I told him I didn't know where he was, and that was the truth.

He didn't call her every Saturday as he was supposed to do within the reunification regimen. And when she called him, he sounded far and distant when he was available to talk to her, which was few and far between. He always hurried off the phone.

For a while, I made her call him every week. At first, she was excited to do so, but I could see the weariness overwhelm her after a while. She'd come back from the phone and say, "Mommy, it looks like I'm disturbing Akin."

I ached for my daughter, and it broke my heart that she wouldn't have a great relationship with her dad. I had never planned for her not to.

And so, Akin faded from our lives, missed call after missed call, missed visit after missed visit, but life went on happily so.

CHAPTER 15

Purposeful Pharmacist, Bread Seller, Care Model Harmonizer

What began with the pharmacy shop grew.

One hot afternoon, the sweat dripping from my brows because the electricity was out and the fans had stopped rolling, I swiveled in the chair that I had somewhat claimed as my own in my parents' shop. It was actually Dad's shop, but Mom was there more than he was, and I thought of it as theirs, not his.

I had worked in the retail pharmacy store since turning 14. I was fascinated by drugs and how they worked. Drugs is how medications were referenced in the Queen's English. Beyond the drugs, I was fascinated by the way money worked, by the way business unfolded. I loved being in the store when the new consignments came in, when we determined how much the new stocks would be sold for. I especially loved sticking the price label on the bottles and capsules.

I was barely 16 when I became supervisory authority for the salespersons and pharmaceutical contracts. The first time I wrote the checks for the suppliers, I felt on top of the world, like the world was an oyster and I, a pearl. A kind of joy filled me from the insides, a kind of exhilaration.

There was a lot said and done and achieved in that little store, and I have forgotten half the things I did, but an occurrence stands out, stays in a place of prominence in my heart.

It was that hot summer afternoon. I had finished secondary school, was waiting on my admission to the university, and had begun to spend my whole days at the store.

I wasn't a doctor, was in no way interested in medicine as a profession, was a future engineer, but at that moment, all of 16 years, with the expectation of the interrogating patient weighing on my shoulders, I wiped the sweat from my face.

"You just finished secondary school, you say?" He was a repeat customer, someone who was very familiar with Dad and now a little bit more familiar with me.

I nodded and stood from my chair because I liked being on the same eye level as the people I had conversations with.

Professor Agbaje shook his graying head and adjusted his bifocals. He had been coming into the shop for years now, to fill his prescriptions for hypertension and diabetes, two conditions he attributed to the stress in his professional life. He was a professor at the University of Ibadan, a widower with grown children, and he often lingered at the store for longer than he needed to. I knew he was lonely and lived a somewhat solitary personal life.

"And you are now responsible for this team of four pharmacy techs?"

I nodded again. "Yes, sir."

"And they tell me you even negotiate the supply chain and drug prices in your parents' absence with drug manufacturers like Roche?"

A flush of pride came to me. I indeed negotiated drug prices, and I absolutely loved it. A typically quiet and introverted person, there was no sign of that when I was negotiating, or when I set a pharm tech right, or when I did anything for the store in the capacity of a manager.

Prof came closer to the counter, a smile tugging at the sides of his lips. When he got closer, I realized that he wasn't quite as tall as I had imagined him to be. He must have been tall once in his life and had the mannerisms of someone who was used to ducking to clear entryways. But he had lost height with old age the way most elderly people did.

"How do you know what to prescribe for patients' complaints? Pray, tell."

I was up for the challenge; He wasn't the first to ask me how I knew what to do. The thing was, pharmacy techs were expected to know a little bit about everything, to be able to diagnose simple conditions based on the patient's complaints and prescribe drugs appropriately. Unfortunately, it was a highly unregulated industry in Nigeria, and still is as I write this.

I knew my way around the store. My keen mind and eternal quest for knowledge had turned me into a sponge. I soaked up everything and knew almost as much as my Dad about the basic drugs.

I smiled back at Prof as I responded, "I use the 80/20 rule, sir. Most people that come here are in the 80% category.

They have complaints such as aches, pains, colds, etc. They are typically fighting malaria or a chest infection, depending on the season of the year. If they fall into the 20%, which is, of course, more serious, you can easily tell, and that is when we tell them to go to the hospital."

Indeed, we often had quite a number of patients come in who were sicker than they thought they were. They'd come into the store out of breath, sweat-ripened, basically struggling for breath, and they'd ask me for a Paracetamol. I'd had to send so many people on their way to the hospital to get emergency treatment. Luckily, the most respected hospital, University College Hospital, UCH, was only a 10-minute drive from the store.

Mom, who was at the back of the shop, kept reading her book, not acting like she was listening to our conversation. But I knew she was listening. When she turned briefly to us and blessed me with a small smile, happiness flooded my heart.

"Good job, young lady." Professor Agbaje complimented. "I am amazed at how well you grasp things, even more amazed that you put in the long hours here and are not grumpy for it. You must really enjoy what you do."

"Yes sir, I do."

"That's a rare thing to see in young people these days." He shook his head, "Now, fill my prescriptions for me, will you?"

***

Dad's chemist wasn't the all of it for my business streak and entrepreneurial tendencies.

A few years later, I was a full-fledged student at the University of Ibadan. I had a knack for data and figures and often made an A with little effort. As I sat one morning in a math class with Moji, one of my best friends, we whispered business ideas to each other as the lecture proceeded, for us, boringly.

"Who wants an A? Who wants a first-class?" I whispered to Moji, and she had to contain her giggle behind her hands. "It's not like you need a first-class to be successful in life. And who has the energy to put in the hard work? It's not like we want to be lecturers. Or are you planning to be one?"

Moji made huge eyes at me, like I was crazy. "Lecturer, no way! How about we get into the real world and go make some money! Some real money!!!"

Why couldn't we begin to make that money now even though we were young and still students? As they said, there was no better time than now.

"Let's continue this conversation after the class, okay!" Even though I wasn't interested in being the best in the math class, I still wanted to do well enough, and this particular lecturer went bonkers if he caught a distracted student in class.

We didn't leave immediately when the class ended and continued the chatter. An idea struck.

We had left over capital from having contributed some money to make a birthday cake for a brother in the Christian fellowship. "Why not use it as seed money to begin a business? We could start right now!" As I spoke, excitement coursed through me.

Moji caught on fast, "So we begin making money now, instead of later." She laughed the hearty way she did, "Seems someone is in a hurry to be wealthy."

I elbowed her, "Like you are not." But I really was not that enthralled at the idea of pocketing some extra money. I was more driven to see and feel our seed capital multiply.

"Okay, but what do we invest in? What do we sell?"

I smiled at this easily excitable friend of mine, "Relax already. Yes, we'd have to add more money. Let's say two hundred naira apiece..." I adjusted my chair to allow another student to pass, "And we can sell bread. You know there is no bread in the hostels, and we have to go outside the school to get some..."

Moji jumped in, "And how stale they are!" She shrugged with revulsion. Moji loved bread, but the ones we got to buy were not so great, "I'd give my right arm and foot for a fresh loaf of bread. And I know so many others who would."

"So, how about we talk to a bakery outside the school, contract them to bake bread and deliver straight to us, and then we distribute."

"Yes!" She shrieked, "Let's do it."

We sat for a while, strategizing and drawing up details for a business plan. And then it hit me, "But how do we distribute? We are in classes most of the morning?"

And so, we went back to the drawing board to think up better strategies.

I'd like to say that it was a smooth sailing business from the very first day, but it wasn't. There is so much you don't know about business until you are up to your neck in it. We dealt with bakeries that wanted payment upfront and then wouldn't deliver the requested amount of merchandise. We had bakeries that disappointed us. And we initially had a difficult time getting the fresh bread to our consumers.

Until one bright afternoon.

It was commonplace to have young mothers from town come into the hostels with their young children to pick up menial jobs from the students. In a hostel that didn't have laundries and that often suffered water shortages, they were a godsend. They fetched water from the neighboring hostels with running water and washed clothes for a fee.

Over time, I had become close with one such young mother and her two sons, and she often sent her sons by themselves to do my laundry. Moji and I were complaining about how difficult it was to get our products out on time when one of the boys, a precocious ten-year-old, spoke up. He was at that time done with his primary school education and was waiting on secondary school.

"Aunty Folakemi, you know you could hire my brother and me to distribute the bread for you while you are in class?"

I halted my conversation with Moji and gave the young boy my attention. "Come, let's talk."

So, we sat down and talked at length. He was young, but he was a shrewd businessman. He didn't want to be paid a salary, asking instead for a commission on his sales. That way, he was asking to become a partner in our little business.

We made him a partner because there was nothing to lose. If he made some money, he got paid, and if he didn't make money, he didn't get paid.

We actually made a lot of money. I had not started the business because I was hurting for money but because it was a brilliant idea that shouldn't lie fallow. It was also very empowering to do something novel, to prove to myself that I could do the things that I put my mind to. It was purposeful. It was entrepreneurial. The first ever of its kind, it birthed the rise of student sales in their dormitories.

***

Blessed with a razor-sharp mind, I wasn't the kind of person to burn the midnight oil for studies. Moreso, I had been interested in academic success only to the degree of achieving the top band in the tier-2 honors (second-class upper). First-class honors seemed meant for true nerds and was not on my purview.

I carried this mindset from year two of college and did just enough to succeed, which I did so exceptionally well.

In my fourth year of school, I received a letter from Dad, him being still in Saudi Arabia at that time.

He wrote regularly but this one letter was different. He'd ended it by expressing a desire. He'd be so proud if I could secure a first-class honors degree.

"And I think you can," he concluded.

I was very smart, but because of that, I hadn't learned how to study. I didn't need to. And now, I only had one full year left. I looked at my Dad's letter, and I looked at my grades. And I realized that I so desperately wanted to please my dad, the quiet but ever-reliable presence in my life. He was a man of few words, but his heart was as big as the heavens, and for him to express his love for me so succinctly on paper put fire under my wings.

I sat down and took stock. If I took two extra classes, and I had a perfect A in all my classes, I'd make it into first class, but barely so.

My Dad's words rang in my ears every step I took, my heart now on a changed course to a first-class, I decided to go for it. It was a huge risk, but one worth taking. I'd have to study real hard to get a chance at the perfect A in every single class.

And so I studied, and studied real hard, for the first time in my life.

When weariness set in, I'd remember my Dad's effusive letter and I'd find the strength to go on. He was going to be proud of me. He said he was sure I would do great things with my life. He had expressed pride at the way I managed to keep myself from defilement. He knew I would raise godly generations of more children for his family lineage.

And I did get that first-class honors. For my dad, I did it.

An enduring lesson in the power of strong positive parental influence.

***

God is an intentional Father and maps the perfected path for His own. I thank God for the "can do" attitude He blessed me with. This attitude was the reason for the blossoming of my parents' pharmacy store under my watch. It was the reason for the success of our bread-selling venture and for my good grades at the BSc and MSc levels.

During my Master's Degree, however, I surrendered my "I can do it if I tried enough" attitude to "I have to be intimate with Him on a regular basis" attitude.

Still borne on the wings of Dad's encouragement and the knowledge that I could do whatever I set my mind to, my MSc at the University of Texas Arlington got off to a good start, but perhaps not nearly as good.

In Nigeria, an A began at either 65% or 70%, and if you were bright enough, you'd have your results crowded with As. At UTA, however, an A began at 90%. I dug in my heels and got studying. I even pulled several over-nighters at the library.

All papers came back with an A, except for the one B grade in my first semester. Because the last year of my undergraduate days had been filled with such excellence, the B grade nearly broke me. It made me question my intelligence, my tenacity. But in the midst of the question, I realized that I was more valuable than my cognitive intelligence. It was in UTA that my relationship with God evolved from "I can do it if I tried enough" to "I have to be intimate with Him on a regular basis. I have to trust Him alone with all my heart and never lean with pride to my own understanding."

I did well at UTA, and that B grade was my first and last B. I would go on to graduate with honors.

One striking thing about my MSc days was that my thesis was on simulation of remote electromagnetic fields substances using the FDTD method. It was for the US Army to identify landmines from afar, and I had never felt so proud, or as American at any point in my life as on the day I was awarded an A passing grade for that thesis.

***

The same restlessness and desire to do something significant would drive me to begin several small businesses while in the US. One of them was a care-connection model, Nanny Harmony. With this business, I matched nannies to families in Dallas. I got some money in the process but nothing ever beat the satisfaction of getting the perfect fit. Busy parents could remain busy and yet have their children in good hands.

One spin off of Nanny Harmony was a house-cleaning business. I'd hire and send house cleaners to houses that required their services.

Yes, I made some good money, running businesses. But the driving purpose of any of the businesses I founded was never the money. It was a burning purpose and desire to make an impact. Driven to make peoples' lives just a little better, just a little easier. Driven to connect all to love.

CHAPTER 16

To Papa With Love

Life has its way of beating down the seemingly strongest strength to pulp.

2009 was a challenging year. We had moved to Minnesota in March, successfully overcome Akin's forgery, and the divorce had finally gone through. I had buried myself so much in work amidst the stress, but my memory had started to reflect the stress and failed at inopportune times. I would forget names, and forget familiar turns that I previously navigated auto-pilot mode. Something had to give. I needed respite. I needed a retreat to rest.

So I took Joy with me for a cruise in July.

But I couldn't get myself to relax, no matter how hard I tried.

That windy afternoon, standing on the top deck, the wind kissing my face and lifting my hair, I cut an idyllic picture, I knew that. Ostensibly, this was the stuff dreams were made of. Only that I wasn't having the best of times; the trip wasn't lifting my spirit as the waters normally did at sight.

I left the deck and went into our cabin, where Joy worked hard at a jigsaw puzzle. She smiled briefly at me as I got into the cabin and then returned her attention to what she was doing.

I sat on my bed, watching my child lose herself in the simple pleasure of life. I sensed in my heart that I should call my childhood pastor, who had by then relocated from Nigeria to the UK. A father through and through. He prayed over me.

Yet, I could not gain my calm, the calm that these yearly cruises had come to mean for me. Not even with these still waters and the deep that calls to the deepest souls in wonder of creation. Not with the worship of my adorable King of Kings that the sight of the ocean naturally evokes. Not with the prayers.

So I called a trusted prayer partner, the same person I'd called when Akin had brought the forged document that stated I had agreed not to relocate with Joy. She always had a listening heart and a deep sensing in the spirit. She picked my call and listened. I couldn't see her smile, but I could feel it. And then she spoke quietly, "It's all well and good that you called me, Folakemi, but I think there is someone else you should be calling at this time. Not me..."

My jaw hit the floor in surprise. Because indeed, she wasn't the person I had wanted to call. So I thanked her, got off the phone, and called the person I should have called in the first place.

The Holy Spirit had orchestrated events because where he shouldn't have, the pastor picked my call on the first ring. And he remembered me immediately.

"Folakemi, so good to hear from you. How are you?"

How was I, really?

I was tired, lackluster, and unenthusiastic. Worn.

"Unable to relax, even though I am on a cruise that is supposed to be relaxing. And the Holy Spirit is asking me to call you, to pray for me. I don't know if you remember me or even know me..."

He said, "I know you; I know you very well. You've been in my heart."

The ship bobbed up and down under my feet, but I didn't notice, for the way my heart swelled in my chest.

"Did someone call you from the church?" He asked.

Yes, someone from his church had called me just before we set sail, and my thought had been that they were simply following up because we had attended their church once before, as we visited various options in the area for a new church home. I told him that.

"No, they weren't calling to follow up. I had asked them to call you because I sensed in my spirit to reach out."

And so he sang in worship and he prayed. He thanked God in recognition that my life had purpose, otherwise, I would have been a statistic. He thanked God for preserving us through the kind of storm that turned others into psychiatric emergencies. He sang of God's mightiness, the same song he would later sing when my younger daughter's birth proved herculean. He prayed for restoration. He summoned for the peace of God that passes all understanding to suffuse my heart and calm me. He prayed for stillness and calm in the midst of a raging sea. And as he prayed, the calmness came over me, overwhelmed my heart, set things right. I found myself drifting asleep almost before the last "Amen."

The sun had come up in my very cloudy sky and my heart was shining again with joy.

***

We had a most beautiful cruise after that.

We enjoyed great food, reveled in the beautiful accommodations, and the history-making daytime and evening entertainments. We were in a floating hotel and got to enjoy five different cities. We walked along the beautiful streets of St. Lucia and Barbados one evening and woke up in Spain two days later.

It was a beautiful, beautiful time. And once I could relax, everything seemed poignant and sweet and painted in the broad, beautiful strokes of the Creator's unmatchable love canvas.

Joy had a great time too, and watching her be a child gladdened my heart. The cruise had extensive kids' facilities, split by age, and she explored them all. She spent a lot of time at the pool while I sat on the lounging chairs. Watching her slice through the water, or as she sat huddled with other children her age, laughing, brought joy to my heart.

Our lives were perfect as it was, I was coming to realize. Single parenting was not all bad after all.

Yet, a little romance wouldn't hurt the heart.

***

Romance did come a little while after that.

Home after the cruise, the peace now a settled thing within me, I longed for the companionship of an adult. I missed having someone to talk with, to share my hopes and aspirations with. I missed being held and cherished. I missed being in love. I missed the promise of a life partnership.

Romance began aboard a Delta flight from Texas to Minnesota, even though the man I would eventually fall in love with and marry was not aboard that flight.

It began with a flight magazine that I flipped through because I had developed a slightly buzzy headache from staring at my laptop screen a little too much. The flight magazine was lighthearted, and several of the stories had me chuckling quietly to myself. And then I came across the ad for a dating service.

It was expertly done and spoke to the professional that I was. The service was targeted at busy professionals who were serious about lifetime companionships. Marketed on the premise that such a busy, focused, and ambitious professional had no time for traditional dating, and if you outsourced your business call center, your housekeeping, dry cleaning, and just about everything else so that execution was seamless, why wouldn't you outsource this most important decision of your life as well to someone whose focus would be an apt lifetime companion to match you?

That made total sense to my intellectually rigorous mind. I took down their number and email address and tucked it away to use. As an executive working insane weekly hours, combined with single parenting, what I did not have was the luxury of dating to fill a social calendar. I wanted to date for purpose. Date for the future. Date with the potential for a life partner only. My time was precious.

It turned out this dating service did not accept women clients. Women were the bait. Men were the payors. That mindset would not have worked for my traditionally conservative, but liberated womanity anyway.

Summer came, and it came with a mailer from *It's Just Lunch,* another dating service. They were having a summer blast with fantastic discounts.

I knew that I didn't feel capable with men. That thing John Gray said about men being from Mars and women from Venus was ringing true for me. I didn't understand men as much as I should in my mid-thirties. I had not dated any growing up. My very first boyfriend became my fiancé and then my husband. I didn't do dating, I didn't know how to do the flirting scene, and I wasn't about to begin now.

So I called "It's *Just Lunch.*"

The girl that interviewed me was tall and pretty, in a model kind of way. She was also extremely patient and took the time to draw me out of myself. But no matter how much she asked me to describe my dream date, I had no physical attributes to give her.

"What kind of a man are you looking for?" She asked again, for the umpteenth time, it seemed.

I shrugged again, "I don't know. I need help figuring that out."

"One minute." She whispered and drew out her drawer. There was a stack of pictures, and she slid them toward me.

Every single shot was the portrait of a man, all kinds of men. Smiling men and more serious ones. African Americans,

Caucasians, Latinos. Some were immediately striking in their handsomeness, some not exactly easy on the eyes.

"Anyone of them catches your eye?"

I flicked through the pictures, and after the tenth or eleventh one, she shrugged, "I don't think physical looks matter any bit to you, does it?"

I considered that for a minute. It dawned on me that I wasn't particular about the shell, the external person. I wanted to know, to hold the heart that lay below the surface. I wanted a good and godly man.

The pictures that I finally chose and slid back across the table to her all had the same thing in common. The men had kind eyes. She noticed it too, because she commented on it.

"Something about these eyes, right?"

I nodded, surprised that she had seen what I saw.

"One other thing. Can you date someone shorter than you?"

I drew the line there. I was about 5'11, which was considered tall for a woman, but I wanted my partner to be at least an inch taller than I was. There was something about nestling into the arms of a man taller than you, to have their arms wrap around you. "No," I said. "Taller!"

"Okay then, Folakemi. I will call you when we find a match and arrange a blind date for you. That works, right?"

***

I was frustrated after three blind dates and put a call through to Stephanie, the girl who was working with me.

"Hey, Stephanie. See the dilemma I am facing. I am a busy woman. I'm a single mom, and I work in finance. I don't have time for dates. I'm not looking for volume social activity. I'm looking for someone who has the potential to be a husband. At a minimum, they should be looking for a wife, right?"

It had taken me all of three dates to realize this, that I was not just dipping my toes in the water to test its depth. I was committed. I was in for the deep swim and there was no use at all visiting with someone that wanted to stay single forever, was there?

"Are you sure?" She sounded bewildered over the phone.

"I am."

"But dates allow you to get out there and have fun."

"See, I am too busy and too old to just want to go on a date so someone can make me feel good. God makes me feel good alright. So, until you find the person who meets the criteria we discussed, let's not bother."

She sighed. "What if that doesn't happen for several months?" She asked.

"I don't mind," I reassured her. "Honestly, I'm not looking for dates. I am not seeking a quick lay. I am not swayed at all by sexual intimacy and not looking for femininity validation."

***

Three months later, Stephanie called me. There was joy in her voice. "Folakemi, if this person is not the person, I don't think I can help you. He fits your bill perfectly, except for one thing. He is two years older than the age range you specified."

I sat in my chair, rooted to my seat by her words.

"But you wouldn't know it, because he acts, looks very young. You'd be surprised at his age, actually!"

As I let out my pent up breath, the air in front of me fanned out in a puff of white smoke. "Sure." I said, "Go ahead. I will go out on a date with him."

***

His name was Bruce, and we went on more than one date.

Bruce was Caucasian, had a smile as vast as the heavens, and a very happy laugh. Two minutes into our date, I lost the low, throbbing anxiety that had gripped me since Stephanie's call. I felt peace through me.

Our first date was the end of July and the second was mid-August. I had had my birthday just two days before the second date and had mentioned this in passing to Bruce in one of our phone calls.

On that second date, he took me to a restaurant in downtown Minneapolis and had planned a surprise with the kitchen staff for a birthday cake.

As the waiter set the cake in front of me, emblazoned with candles, tears formed underneath my eyelids. Even though Bruce didn't know it then, the Holy Spirit had begun a work of healing in my life and He had commissioned Bruce. You see, that date on the calendar had for long been a sad day for me.

Ten years before, two days after my birthday, I had married Akin, only that the marriage wouldn't last and would stack on top of me bad memory after bad memory. For years, the day had been a sad and regret-filled day for me, and I had almost declined Bruce's dinner date, in fact. But Bruce was now converting this to a beautiful day instead of a sad one from that day. Truly God has used him to turn something around.

***

I had dropped Joy off at the hair salon to get her hair done for a couple of hours, while Bruce and I did a third date. Only that we were now caught in a traffic snarl on our way back and were running late. If I returned home first to get my car, I'd be even later.

"Sorry to be late, sweetheart." I apologized to Joy. "Say hi to my friend, Mr. Nelson."

"Bruce, please." He sent a smile Joy's way, and that seemed to calm her down a little bit while I insisted on "Mr. Nelson," and we settled in for a short but quiet drive.

At home, my daughter was quick to scamper out of the car and into the house. She had only managed to say a small thank you to Bruce for the ride.

It was a beautiful evening, and we stood outside of Bruce's car, talking back and forth. He had a deep, deep mind, but his tone was always lighthearted, and he just seemed like a big kid. He had an enthusiasm for life, was well travelled, and there was always this awe in his voice when he spoke of his life experiences.

As we talked, I noticed Joy's face at the window several times. She would look to see that we were still by the car and then go back in. A couple of minutes later, she'd appear at the window again. This was very unlike her.

"One minute, please." I left Bruce by the car and called Joy to come.

She launched into it immediately, "Whenever you have guests, they come inside the house. You're nice to them. Why are you making Mr. Nelson stay outside? Is it because he's white?" This child of mine, all bluntness and no subtlety at that age, blurted out, right there in front of Bruce.

I didn't want it to be obvious that her words had rattled me, so I smiled a slight smile. "Do you want him to come inside?"

The only reason I hadn't invited Bruce inside was to protect my daughter. I didn't want her to fall in love with someone I barely knew. I didn't want her getting attached to someone and then have him disappear from our lives.

That Saturday evening, however, there was something compelling about my daughter's words, that I, despite myself, gave Bruce the permission to come in.

"I didn't remember to tell you when you got into the car, but your hair is very beautiful." He said to Joy when we were inside and settled into chairs. She beamed up like a thousand lights.

Two hours later, my date, a Harvard University-educated Professor, who had a master's degree in Early Childhood Education, who regularly went to Germany, Russia, and other countries to lecture on early childhood education, who was a renowned expert in his field, was sitting on the floor and playing with Joy.

They rolled around on the floor. They sang silly songs. They laughed at each other's inane jokes. Watching the two of them play, one so white and pale-skinned and the other so dark, I felt something shift into place. A family wasn't necessarily one bonded by blood or DNA. It wasn't a matter of skin color. It was all a matter of hearts, hearts bonded, one heart seeking and several others answering.

As Bruce waved goodbye to us at the door, Joy said to him, her face bathed in a huge smile, "Thank you so much, Mr. Nelson. This has been the happiest day of my life. I can never forget that."

Trust children to sweep you off your feet every now and then, and not always in the most pleasant ways.

"Joy!" I exclaimed. "Are you kidding? Do you mean your life has been sad? That I haven't made you happy?"

She smiled, shrugged, and amended her enthusiastic goodbye to Bruce, "Okay, fine. Thank you, Mr. Nelson. This has been the second happiest day of my life."

CHAPTER 17

A Chance To Love Again

As I walked Bruce to his car, I had the sense that he was going to be in my life, in our lives, for a long, long time. For forever.

Even though Joy was only six at that point, I had for years made her a promise that I would never bring a man into our lives that she didn't love, that she didn't accept, that she didn't approve of. I wanted a good man in my life, but I would prioritize Joy over everyone and anyone.

The best blessing God could have given me at that time was a man who would love me and love Joy as his very own, and who Joy would treasure like he had birthed her.

Bruce would be that man.

He had never had children of his own. He had graduated among the best from the business school of a prestigious college, one widely acclaimed worldwide. But he did not attend to study entrepreneurship or business management or anything business-related. He had gone to Harvard to study public health with focused research on fatherhood and early education.

I was surprised, amazed, bewildered that he hadn't yet had the opportunity to call a child his own. Yet he slid into that role so naturally with Joy, like he had been preparing all his life for her, and she embraced him with her heart just like she had been born for him, born from him.

That night, as I walked Bruce to his car, my heart thump-thumped inside my chest. We had only known each other for so long, but I knew that this was the man for me. He would make the perfect father for Joy. And he would make the perfect husband for me.

He was kind, courteous, and knew how to make me laugh.

My heart had started to skip at the sight of him. I felt like a teenager in love for the first time.

***

I fell in love with Bruce. It felt exciting, even exhilarating.

As we dated more and more, as I got to know his heart, I couldn't be happier. I was excited and nervous. He made me feel warm and shivery at the same time. Around him, I felt charged and euphoric. I felt giddy. After dates, I couldn't wait to see him again, even when he had just left.

I'd sit and wonder, at night, thinking about him. I'd wonder if he saw the same night sky I was seeing. I'd wonder if he was having the same sleepless night that I was, if he was thinking about me the way I was thinking about him.

Everything felt exciting and new. Even going grocery shopping with him felt huge and became an exciting venture.

As time went on, I progressed to loving Bruce instead of just being in love with him. I felt that shift less than four months into our relationship. My feelings for him settled. I still felt giddy around him, but I also started to trust him. I became secure in his affection. I saw that he was not a perfect man, because no one is. But I saw what was good, and I was able to accept the good with the less than good.

I felt deeply connected to him, and even though I was no longer up at night thinking of what he was doing, I looked forward to his phone calls late at night. His voice soothed and comforted and wrapped around me like a blanket when I got into bed.

He became my best friend so quickly it made my head turn. Yes, he was my romantic interest, the man I would settle down with and grow old with. But he was also my friend. I could tell him everything and anything, and he'd listen intently, even when I rambled, even when I didn't seem to make sense.

He brought me out of myself. An extrovert where I was more introverted, he took me out and attended church functions that I wouldn't have otherwise attended.

One afternoon, as we milled around the buffet table at the wedding of a church colleague, one of my church members sidled up to me and nudged me playfully.

"Bruce is such a great influence on you. This is the third purely social church function that we've seen you at within two months. You..." She nudged a little more, "We hardly saw you at anything last year. I think we have him to thank for that."

And yes, they did have him to thank for that. Large crowds drained me, and I had become quite the expert at avoiding them. But Bruce was so gregarious, so full of life, such a people person that he started to draw me out of myself. I will never in a million years become a party person, but I can say that I have become a little more outgoing because of Bruce.

And he was, still is, nothing but a big kid. Seventeen years older than me, yet so childlike, so believing, so trusting. And so playful. It was this playfulness, this ability to let go of all adult problems and become a child with eyes filled with wonder that had first endeared Joy to him.

And then, his father's heart. He loved without reproach, without blame, without constraints. His arms were opened wide every single time. Aside from my dad, he was the other man in whom I would see the Father's heart of God so clearly and unashamedly displayed.

I fell in love with Bruce, and then I grew to love him with a deep, abiding love.

***

"Marry me, Mr. Nelson. Don't marry Mom. Marry me instead." Joy would call Bruce "Dad" later, but at that time that he was proposing to me, ring held out, one knee bent, Joy wanted to be front and center of it.

The day was one year after we met, and Bruce and I had become an item. His presence warmed me, and his absence made me wish he was present. It had been obvious from the get-go, to both of us, that we weren't playing, that we were in this for the long haul, that we would be man and wife someday soon.

Yet, it surprised me that evening, when he got on his knees and asked me to marry him. We had gone out to dinner downtown, and I had allowed him into the house after he dropped me off so he could say hi to Joy, who was by then smitten with him.

Joy was wrapped in a housecoat, huddled on the sofa. She had stayed up to say hi to Bruce because she knew he was going to drop me off. Her nanny had insisted that she go to bed, but she hadn't.

"Will you marry me?"

I had turned away just for one minute to right a figurine on the mantel, and upon turning back, there Bruce was, all 6'3 of him, on one knee, his eyes pleading.

There was no hesitation whatsoever. My heart leaped within me, and I fell into Bruce's arms. His warm on-the-cheek kiss melted me and brought tears to my eyes. We had never done more than give each other hugs and kisses, because we were keeping ourselves until we got married. But as we hugged that night, the pit patter of my heart was only an echo of his, and my body yearned for him. All of a sudden, I couldn't wait to be married to this man.

And that was when Joy stepped in. She had gotten off the sofa, and was grinning from ear to ear at the display of love that was unfolding in front of her. She got on one knee herself and hugged Bruce by the legs.

"Marry me, Mr. Nelson. Don't marry Mom. Marry me instead."

Her childlike heart and the evident love she had in her heart for Bruce made the moment all the more tender. But it also added a humorous side to the evening.

"You can't marry Bruce, Love." I smiled, "You have to be eighteen before you can marry, unless you want Mr. Nelson to be taken away to jail."

She was aghast for a little bit, and then she rebounded, "You can wait till I am eighteen, right? Mr. Nelson, say you'll wait."

The father that he was, Bruce had the perfect answer for this young girl who had claimed him for hers. He had been intentional to propose while she was there because he knew he was asking her, as much as me, for my hands in holy matrimony. "When I marry Mom, I also marry you. You become mine. In fact, you are already mine, and I believe that God made the three of us for each other from the foundations of the world. Does that sound right to you, Mom?

He asked me. He had taken to calling me "Mom" when we were in a conversation with Joy. It made her less confused, and that small act had started to knit us together as a family.

"Yes, that does sound right. Thank you, Bruce."

Joy's smile seemed to reach all the way to the heavens. "Thank you, Mom. Thank you, Mr. Nelson. And when you marry us, can I call you 'Daddy'?"

"Yes, sweetheart. Yes."

It was a bittersweet moment. My daughter had lost out on a relationship with her biological father, and I ached for her. But I also was ecstatic that God had brought Bruce into our lives to love me and to parent Joy.

***

We wanted to get married sooner rather than later, so we chose December of that year.

I sought counsel from some dear friends of mine. They were a parent-figure Caucasian couple that attended the same church as we did in Dallas. I knew I wanted to marry Bruce, that I wanted to spend the rest of my life with him, but there was so much to be untangled. Not ever had anyone in my family or that I knew gone through a divorce. I was at a loss and didn't have anyone to turn to for wisdom.

Beyond that, I didn't want to make the same mistake twice. I had had my heart and fingers burned by Akin, and I didn't want Bruce doing the same to me. I knew his heart. In our few months of courtship, he had been vulnerable. He had opened up himself to me. I knew him, the essence of him. But you never fully know someone. And I was scared.

So, I went to see Mama and Papa, as I fondly called them. Papa brought me Earl Grey tea, and spoke softly when I asked questions that bothered me. Mama sipped a cup of coffee that was so black I could almost taste it where I sat.

"He loves you, you know?"

I nodded in agreement, "Yes, he does. But is love enough?"

"And he loves the Lord. Right?"

"I think he does." I sighed.

"You should go see your pastor in Minnesota for counsel," Mama said as softly as Papa. "Better still, have Bruce go see him."

And so, I sent Bruce to see my pastor. I needed a witness.

***

My pastor loved Bruce, and he was very vocal about it.

I had met this man of God during one of my lowest points in life. I had been a broken woman, a woman whose life had not made much sense when he ministered God's word and God's grace to me. God had led me to the church he pastored. I felt cocooned in the warmth of the place, and the love I felt around me was such a tangible thing. I never became a churchy-church person, but I became more comfortable in other church activities settings. I learned to relax.

God had placed this man in charge of me. He had told me that God had given him a mandate for single parents. He was to step in to become the father of children being raised by single moms. And the mother for children being raised by single dads. The day he told me this, Joy had been by my side. Afterward, she stood and hugged him very tightly. And true to his word, he had been an exceptional father figure for Joy before Bruce came on the scene.

And he loved Bruce and could barely wait for us to be married.

The only problem was that the laid down laws of the church that he pastored was against remarriage. He would not be allowed to conduct marriage ceremonies for us as divorcees. As much as he loved me and as much as he wanted me to be with Bruce, he couldn't marry us.

***

We would have a very quiet, but very intimate wedding.

Bruce asked the pastor to walk me down the aisle as the father of the bride. If he couldn't join us in holy matrimony, he could do one better and stand in place of my dad.

"That's a hard thing to do." He said. Even though he was almost as dark as me, a paleness had settled on his face, and I could see a nerve at the side of his face twitching. "That's a hard thing to do." He repeated. "I know I will ultimately walk a child that is not mine down the aisle. I saw that in my future so long ago. What I didn't foresee, what I don't want to happen, is to walk someone else before I walk my own daughter. I won't have a problem with it, after I have done the same for my kids, but I never thought I'd do it before. Never."

I would love nothing more than for this man whose heart yearned after God to lead me to and then hand me over to my husband, but I knew it would be unconscionable to pressure him.

"Let me pray about it." He finally said.

***

The Holy Spirit told him to do it.

And so, on a glorious winter day, one made for hot cocoa and marshmallows and family stories told by the fireplace, Pastor Sola Olowokere walked me across a small room filled with pansies and violas and snowdrops and daffodils, and into the arms of Bruce Nelson.

We exchanged our solemn vows to one another, and I felt full, complete, content, like I had come home.

***

Joy really fell in love with Bruce. This was something I had specifically prayed for in remarriage. I wanted a father for Joy, and we found it in Bruce. The way Bruce accepted and still accepts Joy is off the charts.

One night, a few months after we were married, Bruce turned to me in bed. It still felt a little odd but very comforting to sleep with someone in a bed, to wake up to my husband, to have his arms around me as I slept, to have my face peppered with his kiss.

This night, his arms snuggled around me, he whispered in my ears, "Are you really sure that Joy is not mine? That she doesn't share the same DNA as mine?"

A few minutes ago, I had been asleep, warm in the arms of sleep. I had only started to fall awake as I felt Bruce's arms come around me. And now I was fully awake at his words.

I smiled and turned to my husband. It was amazing what God had done here, what He was doing. I knew for a fact that Joy wasn't Bruce's. Bruce knew for a fact that she wasn't his. But sometimes, we wondered if it was possible for two hearts to meld together so quickly, so infinitely, so totally. From the day he met her, from the day Joy had told him that his playtime had given her the best day of her life, Joy had fallen completely and irrevocably in love with Bruce. And Bruce had done the same with her.

"We are sure she is not biologically yours, sweetheart." I told him that night, "But I know that her heart is yours, just like your heart is hers. She is your child, Bruce. She really is. God has secret spiritual DNAs."

CHAPTER 18

Joyful Praises

On the floor, amidst an avalanche of toys, were the two most important people in my life. Joy was eight, Bruce in his early-fifties, my child and my husband. Looking at the external shell, they were as different as day and night. One so young, one much older and wiser. One with skin the color of caramel, the other with pink, beautiful skin. But in the tangle of their arms and their raucous laughter, all I could see, all I could hear, was love.

The sound of their laughter was the most beautiful thing. And the sight of both of them in their play was the most precious thing in the world. This was how a family was supposed to be, to look like, to feel like. People whose hearts were bound in love for Jesus and one another.

Even though I was not an overly emotional person, tears came unbidden to my eyes. They were tears of happiness and gratitude. Three years ago, I couldn't have envisaged, couldn't have imagined that we'd be here. Had it been only three years that I had been so overwhelmed, so out of it that I, for the briefest of moments, had wanted so badly for life, for the pain, for the rawness I felt inside, to stop.

And just three short years later, borne on the arms of God's grace, kept by His love, we were out on the other side, living life as it should be lived.

That evening, as I watched my husband, who was but a child at heart, and my daughter arrange and scatter and rearrange Legos, I remembered the scriptures in Romans 16:20: "The God of peace will soon crush Satan under your feet. The grace of our Lord Jesus be with you."

Indeed, He was the God of peace, and He had brought His peace flooding into my heart.

Standing up to go to the bathroom, Bruce noticed me standing there for the first time. He broke out into one of his thousand-watts smiles. I loved it when he smiled. The sides of his face crinkled up with smile lines, and light flooded his eyes. He noticed the tears in my eyes.

"You okay?" He asked.

I nodded that I was, and I smiled a little smile of mine, "Maudlin thoughts."

He cocked his head and asked again, "You okay?"

"Yes. Happy tears...happy tears."

***

I firmly believe that God had determined from the very beginning of the world that Joy would be Bruce's daughter, whether she was born from his loins or not.

I also firmly believe that the same God had determined that Grace would be Bruce's first biological child.

According to the experts, he wasn't supposed to be a father, but God had other plans.

As a young man and then later as a middle-aged man, he had so desperately desired to have biological children. He tried to be a sperm donor. He wanted to help others build and create families; he wanted to give others the gift of children. But each time, the experts would medically reject his application. Told him that his chances of fathering a child were very slim. They accompanied that with all sorts of medical jargons; low sperm motility, non-viability.

For the first two years of marriage, life with Bruce and Joy was full and fulfilling. Our lives had the ups and downs of any family life. We worshipped God together. We pursued work and school. We went to church and had a great family there. We were happy with what we had built. A baby never even crossed my mind. I had been on birth control all the while, and then we decided that it was time to take it out. We were going to try for a baby, but we were not going to pressure ourselves about it. If it happened, it happened.

"All in God's hands," I told Bruce the day after I had the IUD taken out. I wasn't pressured and certainly didn't want him to feel so. I wanted him to know that he was and would always be more to me than a hundred children.

Two short months after going off birth control, a home test confirmed what my body had been telling me for days. I was pregnant.

The news brought Bruce to his knees, all 6'3" of him. The emotions rocked his body, and he gazed up at me in somewhat of awe.

"You are positive?" He asked, "You are absolutely sure?"

In response, I showed him the positive home test kits. The delayed emotions came to me then, the ones I had been trying to suppress. Gratitude, exhilaration, awe, a spinning of the head; every emotion I felt at that moment rose to the surface and overwhelmed me. I knelt with Bruce, shaking like a leaf. As he held me in his arms, as we laughed and cried and jubilated together, as we prayed and dedicated the child right there unto Jesus, all was right with the world.

The pregnancy was not an easy one, but Bruce, over the moon with joy, made it all easy for me. Breakfast in bed when I wanted it. He laid out my work clothes for the next day the night before. He rubbed my feet when they were swollen. He laid beside me in bed, one hand resting gently over the arch of my swollen belly. And several mornings, I'd wake up to him just looking at me with love and awe, ready to help me get ready for the day, and to walk me to my car for my drive to work.

***

I couldn't tell who was more excited; Bruce or Joy. The one excited to become a father and the one excited to become a big sister. Between the two of them, our house went from a house to a home and then to a haven. Warm hugs, sloppy heart-rending kisses, and bated anticipation.

They could barely wait.

I was hoping for a little boy, because I subconsciously thought it easier to raise boys. Boys seemed easier to handle. Boys could not as much be at risk of becoming the victim of rape and molestation as girls were.

"A little girl, mummy. A little sister for me, please." Joy would plead with me, like I had a say in the gender of the baby. By then, she was nine, old and smart enough to know how babies' genders were determined. Just the summer before, I had assisted her with a school project on how babies were made.

"You know I can't promise, Love." I would tell her, but my heart would beat out a silent staccato of "boy" each time we spoke about it.

But God, who knows the end of the world from the beginning, who knows how to separate our needs from our wants, gifted me with the gift of a perfect baby girl, one I would give my life for, one who was the perfect addition to our family.

My pastor, who by then I called Papa, who was by then much more than a pastor but a father figure to me, had daughters of his own. The first was named Favor, just like my Joy was. And the second daughter was named Grace.

"You are pregnant with Grace." The Holy Spirit told me one morning, loud and clear, almost like He was in the same physical room as I was. "Your baby's name is Grace."

The voice of the Holy Spirit was warm and comforting, like sweet syrup, and it enveloped me, every inch of my body. But the message He had sent through was unmistakable, and it wasn't the one I wanted to hear. It came with a sense of Grace being a girl, and I didn't want a girl.

"If my child is a girl, it is your fault," I told Papa the next time we saw each other. Of course, the rational part of me knew that he was not responsible for what was going on within my body. Yet, the irrational and highly emotional pregnant part of me wanted nothing to do with a girl. I had never really wanted girls, and Joy had been a surprise and a mystery.

Over time, she became less of a mystery and became my world, and I wouldn't have traded her or exchanged her gender for all the money in the world. But I didn't think I had in me the emotional fortitude to mother two daughters.

"I will hold you and Joy responsible if this ends up being a girl."

He smiled at me and shook his head. "Joy and I don't make babies. I hope you will remember that."

"It's both your fault. Joy is busy praying for a girl, and you have both a Joy and a Grace, and here am I, the Holy Spirit talking to me about carrying a Grace within me. I just know..."

Very lovingly, but still smiling at my uncharacteristic self, he simply said, "And if you do so, we'll simply rejoice. God doesn't give us gifts He knows we cannot handle."

✳✳✳

Grace came into the world after an intense, intense labor.

I had been pregnant for almost 43 weeks, with a very active baby. Most babies turn heads down by 34 weeks, getting themselves ready to be born. Not Grace. At 38 weeks, she was still head up, and we waited with bated breaths to have her turn the right way. We waited in prayers and fasting and with hope filling our hearts each time I went to be scanned. In the 38th week, she finally turned the right way down, but she didn't move all the way down into the birthing canal and by the 42nd week, would not bulge still. So I had to be induced.

The labor lasted 41 hours. We had everyone praying, our church family, Papa and his family, Papa's mum, my mom, and all those we called friends. Joy had refused to go to school, and looked like she was in every bit of agony as I was. She wept when I screamed. She held my hands and wiped my brows. She hugged and she consoled and was a blessing.

Bruce held it together when he was in the delivery room with me, but I would later learn that he fell apart each time he stepped out of the room, when he didn't have to be strong for me. He so desperately wanted to see his baby born, but above all, he wanted me to be out of the pain. He wanted it done and over. For my relief.

Grace was indeed a girl, just like the Holy Spirit had told me she would be, and in answer to Joy's prayers for a little sister of her own. She was perfect, this little baby of mine, and my heart ballooned inside of me, filled with so much love, so much tenderness, that I would need all the words in the world and then some to describe how I felt.

Holding the tiny bundle of joy, there were no words to describe how I felt, how I would continue to feel forever as I am called Joy and Grace's mom. A deep abiding well of unconditional love, the fiercest need to protect my daughters at all costs, the knowledge that I would trade all the happiness in my life to secure the flow of unabated joy in their futures. As I held Grace to my breasts the first time, as I watched her suckle, and as I brushed back her curly mass of hair, I didn't understand why I wouldn't have wanted a daughter.

Because she was perfect. And she was all, and more than I could have ever hoped for.

***

Love settled in around my family.

Family meant that you were almost always joyful, but you also had the permission to be sad without shame. It meant crying and laughing together. It meant having inside jokes that no one else but your family got. It meant waking up to go to the bathroom in the middle of the night and taking a detour to check in on your sleeping children, watching the rise and fall of their chests, getting back into bed beside your husband and feeling gratitude fill your heart for these precious people. It meant disagreeing so fiercely over something, and yet reaching out a hand to clasp the other person's hand and saying, "I love you," and meaning it wholeheartedly.

Family wasn't about age. Or color. Or backgrounds.

Family was love, and God-centered relationships, and commitment, and forgiveness, and then more love.

With Bruce, Joy, and Grace, I got to experience family the way God always intended.

***

Grace was a baby of light, and she brought joy to so many people. Of course, first and foremost to us, her immediate family.

Mama Nelson, Bruce's mom, who had since relinquished the idea of a grandchild ever coming from Bruce, was over the moon with joy. She would hold Grace in her arms, rocking quietly on the rocker, her eyes closed, a warm smile playing on her lips.

Grace also made my sister extremely happy. My sister had been sick for most of her adult life and had preserved and triumphed for most of it. She was my confidante, my go-to person to share good and bad news with, and when I had first shared with her the good news of being pregnant with Grace, it had felt almost like she was pregnant with me, for the joy she felt. She was euphoric.

When Grace was three months old, we went to London to see my sister, who had recently come out of hospital and into a recovery home. The doctors had given her a terminal prognosis, but she was alive and was excited to meet her littlest niece. She had loved Grace from the time I told her I was pregnant, but she fell in love with her all over again when we placed Grace in her arms.

She'd had a stroke, had aphasia, and couldn't speak, but her eyes were bright. And with Grace in her arms, she raised her voice and sang a worship song. Not in the clearest of voices, but she sang nonetheless. This was a woman who had been told would never speak again until she passed away.

When we returned to the US, I'd call her over the phone, and she'd recite beautiful scriptures to me, Joy, and Grace. She couldn't and wouldn't speak normally again for the rest of her life, but she sang and prophesied scriptures.

For the next seven years that she would live, without the use of words, my sister and Grace just had this incredible connection that was like no other. It was love without guile. They sang together on a video call even after the last stroke and days before my sister would call heaven home.

***

What I love about my family is that it has given me, given us, an opportunity to model Jesus to our children the way God asks.

To be counted worthy of raising children for Him has been such an overwhelming blessing. It is what gets me up every morning. It is what drives me to my knees in prayers and supplications, and not just for my children, but for the other children God has placed in my life one way or the other.

To raise children not according to my feelings but according to His word. What a blessing.

CHAPTER 19

Purposeful Parenting

Semantically speaking, I have a child who is a Nigerian American and another who is Nigerian-German-Scandinavian-American. But when I think about my children, the furthest thing from my mind is their race or the color of their skin. To me, they are and will always be Jesus' children, the children of God, loved by Him before He gave them to me as a caretaker and husbandman.

These children were carried within me and birthed by my body. They have been cared for and nurtured by my hands and will be so nurtured for as long as I live. But they are His first and mine second. I am nothing but a hired hand for Him, the one who loves them so lavishly that He gave His Son for them.

***

Children are precious and protective of their family. They don't like to see hurt. But it is not the responsibility of a child to protect a parent from heartache. Rather ought to be the other way around, for parents to take their children's pain and own it. For me to take my children's pain and make it mine. To wipe their tears and rather cry a river on their behalf. They are not supposed to be the ones to protect me.

This was a lesson I taught Joy when she was around six years old.

It is a story of racism that was triggered by a bully.

Joy loved school; she still does. Even when ill and told to stay in bed for the day, she'd agitate to go to school. I loved education too, and greatly appreciated the gift that great educators brought to their communities. I was very involved with her learning curriculum – both what she learned and how she was learning it. As other commitments permitted, I'd pay unscheduled visits to the school to express gratitude to the learning village, and never failed to be present at parent-teacher conferences. Work could be done at night or early morning, but motherhood was paramount at all times.

One unseasonably warm afternoon, I drove into Joy's elementary school, taking the opportunity for a quick visit after a cancelled meeting at work that afternoon. As usual, I peeked into the administrative office to say a quick hello to the pleasant admin staff and if present, the school principal and associate principal.

The associate principal was warm and buxom, had a perpetual smile affixed to her face. She smiled when I swung open the door to her "come in, please," and rose from behind her desk to shake my hands. Her room was crowded with the most fun of an educator's life – files, dictionaries, sports uniforms. I could never work in an environment that was so filled with children's artifacts, but this is what they did and they did it so well.

Her palms were soft and warm and moist. "You came in to see us today, Ms. Oladimeji." Maintaining that name after divorce saved a lot of explanation that a single mother will avoid. "If it's about the bully issue, I'd like you to know that we handled it. It's all sorted out, and I want to assure you that it was a rarity, and would never happen again."

Her face had become animated as she spoke, and she gestured emphatically with her hands.

But I had no clue what she was going on about. I held up a hand for her to stop, "What bully? I don't know what you are talking about."

She stopped, and her eyes bulged out, almost out of their sockets. "Joy didn't tell you?"

"About what?" I almost couldn't believe my ears. Joy and I had an honesty, no-lies policy. I couldn't believe my ears that something had happened that she hadn't told me about.

The associate principal put a hand to her mouth, realizing she may have shared more than I knew.

"Please go ahead." I insisted.

"Joy was not to blame, I can assure you. She was the victim here."

"Please tell me what happened."

And so she did.

There was a boy of the same grade who was a habitual bully. Bullying seemed to fuel his young and untamed mind. His parents had been invited on several occasions to address the matter, and although his behavior would get better for a little while, it was a matter of days before he lost control again. The school administration was doing their best to train and tame this mind.

By happenstance, one otherwise cheery day, Joy found herself sharing the playground with the bully and on his approach, he asked her to leave a play area for him. In her classical quiet but solid demeanor, Joy quietly but forcefully stood her ground, telling him in a quiet but firm tone, "No," like not many had the courage to do with this boy.

The bully was shocked to hear this shy, diminutive little girl tell him no.

"Get off now!" He'd said in a louder, more belligerent tone. But Joy stood her ground and did not answer any further.

"You are nothing but a black nigga! No wonder you are so dumb!" He'd shouted in defeat as he walked away. But his words cut to the very core of my child's heart, and she'd collapsed into a mess of tears.

Her class teacher had met her crying and after several minutes of asking, Joy had told why she was crying. The matter had been escalated to the school administrators. The boy had been told to apologize, and his parents had been called in and issued an ultimatum; if he was ever involved in another case of bullying, he'd have to be suspended and potentially expelled from the school.

I felt pressed to my chair, unable to shift myself out of it. Why would my own child not have told me about this saga?! I had frequently experienced racism, and it was a burr in my side, a pain I never wanted a child of mine to ever feel.

Texas had not prepared me for the experience in Minnesota. I had lived in a city, had had no business venturing into the rural areas where racism happened and was quite blatant. And then we'd relocated to Minnesota, a supposed home of the liberal and free. I had thought that Minnesota would be even more welcoming of racial diversity than Texas, but how mistaken I was.

When we first relocated, I encountered a lot of warmth until the realization of locals that I was not a qualified charity. Many people warmly received Africans and African Americans as needing handouts, but the moment of realization that one could be their equal in status, then the gloves came off.

I remember a particular incident involving a new subordinate. On the first day of her transfer, I'd heard her voice, low and throbbing with anger as she confronted my boss, our boss, "How can a Nigerian be smarter than me? How can you put me under a Nigerian girl, a black woman?"

I wasn't supposed to overhear, but I did anyway. And my boss at that time, who hadn't known I'd overhead, had also told me later. He was just open that way. Unwise, but not with guile.

At another job, my role got "eliminated" because there was no performance reason for any different rationale, although they turned around and replaced the eliminated role. This happened after my then boss had made insensitive jokes about how she enjoyed hunting geese but how she really missed hunting the way their forefathers did. And by God, she'd been referring to how white men in the past set loose black slaves and then hunted them.

It was also after she'd come out bluntly one day to tell me, "Oh, I think I'm just struggling. I've never had to work with a black woman at your level before."

I had documented so many instances of this subtle micro and macro racism that I wrote a letter to the HR leader following the "role elimination." To keep a mutually amicable exit, I was paid handsome compensation. It took a little while to find another job, but I actually earned more that year than if I worked throughout the year. God's recompense.

And then, I went to a different employer, and I had the time of my life. It was very homogeneous and heterogeneous at the same time. We were of different colors, from different places, so there was diversity. Yet, everyone was regarded as the same, equals in the eyes of God and under the law.

Before then, I had seen and experienced so much racism that I never wanted my child to, and because there was an open-door policy between Joy and me, she knew all about this.

So, following the associate principal's sharing, I was perturbed but did not bring up the school issue directly with Joy throughout that evening. I offered a few innuendoes with the hope that Joy would come forward by herself, to take me into confidence. But she didn't.

The next day, I sat her down.

She didn't want to be sat down, didn't want to really talk about it, "Well, he didn't really bully me. He didn't do anything to me, didn't shove me or anything." But she wouldn't look up at me.

"Joy?"

She rambled on, "Yes, he bullied other people, but not really me." She was lying, and she knew it. She would not meet my eyes.

"Are you sure?"

"Yes, Mom." But her lips were trembling, and she was holding on to the sides of the chair, as if for dear life.

"Are you sure, Joy?" I asked again. "I just want to understand what happened. Something happened with that bully situation that you are not telling me about, and I heard all about it in your school yesterday."

The tears filled her eyes then, and she looked at me for the first time since the conversation began. Her lips trembled even more as she spoke, "I'm sorry, Mommy. I didn't want you to be hurt that I was called a nigga."

The anger fizzled out of me, and a deep, deep sadness came in its place. What a world we lived in, a world where six-year-olds knew that the world was evil and tried to protect their parents from evilness.

Yes, she had lied, but she had lied to protect me. My heart went out to her. What an agony it must have been, to be emotionally hurt and yet choose to handle that hurt all by yourself instead of turning to the one who could comfort you, because you knew your hurt would hurt her too.

My sadness brought tears with it. I wiped them away and sat closer to Joy. "Thank you. You shouldn't have lied, but I also realize that you lied to protect me, because you didn't want me to be hurt."

She nodded enthusiastically.

"But you know something, Love?" Her eyes were white and round and fixated on me now. "It's not your job to protect me. That's God's job. You're not my husband, and God is. That we don't have a man physically living in the house with us doesn't mean we are not protected. Protecting us physically and emotionally is God's job, and we have to trust God with it. Do you understand?"

She stared at me with tear-stained cheeks, but a glow had come into her eyes. "I think I do, Mom."

"Thank you. So, you tell me everything that happens, even if it has the capacity to hurt me. God always has my...our backs. He will always help us through it. But never keep something from me because you don't want me to be hurt. Never! Understood?"

"Yes, Mom. Because it's not my job."

That lesson deeply impacted Joy, and it was a lesson I'd teach Grace when she joined the family. It isn't their responsibility to take care of adults physically or mentally or emotionally. It is mine, us as parents, to take care of them, to be the caretakers for Jesus.

***

The second time Joy experienced racism, she didn't hide it from me, because she had internalized my lesson, now knew it wasn't her job in any shape or form to shield my heart. At least not while she was a child. Studies abound on the toxic effects that parentification causes on a child throughout the rest of their lives.

Joy was in middle school, and there was a boy originally from Russia, who shared a school bus ride with her. He had a squirt bottle and often had left over water in it after the school day, for no reason than to torment Joy. On their afternoon bus ride back home, he'd suddenly squirt at her when she least expected it.

He did this for a while, and she tried to handle it on her own, until the day he called her a "nerd nigger."

Joy said her jaw hit the floor in surprise, and even more so when she turned to the front of the bus to see if the driver had seen what just happened. The driver looked straight at Joy, perhaps to let her know that he had seen all that transpired, and then he looked away, like he hadn't seen anything.

"How on earth is someone black and so smart?!" The bully had spat at her. This was a twelve-year-old boy, and it is hard to understand how someone so young could be filled with such anger, such hatred, such malice of an entire race of people.

Because that was what Joy saw on his face as he raged at her. Anger and hatred, directed toward her simply because she was black and smart. What might he have heard recited at the family dinner table? Seen on preferred family TV channels?!

She said she looked again toward the driver, and that he did the same thing again, which was to look at her and then pointedly look away. All while this Russian kid and his friends laughed at Joy's expense.

She returned to her book, wanting to disappear into it, not wanting to cause any more stirs on the bus.

But she told me immediately I got back from work, and as she recounted the tale, her voice was tinged with anger and bitterness. "How can I be suffering because of the color of my skin? It's just unfair!" She wailed. I didn't want my daughter to ever turn bitter. Darkness does not drive out darkness; only light does.

Her emotions wrapped themselves around my heart and weighed it down. I felt like I was in that bus with her, in that situation with her, being squirted, being called a nerdy nigger. I wanted to take my daughter and run, to go far away to a place where everyone was pleasant, and bullying and racism didn't happen. And yet, I knew that there was no perfect place on Earth, that problems would always follow human beings for as long as we were human.

By this time, Bruce was a part of our lives, so I didn't have to handle it alone. That night, seated around the dining table to a dinner of mashed potatoes and grilled chicken, we spoke at length about what to do. We even looked up ideas on Google.com to see how other families had handled such issues.

The general consensus was to not do the job for your child! Because you could talk to the school, and the school could talk to the driver (who obviously didn't care), or the school could talk to the bully, and the bullying would intensify. The bully would feel empowered; your child would be labeled a tattletale and seen as one unable to fight their own battles.

From the wisdom of internet parenting, we eventually settled on a plan, one which would require Joy to stand up for herself.

She would get on the bus before the bully and deliberately sit on his preferred seat. And when he came to her, she would act like she couldn't, didn't see him. When he stood in front of her to confront her, she was to stand up, place her hands akimbo, pop up her feet at a 45 degrees angle, in a posture of power and authority. And then she'd say to him, in a firm, loud voice, so that everyone on the bus could hear, "Never you in your life squirt me again." At this point, she was to point a finger at him.

We had to practice this over and over and over again, simply because Joy was not a naturally confrontational person. We looked stupid, I guess, Bruce and I taking turns acting the roles of Joy and the bully, training her how to address this peculiar situation.

"But what if the cops arrest me?"

I laughed, "The cops don't arrest someone for standing up for themselves, Love. And I've told you before and am telling you again now, if the cops ever get called on you for doing something I told you to, I am going to defend you. I'll go to jail rather than you go." And I meant it. I will never tell my children to do something illegal, but if I ever gave them advice and it turned out bad, I would defend them with my life if need be.

"What if I embarrass Faith?" Faith was her best friend, and they rode the bus together.

"Trust me. Faith will be happy that you solved this bully situation for everyone!"

She nodded then, but I could see that she was still a little cautious and unsure. I pulled her into a hug and kissed the top of her head, amazed that she was shooting up so fast. I wondered how soon it would be before she was as tall as I was.

The next day, I left work early, as did my husband. Our plan was to get to the school on time and drive behind the bus, surreptitiously, of course. It was a backup plan if things got out of hand. While waiting for the bus to pull out, we actually got to meet the school resource police officer and security guard, and we chatted her up to let her know why we were there.

I remember her laughing and nodding her head. "That's a creative way to sort the problem. And I love it!"

And so, we drove behind the bus as it pulled out, waiting for what was to unfold. We couldn't really see what was going on on the bus, but what a tale Joy had to tell when we got home.

"So, I sat in his chair as you said to do. And everyone was asking me, 'Why would you do that, Joy?!' But I didn't respond, just sat there till he came on the bus...'"

She paused to catch her breath, and her face was suffused with joy and laughter. "You should have seen his face. He was apoplectic, it seemed..." I wondered how she knew what apoplectic meant, but then she'd always had a keen mind.

"When he told me to get up from his spot, I stood up, and then I told him...I wagged my fingers and stood with my other hand on my waist as we planned...and I told him never in his life to squirt me with water again or call me bad names. His face just dropped. Just like a coward."

I sighed, closed my eyes, and opened them again, to the beaming face of my daughter. I was exhilarated for her.

"And kids on the bus were happy. They started clapping and calling my name, saying, 'Go, Joy!' I didn't even know some of them knew my name. Everyone was just so relieved that I had called him out. And Faith, well, she wasn't embarrassed. She was so happy. She told me that this boy and his friends had actually been planning to embarrass her, to pressure her into confessing that she had a boyfriend, when she didn't. So Faith was very happy with this turn of events."

It wasn't only Faith that benefited from this incident because the boy in question and his gang had been bullying so many of the other kids for a long time. Joy's confrontation seemed to turn him into another person, a gentler, less controlling person. And as for Joy, I could see her confidence birthed anew. I could see the strength that had been birthed in her for being able to fight and win her own battles.

The bully never bothered Joy again, and I started to see confidence settle around her like a cloak. After that incident, I saw her volunteer for more public speaking assignments in school, and watched her come into her own in conversations. I watched my daughter grow in leaps and bounds.

The lesson of standing up and confronting whatever confronted you yourself is one that we now teach to nine-year-old Grace. It is a lesson all parents need to teach their children. It's a lesson even parents can bear reminders of in our own lives too.

***

"It's okay to fail, Joy. I won't be mad. I won't be disappointed." I told my fourteen-year-old child, this child who was so brilliant and dazzling and driven.

I could see that she was struggling and overwhelmed, and I knew without a doubt that she needed to hear those words from me. I knew that she needed my permission to relax.

I have always had high academic standards, and was the one who went above board to ensure that Joy's education was the best it could be. When she was a very young child, when Akin and I had the responsibility of planning her future, I had pushed for her to go to private schools and eventually to attend a prestigious college. To which Akin had adamantly refused. Why should she attend private schools? Why wasn't a public school good enough for her? But I had always known that our child was a shiny bright coin and that she needed to be in the right environment to come into the fullness of her potential.

I fought for her, and always pushed her to live to her potential. She was precocious, reading and solving math two grades ahead of her age group, and while some families held back their children a year so that they could be top of their class, I did the opposite. There was no need to hold her back, and no use even having her in the same class as her age mates. Because it bored her that they were studying things she had studied and mastered on her own already.

I was not one to be complacent with her doing just good enough academically; and often encouraged her to be better and do the most that she could.

In first grade, there had been no gifted program for first graders, but after seeing Joy's extraordinarily high test scores, the lion mother in me approached the school administrators and sold them on the idea of extending the gifted program to first graders. They graciously did, and I am happy to state that several other gifted first graders also benefited from that program.

That program set the tone and pace for Joy's education.

I was originally amicably labelled the "Tiger Mom," after a popular Yale Law School Asian author that elevated parenting as practiced by the Chinese, the Indians, the Japanese and the West Africans. We, as a family, agreed I could neither be a tiger, nor a mother tiger. Why? Because I was progeny to a lion. The Lion. Lion of the tribe of Judah. Aslan's blood runs in my veins. Hence, "Lion Mom" it was. A lion as gentle as to nurture its own and wild as to destroy the gates of enemy forces.

In fourth grade, the school had to provide Joy with an advanced online math program that she could work through at her own pace, but it was not enough, and by fifth grade, she was bored...again. She was placed in the advanced portion of an already above-grade level curriculum, and the school was thinking to simply let her be and let her have an easy year. But Joy didn't want an easy year. And I didn't want an easy year for her either. An easy year, indeed a year filled with boredom, was a retrogression in any child's love for academics.

We hired a private tutor, and advocated for her to test out of class. Surprisingly, Joy tested out of class not only for the one class, but for a handful of others that year alone.

So Joy had grown to be as hardworking, perhaps even more hardworking than I was.

But to see my fourteen-year-old daughter run herself ragged tore at my heart. That year, she had kept pushing to determine where her limit would be, and to live up to the full potential that she had. She had taken on so many courses and so many projects her slim shoulders were practically sagging under it all. She had not let up on sports or other activities either, and went from one championship to another. She became the Minnesota state champion for Xcel gymnastics on balance beam that year, and played piano two years in a row at the Minneapolis Convention Center, as a winner of the state wide piano teacher's guild competition.

It was definitely okay to fail.

She looked up at me, at my words, her eyes huge behind her glasses.

"But I don't want to fail." She wailed in that whiny voice teenagers seem to have trademarked.

"You have my permission, Sweetheart. You have done your best, and sometimes our best is not enough! Go ahead and let it go. Fail."

"Thank you, Mom, for not pressuring me! But this is now a personal thing, no longer about what you expect or don't expect. I don't want to fail."

That day, I learned from Joy as much as she learned from me. She learned from me that all God required us to do was to put in our effort, to do our best. She also learned that we did not always have to get it right, that it was okay not to always get the top scores.

On the other hand, my daughter taught me that whatever we taught children from their early years became their gospel truth. She taught me that our examples and our words as parents were more impactful than we often realized, that children magnified what we said and did, making it all their own. This is how we pass on the good and sadly, also the bad. We are models being watched.

I would never need to push Joy again to strive for her best; the seed had been sown, watered, and was blooming.

That year, she did well despite her workload. And even though I never pushed her to get As anymore, she did, because the drive for excellence had been well internalized.

***

We had been believing God for a scholarship for Joy, particularly the SMART scholarship funded by the Department of Defense. She was a semi-finalist for one funded by the NSA and was to go do her background check to be qualified as a finalist when COVID hit, and that entire year was canceled.

It was a body blow, but as with many people in the year the pandemic broke out, we picked ourselves up, encouraged ourselves, and moved on.

She would be shortlisted for the SMART scholarship twice, even though she never made it all the way to the finalist's level. But to see her succeed so far was a joy, an exhilarating kind of joy. We would later learn that her choice facility had planned from the beginning of the year that the SMART scholarship for 2022 would be dedicated to Ph.Ds.

So, we haven't quite gotten the scholarship we want just yet. But in everything, Joy's faith and mine stand strong. We are still paying out of pocket for her very expensive tuition, but she at 19, has achieved things I hadn't at 19. And she burns with an inner fire, a fire that is aglow for Jesus, and one that is propelling her toward her future.

For this, I am grateful.

✳✳✳

And forgiveness? I would learn all about it anew from Grace when she was only three years old.

Because I could afford the preference, even if that meant cutting other things, I always had someone living in to take care of my children while I worked. Daycare centers were and are often completely fine, but the personal touch that a nanny brought was worth my sacrifice. I got to see the nanny's interaction with my child, and how she loved on that child. I got to see their connection or lack of connection. Also, I got to avoid the risk to my job commitment when a daycare center would suddenly close or have weather-related shut downs.

So, nanny care it was. And live-in nanny care specifically. Family they were.

One early evening, I returned from work exhausted, as I usually did. I parked in the garage, sat in my car for a couple of minutes to catch my breath. The quietness of the garage washed over me, and the smell of simmering stew somehow wended its way from the kitchen and into the garage. I felt at peace. I felt at home.

Until I eased open the door, and Grace's ball went whizzing past my head. Obviously, she hadn't known I was going to open the door and hadn't envisaged that she would just nearly miss me with the ball.

"Sorry, Mom!" She piped up. At only three, Grace had a vocabulary that could rival almost any adult's. While Joy was more mechanically oriented, Grace has always had a love for words. She would later parlay this love into becoming a published author at age nine. "I really wasn't aiming at you but at Aunty."

"Aunty" was the nanny, and true to what Grace had just said, "Aunty" was just a hand's length from me, obviously the target of the throw.

My daughter's words caught me off guard. Had I managed to raise a daughter who was so insensitive, who threw balls at her caregiver?

"Not on my watch, Grace! Not in my house. How dare you? How dare you throw stuff at an older person, and the one who takes care of you?"

My daughter went from smiling in one minute to being crestfallen in the next. Her face fell, her shoulders stooped, and the tears came to her eyes. She did not utter a word any further.

"But we were playing." It was "Aunty" speaking now. "She and I were just playing. We were practicing catch!"

Grace went to the foot of the stairs, was now seated on the lowest stair, her arms crossed around her tiny body, her face awash with tears.

My anger dried up within me, and remorse filled me instead. I had just shouted and assumed ill about a perfectly normal situation. For a moment, I had stepped out of myself and not trusted in the lessons I had taught for years. I had just accused my daughter of maltreating the hired help, which she obviously hadn't been doing.

I went to her and sat beside her on the staircase, attempting to put my arms around her. "I am so sorry, Grace, so so sorry."

She rebuffed my hug. "You don't trust me, Mom!"

"I am sorry, Grace."

She shrugged and folded her arms even tighter. "Well, I am not ready to forgive you. Not yet!"

She was only three, but she was showing me that some hurts were so deep, so egregious that the forgiver needed to go deep within to find reconciliatory forgiveness in their heart for the wounder. And I appreciated it, understood it.

"I understand, Grace. And I am truly sorry."

I sat on the sofa and waited for my daughter to forgive me. It took less than five minutes before she was off the stairs and nestled into my arms. "Now, I forgive you, Mom!"

And the forgiveness was even more worth its weight in gold because she had forgiven me from her heart. And so, these days, I don't expect automatic forgiveness from people when I offend them and apologize. I now give time to allow the person work through their complex emotions and come to forgiveness without any badgering, but in their own space and time.

This was the lesson my three-year-old taught me about forgiveness.

***

Grace loves hard and long.

She was born several years after my sister was diagnosed with lupus, never knew my sister in a healthy body, but Grace loved her with every fiber of her being. Separated by time, age, and distance, these two people were perfectly content to video call each other and just stare at the screens without saying any word.

My sister couldn't speak due to aphasia, but she and Grace got along just well. They sang together. They recited scriptures together. They were happily besties.

When my sister was hospitalized for the last time before she left her earthly shell behind, Grace prayed as I had never seen her pray. For years, she had prayed and thanked God with faith for Yomi, my best friend, who was also going through health challenges. Someone also beloved by Grace, my seven-year-old turned to prayer.

For these two women to lose their earthly burdens within months of each other almost damaged Grace, but for God.

"He didn't answer! He didn't!" My sister had passed on first, and Grace had shuddered with repressed tears when this happened. When Yomi died a mere 89 days later, Grace couldn't hold it in anymore.

She wept with abandon, lay flat across her bed, and wouldn't get off. When we spoke to her, when we tried to console her, she was inconsolable.

In less than a week, her grief began to manifest itself in hormonal imbalance, stomach cramps, and a host of other pesky illnesses. And thus began the long, winding road to specialists and medication and recovery.

I started to deliberately speak scriptures over this child of mine, who was so heartbroken that she didn't know what to do with herself. I gave her back to God, handed everything that had to do with her, physically and emotionally, back to the one who had molded her and placed her in my womb.

"Jesus is good in everything!" I started to tell her, and made it a habit to remind her of this. "He does answer prayers, but sometimes not in the way we expect. And even if we don't get the answers we want, He is still good."

I had always taught my children that God was good and remains good till the end of the world, but that would be the first time Grace's faith would be so confronted. So, I needed to remind her again and again that Jesus was good, even when we didn't understand what He was working out.

This was the time to drive this lesson home again and again.

It was a long journey, but my daughter's faith rose again, and she started to believe in the undoubted goodness of God again. And slowly but surely, all of her physical ailments resolved themselves, to the surprise of her attending doctors.

***

The Uvalde school shooting would touch our hearts the same way it would impact millions of families with little children all over America. School security became tighter, and parents' hearts skipped a little faster when we dropped off our children at school, only loosening slightly when they were back home safe in the afternoon.

Grace's school especially felt vulnerable, having been threatened with religious/tribal encounters only weeks before Uvalde happened. With Uvalde, their security protocol underwent a massive overhaul, for which I am grateful to the administrators and an amazing school principal.

However, picking Grace up one afternoon, she had misunderstood where I was, and inadvertently made a beeline for me directly from the playground instead of going through the reception and exiting through newly sanctioned procedures.

Two school staff were seated in the reception, seeing the children going and coming, and one of them heaved to her feet to call out to Grace.

"No! No!! That is wrong." Her words were in and of themselves okay because she was in correction mode, but her tone was something else. It was loud and grating and carried with harshness.

At her words, Grace self-corrected and turned toward the reception. I took the last few steps into the reception myself, and there Grace was, now being chewed out by not just the one school staff, but additionally by an accomplice staff adult that had joined the chastisement. They were yelling at my daughter who simply stood there, crestfallen.

I put my anger in check but spoke up. "Ladies, I think that should be plenty enough. She made a mistake, an innocent error and has received your correction. But I don't think she needs the intimidation by two adults, when she could have been corrected firmly but gently." I pulled Grace tighter into my embrace and flung back the stray lock of hair that had fallen out of her ponytail braids and onto her face.

"One adult is good enough to correct a child."

No one was going to have the permission to make my child feel less than she was – God's beloved.

Words don't break bones, but they can do a lot worse damage. They can corrupt the mind. And they can embed the evil grains of trauma into an innocent soul.

One of the women looked at me, and then turned her gaze to the other woman, who was looking everywhere but at me or Grace.

"I guess you...she can go home now."

And so, we went home, my child's hand in mine as we traversed the short distance between the reception and the waiting car. Grace was not smiling, but she wasn't frowning either. For me, the knowledge that my child knew that she was loved and that we had her back, no matter what, was a comforting one.

Shame should have no place with children.

***

All children do wrong from time to time and get to be corrected in love and set right. But once, when I myself was the source of worthy correction that meted shame, I took action.

My usually vivacious child, who enters the room words first, who bounces off the walls in excitement when she is with family, had become subdued from the correction. She had gone deep inside herself, and would only respond when spoken to.

"Come here, Little Bear," I told her, gathering her up in my arms for a tight, tight hug.

Her hug was tentative at first, but when I squeezed her with all of the love in my heart, she returned the favor.

"You know there is nothing to be ashamed of. You were wrong. You were corrected, and you've been forgiven. And we are back again on a clean slate. Never ever forget that when I forgive you, it is complete, no strings attached, everything forgiven."

She nodded against my chest, this little child of mine who was not exactly so little anymore. As I placed a kiss on top of her head, I wondered how the time flew by so fast, how a toddler could be in diapers just a couple of years ago and be all girly and sparkly and almost grown already.

And I also realized that my job as a parent is to always deal in grace and mercy, just like Jesus did for me. This is what we are all called to do.

***

I am a fervent believer in the fact that children hear from the womb. They hear our words, whether these words are words of life or death. Having learned this long before I even became a mother, I deliberately, intentionally spoke words of life to my children when they were in the womb.

With Grace, I'd listen without fail every morning by 5 am to prayer hour, and sometimes I'd play soft Christian music on my phone and place it right across my belly, for her entertainment and edification.

At 34 weeks, Grace was breech, and we did all we could to make her turn. I engaged a chiropractic doctor and did the hip exercises that abound on internet pregnancy forums. But Grace, purposefully created Grace, porpoised in and out of being breeched and did not fully engage in position.

At 42 weeks, she chose breech, and I was advised that it was safer to do a C-section. I politely declined and went back home. The next morning, as usual, I was on the prayer line when I felt her hiccup, and this hiccup was different from the rest. It came from the vaginal area, much lower than where I had placed the phone, and I knew, just knew that she had turned again right side up.

So back to the hospital we went, and the ultrasound confirmed my hope and desire although with a cervix that maintained persistent refusal to efface. Now at 42 weeks that medical staff could safely and legally apply Cytotec to prompt progress and induce labor, we went right in.

Grace is a great little gymnast today, but she has been one right from the time she was in the womb. And right there during the labor, she had started to make her way yet again to flip the wrong side up. The anatomical possibility of her adventures defied logical explanation and it would take 41 hours of active labor to have my girl in my arms.

Grace is now closing in on double digit ages, and the prayer telephone line remains a source of anchoring for her, as much as she was comforted by it when she was in the womb. She'd be sleeping, but her spirit would be consciously tuned to the 5 am prayer. Sometimes, she'd even ask to listen to it on speaker phone stating that it comforted her soul.

Indeed, children do hear from the womb, and the words we speak to them, and the atmosphere we surround them with do matter. Oh, how much it does.

***

It's incredibly hard not to spank children. I will be the first to admit this.

I spanked Joy for the first eight or nine years of her life, and I have since concluded this; We spank because it is convenient. You spank, they listen, you move on, your anger resolved. But with the spanking, you leave emotional scars that might follow these precious gifts into their adult years.

When she was nine, after a spanking that satisfied my anger more than corrected Joy's errant behavior, she came to me for a discussion.

"I'd like you to sign a contract that you will never spank me again."

Her words caught my attention, and my first reaction was to raise a hand and stop her in her tracks. But I took a minute to digest her words.

She went on, "We will list all the things you don't like me doing, and I will try my very best not to do them. I am trusting God to help me! And then you sign that you will never spank me again."

My heart in my throat, but certain that the Holy Spirit was ministering to me through her, I allowed her to draw up the contract, and I appended my signature.

I would learn in the following months how much harder it was to parent a child without resorting to spanking. I would also learn how impactful parenting can be when you ditch the spanking rod and replace it with the true biblical guiding rod, with an ounce of listening. I matured as a parent, because my discipline started to come less from a place of anger and more from a place of love and sacrifice.

Without a physical cane, you sat and listened, weighed the discipline/punishment options that fit the behavior, and curtailed yourself from becoming the person to inflict emotional scars on the people you loved.

Grace doesn't know what it means to be spanked now, because she has never been spanked.

Yes, Proverbs 13:24 says, "He that spareth his rod hateth his son: but he that loveth him chasteneth him betimes." But I would grow to understand that the rod was the Word, the rod of guidance, not the rod of abuse.

This is the way I have chosen to parent, to use the word of God as a guiding rod, to bring them back to the Word again and again. And I am ecstatic at the world changers I am privileged to so nurture, both in my direct biological lineage and in every circle of influence at which God brings me a child to nurture.

By the world's definition, I have a child who is a Nigerian American and another who is Nigerian-German-Scandinavian-American. But these kids are not really mine. They are Jesus' children, the children of God, loved by Him before He gave them to me to nurture. And I'll make sure to do an excellent job for Him!

Will you join me and make a commitment to raise champion generations with love and sacrifice? It all really starts with family.

CHAPTER 20

Family Is Everything. It Is Where Love Is Patient And Kind

What do you find unforgivable in your relationships and what are you able to forgive?

As believers, we have been called to forgive all things. But what does that really mean?

Can you forgive a sister who sleeps with your spouse? Can you forgive a mother who disowns you? How about a spouse who lusted after another woman, and right in your presence too? Or a spouse who cheated on you?

Let's take it a bit further. Will you forgive your spouse that cheated throughout your marriage, and was neck-deep in sleeping with prostitutes?

The interesting thing is that God has called us to forgive every single one of these things. But what does forgiveness really mean?

It is important to understand that we have been called to forgive all, but we have not been called to reconcile all. We've never been called to do that because it is not in our power to do so.

Forgiveness is between the offended person and God. You release the justice to God because you trust Him that He is the only one who can make it right, who can heal the trauma, and make you whole again. The offender can restitute all they want, but they cannot make you whole to where you were before you were offended. They cannot heal your trauma or your pain. Their actions can show that they are sorry, and this can help the hurt, but only God can reconcile that hurt.

Forgiveness is like the vertical arm of the cross; it is the part pointing to heaven, the part that says, I release this person to God because I know God can make me whole again. It doesn't mean saying that the offender did not offend you or hurt you, or that they are going scot-free. It simply means that you are releasing it all to God.

Reconciliation, however, is a different ball game altogether. It requires the offender to repent, and this is the horizontal arm of the cross of Jesus Christ. This horizontal arm also represents our relationships here on earth, between brethren, between spouses, and between parents and children. This arm does not get fixed unless the offender repents, turns his way around, and chooses a new direction.

We Christians often miss this. We think forgiveness means that we can live with an abuser, and tolerate improper situations. But we were never called to that.

In my marriage, this calling has meant forgiving my husband for cheating on me with prostitutes, but it has never meant that I would reconcile with him unless he repented and turned his way around.

This chapter is about that story. It is a story of forgiveness and reconciliation, of me forgiving what I never thought I would, of how God helped me through my trauma, of navigating a journey I never thought I would be on. It is a story of how we have journeyed toward reconciliation.

This chapter is also a story about family, of the unique, beautiful relationships between siblings.

***

It had been a month of holding it to my chest, of this crazy, terrible secret that I could no longer keep a secret. The weight of the secret was threatening to burn a hole through my chest, and I often woke in the middle of the night, hyperventilating, feeling like I was drowning in an ocean I could not get my head above.

One evening, in my prayer closet, weeping more than I was praying, I finally reached for my phone and called my psychiatrist brother, who was on the other end of the world, but who was the person my heart had instructed me to call.

"Brother Dele." My voice was thin and ragged, a testament to the fact that I had been crying for days on end.

The panic came into his voice immediately, tinging the timbre of his voice from its normally pleasant tone. "What's the matter? Is everything okay, Kemi?"

I swallowed a huge mouthful of air, "Promise me that you will keep this confidential, that this would not be heard by anyone else." Even as I made him promise, I knew that there was a huge chance that he would tell his wife. That was how marriages worked; that was how they were supposed to work. You were supposed to be your spouse's best friend, to bare your soul to them, to have them know everything that there was to know about you.

Unfortunately, I was discovering that this wasn't the case with my own marriage. I had just realized that mine had secrets stacked on top of each other. Treason, betrayal, and many things unimaginable.

But then, how does a husband sit his wife and tell her how deep in sin he had been, how bound he had been, just how badly he had been hurting her?

"Bruce has been cheating on me!" I blurted out and waited to let that sink in, and then continued in the rush of the same breath, "And not just with normal people! He's been seeing prostitutes!"

Even as I spoke the words, the trauma overtook me again, the same way it had taken me each time I thought of my husband's infidelity. Days after I found out, I couldn't bear to be in the same room with him. I still loved him with a desperate love, but I also felt completely repulsed by him. For the past decade and more, he had been the one person I thought I could reliably turn to when I needed comfort, and with a pang, I realized that I couldn't turn to him now. He was the source of my pain.

And so, we lived in the same home, breathed the same air, but I felt a thousand years removed from him. By God, I came close to hating him. Maybe I did hate him at that point.

My brother was gentle and kind, the response I had prayed for, but hadn't really expected. One of the reasons it had taken me so long to reach out to any support system, any sibling, was because I had been treated differently than you'd hope for at the time of the divorce from Akin.

The support I'd received then was lackluster at best from everyone for the most part. The pastor who joined us in marriage had bluntly said to me, "Was it not you who told us God spoke to you? What has happened now?" When music fades, how easy it is to forget that marriage is a threefold cord that requires the participation of the two married ones, and not just the hand of God.

Also, one sibling had written to me at the time, stating that they didn't know what to say, whose side to take, that it was a matter of "he said, she said," and that they were unable to actually see where the truth lived. That broke an already broken heart into smithereens. Family was supposed to have your back, no matter what. It was as simple as that! Family chose you over your spouse, except you had proven time and time again to be a liar. Even if you were a liar, you still had their blood. You were family, for God's sake!

But even with my broken heart, I had worked to understand, to see the whole thing from their viewpoint. I realized that they were in uncharted waters, that there were no handwritten manuals on how to act toward a divorcing sister, and they were lost for what to do.

So, as I poured my heart out to Brother Dele, that I would be met with grace, with compassion, with understanding this time, made it all the more emotional.

There was a moment of silence, and then more than just one moment. Several moments of silence, and then he sucked in a deep breath.

"Kemi, I have never lived through your reality, and I never will. But I love you with the whole of my heart. Let whosoever has been through a betraying spouse come forward to cast blame on you. God sees them. Let whosoever has not been through it also come forward and cast their own blame. Let them come forward to judge and castigate any decisions you choose to make. God sees and judges them. I can't imagine myself in this situation and what decision I might take to leave or to stay with horror. I don't blame you for any decision you choose, my sister! Please know that I don't. I am solidly behind you, whatever you choose to do!

"I support you completely, Sis, whatever you choose. But here is what I want to say; You're not stuck, never forget that. Your safety and health are much more important."

***

It had been a terrible month!

I found out about the addiction in a spectacular, roundabout, God-ordained way. For months, we had been having incessant quarrels. In and of themselves, they were small and insignificant, and we were going through so much upheaval at this time. My sister was ill, as was my best friend, and I had the pressure of nonstop work to crown it all. So, I was more irritable. He was more irritable than usual as well. So, we butted heads and had these little arguments.

But the arguments were getting to be quite a lot, so that we were constantly forgiving and re-quarrelling. We thought we loved each other and couldn't continue to let the detritus of everyday living chip away at our love. So, I started to seek help professionally and to connect the dots.

Whatever the search filter I was entering in Google inquiries directed to a trend of possibilities of betrayal in the relationship. Said more accurately, abuse in the relationship. Hidden sexual addiction, or as Dr. Omar

Minwalla, a leading expert on addiction would call it - living a basement life of lies – is spousal abuse.

Don't be fooled. Sexual addiction has little to nothing to do with one person's sexual appetite exceeding their spouse's – I initiated more than 60% of our sexual intimacy at that time. It has little to nothing to do with one person withdrawing sex from another – my husband will be first to tell you there was never such a denial in our relationship. Sexual addiction has little to nothing to do with mid-life crisis. But it has a lot to do with intimacy anorexia; it has a lot to do with control, shame, and abuse. It has a lot to do with society's elevation of everything sexual. It has a lot to do with mental sickness from learned evil behaviors that reprograms a human brain. It has all to do with SIN. Calling it an addiction is just a label. It becomes addictive from learned evil behavioral patterns that the person has adopted by choice. Although it always has a trauma root, it is also always a choice. By intent.

Most recently, we had attended Restoring the Foundations (RTF) in Dallas, where the Holy Spirit had persisted on our hosts that a deep sexual sin was being hidden by him. He didn't tell me this, as it occurred during his individual sessions. He eventually yielded some to them after four days of persistence. The devil is a hardened evil. Eventually, when he acquiesced, he lied about the occurrence as being once, and he lied about the degree as not including intercourse. But I knew something was off. Very off. After RTF, he honed his deception skills and became an expert liar even to our RTF host couples to the point of their confusion of my role. You see, it's easy to pick out a liar who sounds mean. How about a liar who is soft, calm, and charming? A liar who precedes their false witnessing and evil report with pleas to the listener not to withdraw love from their victim. A liar who spends 80% of the discussion embellishing on their love for their victim, and elaborating how perfect their victim is, and then spends 20% adorning her with the evilest false witness. How about that? Can you detect the deception that is cleverly marinated in a mast of just enough omissions, partial truths, distortions, minimizations, exaggerations, justifications, rationalizations, allowing others to misperceive, avoiding truth by shifting topic/distraction, staying superficial, and "forgetting"?

So, I researched, and learned more. Starting with questioning my part in the play since even our hosts were being confounded after having such deep convictions. I started to see a trend with the discoveries, from one article to another. I contacted a number of the authors and the first to broach sex addiction was Dr. Weiss' assistant. She had asked if Bruce had stopped masturbation and I said yes, and she responded he hadn't and guaranteed me there was worse. The naïve me forwarded the email to my husband, telling him to be honest with me. Of course, you guessed it. He lied. "She is completely off. That's why she is the admin person and not the therapist!" And I had agreed with Bruce. The idea at that time was ridiculous. It seemed just too farfetched and impossible.

And so, our arguments continued. Until I decided the fee to see one of the absolute leading experts in marital issues, was worth the trouble to diagnose for myself.

We were scheduled for a beautiful Friday afternoon on a Fall Day. As we returned from Austin, running late for the appointment with Dr. Weiss, I called Dr. Weiss to let him know we were late, that we were in the middle of an argument. Truth be told, I didn't want to even go into that session anymore. I just wanted to climb into bed and let this all just go away.

"Not to worry. I want to watch how you argue. It gives me additional insights into your relationship to diagnose root causes of any issues."

We set up the Tab to catch our argument and joined him on zoom. I felt awkward at the very beginning, wondering where on earth this was done; arguing on video with your spouse so that your therapist could see what made your relationship work the way it did. But in less than five minutes, I forgot that there was someone on the other end watching us. I was fully in the moment, incensed at something Bruce had said.

But Dr. Weiss encouraged us to proceed. By this time, we were home. He offered an extended session to get to the bottom of the matter.

"Just so you know," Dr. Weiss began, "Your quarrel...the way that you both quarrel is pretty normal for couples. As I watched you get angry at each other and try to resolve the issue you had, I noticed that none of you used any obscene words, so great job on that."

What a relief, I thought. It was normal couples' stuff, after all. I felt a little nod of satisfaction that we were quarrelling fairly, if that was something to be proud of, but Dr. Weiss' next words took the wind out of my sail.

"But there is a deeper issue I want to address. And this has to do with Bruce!"

My heart was thumping inside of my heart, and I raised a shaky glass of water to my lips, only to find that I wasn't thirsty. I placed the glass back on the coaster.

"I am convinced that you, Bruce, have secrets you are grappling with that Folakemi does not know about. You check all the boxes of being a sexual addict, and not just masturbation. You are hiding things of grave consequences from your wife. You are a coward."

I lifted the glass again, put it down again, my heart now no longer thumping in my chest but in my throat.

"I have no addiction! I am not addicted to anything!" Bruce's voice was throbbing with indignation, and I wanted to be angry along with it.

That was when Dr. Weiss tore into him. Dr. Weiss' voice was low, never rose, but it was forceful, powerful, as he told my husband he knew Bruce had gone well beyond masturbation or non-intercourse. He asked him pointedly how often he had sex out of marriage and Bruce denied it, yet Dr. Weiss repeatedly called him a liar.

I found my voice then, "Don't do that to Bruce, Dr. Weiss. As much as I respect you and value your insight, I draw the line at the tone you are taking, the way you are tearing into my husband."

Dr. Weiss smiled. "Are you the expert, Folakemi, or am I the expert?"

We went for a walk after that encounter. Bruce repeatedly said no one had ever reached into him like Dr. Weiss did and that he liked Dr. Weiss. That seemed so strange to me.

***

I turned in for the night early, my heart heavy. I didn't believe what Dr. Weiss had accused Bruce of. Once, Grace had asked if we were okay, to which we had both nodded.

When Bruce came in for the night, he sat on his side of the bed, his back turned to me, as mine was to him. And then he said Dr. Weiss was accurate, except for the extent. He confessed some and hid the rest...until a couple months after that day, that he confessed, very softly, very calmly, the extent to his betrayal, included all but unprotected intercourse.

"It's true, Sweetheart! I have struggled with sexual addiction for a very long time, even long before we were married."

His words were no longer words; now, they were weapons, sharp, barbed hooks that found their way from his heart and mouth, and into the soft earth of my heart.

"It doesn't happen every time. There are even months when absolutely nothing happened, and then I feel this compulsion, this overwhelming compulsion..."

As his barbed words lanced my heart, again and again, I found myself flailing my arms, striking at the pillows surrounding me. And then a strange keening sound began to issue from my mouth, quite unnatural sounding, piercing and shrill.

***

We would make the rounds to learn from many experts. The lovely Susan Allen, Marsha Means, Bob & Audrey Meisner, Dr. Sheri Keffer, Debbie Laaser persisting the legacy of her husband, Mark Lasser, Connie Spiegel, Anne Blythe, Charles and Carin Dusse, and name almost any leading CSATs, and even to engaging with the Wisdom of Trauma movie pros - Zaya & Maurizio Benazzo in Europe.

I found myself poring over journal upon journal. I was speaking with experts at all costs, digesting every mental diagnosis code in the DSM, weighing whether I was entwined with a sociopath or a psychopath. My heart thought it knew Bruce; the essence of me knew the essence of him. But these new layers to him, this huge secret he had been carrying, threw a cloud over everything I knew, over everything I thought I knew.

We attended a three-day intensive retreat with Ella and Jeff Hutchinson. Ella said it was extremely rare and unusual and promising for the addict to have come forward with a disclosure themselves as Bruce did. The typical situation was discovery, not disclosure. That was the first glimpse of hope, something I would need on the long, tortuous journey ahead of us.

Bruce seemed relieved after the retreat. He has completed a therapeutic disclosure, with polygraph to boot, and passed. I could also see the relief in his eyes, the relief that came from finally shrugging off a heavy burden, perhaps his heaviest burden yet.

One minute, I wanted to make our marriage work, to give it all it required, to offer Bruce forgiveness on a platter as it was. And the very next minute, I couldn't wait to be gone from the marriage, to shrug off a husband who could be this deceiving. I was trying to stop myself from becoming a pseudo psychologist but couldn't help myself. The load, offloaded his back, seemed to have hopped on mine.

I wavered between pity for him and disgust at him. I still loved him, because love doesn't just up and leave, but I found myself to be afraid of him, to be wary of him. He was an unsafe partner. How could a man who was so good to me, so good to our children, so vivacious and bubbly and the outward fit for a Christian have such a basement life?

It just did not make sense.

***

Yes, we have been called to forgiveness as Christians. We have been called to release the justice to God because we trust Him, that He is the only one who can make it right, who can heal the trauma, who can make us whole again. Only He can, regardless of what the offense might be, or how repentant or unrepentant the offender is. The repentant brings only an added hope of reconciliation, but they cannot heal the hurt that God can.

When psychology and science couldn't explain to me the how and why of Bruce's deception, I turned to the only person I could; Jesus. I knelt at the foot of the cross, and in a flood of tears and a river of desperation, I handed it over to God. I was going to walk with God through the following weeks, whether it would lead to the healing of or the dissolution of my marriage. I didn't know what the future held, but I placed my little hands into God's bigger hands and let Him lead the way.

I believe that the Holy Spirit had been orchestrating Bruce's deliverance for years and that things had just boiled over at the exact moment it was supposed to. My husband needed to be found out before his healing from the age-long bondage that had held him down could commence. Whether our marriage survived the upheaval or not, God had never stopped loving Bruce and wanted to heal him, to free him, to give him back his life as it should be.

I saw the broken heart of my husband. I saw him reaching out to God, and I saw God reach out, scoop this child of His up in His arms and work to reinstate him.

But that was between Bruce and God. It had nothing to do with me.

My heart alternated between being a rock of unforgiveness and then a soft bed of forgiveness. I wanted to slick back my husband's brown hair and look into his eyes like I had once done. But I felt betrayed to the core. I worked with God on forgiveness, and I did forgive Bruce. But I didn't know if I still wanted a future with him. Even that, now, only God knows.

Bruce tried to help me on the forgiveness journey. He was going to do all he could to win me back. He signed himself into a Christian-based sexual addiction workshop and started seeing a therapist. Because we had an honesty at all cost policy with our children, we had to sit them and tell them what was happening with Dad and where we were with our marriage. He would apologize to them again and again.

He started to restitute; he still is restituting and has long ways to go. But I came to realize, as he also did, that Bruce could not make me whole to where I was before all this started. He had no power to heal my trauma or pain.

***

I am still in love with Bruce. As he works and journeys toward becoming a bonafide child of God, a true husband and father, and the man he was always destined to be, I am allowing God to continue to work the work of forgiveness in my heart.

I think we will make it through. Would this be simply because Bruce asked for my forgiveness? No.

It would be because he has given God the wheels of his life, and is working at healing the past trauma in his life that triggered the addiction. It would be because Bruce is proving himself to me and the children that he wants to be here, that he would move heaven and earth to be here.

But the future, I leave in God's hands alone. It is left to Bruce to earn trust and completely turn to the healer alone. There are days I still struggle, but at those times, the agonizing pain that lanced my heart a year and two years ago has been replaced by a quick surrender to God and a practice of the Immanuel prayer. Instead of pain, there is a shard of light, a brightness that is assuring of God's presence.

I am not stuck by religious bigots' opinions on divorce and separation. But I am free. Free to love and be loved. This load of hurt and sadness, of treason and trauma, this unimaginably heavy burden, is what I dropped at Jesus' feet when I blurted out my tragedies for the first time ever at Grief to Grace, and to strangers, nonetheless. This was the #4 tragedy of my life that brought it crashing to find the love of Jesus Christ. Preceded by the death of both moms, and then the miscarriage of our almost 16 weeks child. Succeeded by the disconcerting failure of human frailty in clergy, and then by the deaths of my sister and my best friend. These devastating calamities were the true guiding light that led me to re-finding my Savior. My love. My all-in love.

✱✱✱

Family indeed is everything. Less than six months after Bruce's disclosure was when my sister called heaven her new home and we would all be shaken to our roots.

I later got to understand, by the help of the Holy Spirit, that it was simply her time to go. I would hear the whisper of the words, "She has pleased me," in my heart in response to my "why now" questions.

After she passed on, I couldn't help but ask why now? Why not at 24 when she was first diagnosed with SLE? Why not at 36 when she had brain cancer? And why not at 40 when the stroke took away her ability to speak? Why at 48? And how could she have been felled by something as innocuous as choking on food, when she had fought for so long and so hard?

At the words, "She has pleased me," relief started to steal into my heart, bit by bit, and then in increments. As time passed, I would no longer mourn Sister Ronke with the desperation I had initially done. I became able to smile at the memories I had of her, of our childhood, of the love we had shared.

I realized that she had had a purpose that was fully fulfilled in the Master's grand plan. She lived for purpose and left on accomplishment. Life is fleeting, but heaven is real, and heaven is forever.

Preparing for the funeral in the midst of a pandemic lockdown was tough and toughened our family bonds.

***

I enjoy a unique relationship with each of my siblings. The only time I had ever felt separate from them was at the season of my hardships with Akin, and I no longer fault them for their reactions at that time.

I remember lots of laughter as children. When I think of Sister Ronke, the first visual that comes to me is her hiding a sticky smile behind her palms, her eyes crinkled at the sides with barely suppressed laughter.

I remember nights of storytelling, of huddling under the covers with my two big brothers, elder sister and younger brother. I remember this feeling of completeness, of all being right with the universe when they were around.

As we grew up, Sister Ronke was my best friend, but the twins, Brother Dele and Ayo, were my heroes. I adored them, practically worshipping the grounds upon which they walked.

"One day, I'll marry a man just like you." I remember telling Brother Ayo one sun-drenched afternoon.

He removed his glasses to wipe the sweat from his face before speaking, a huge smile on his face. "That's fine and all, but he's got to be just half as smart as I am."

I proceeded to swat at him, but he was already ducking.

We teased each other mercilessly, but it was all in good faith, and all in love. We were the siblings who would take a bullet for the other, the siblings who would go to hell and back for the other.

Brother Ayo was the calmer of nerves, the one who made all your jitters go away when you approached a difficult exam. He was the one with the most soothing of voices, the one who just seemed to know what to say and how to say it.

I remember being all of three years old and being teary and furious when some of his friends unintentionally hit me with a football they were kicking around in the backyard. I remember being so infuriated and sad at the same time, swinging my slate at my brother, hitting his head, and barely missing his eyes.

He plucked the slate out of my hand quietly, set it on the patio beside us, and proceeded to hug me, calming my nerves, wiping my tears. Less than ten minutes later, I was kicking the ball with my big brother and his friends.

Sean, my younger brother, is my gift from God. He was the one I wanted to protect with every fiber of my being as we grew. I wanted to be everything to him that my elder ones were to me; his protector, his nurturer, his confidante. Today, his Yale-Law-School-honed lawyerly smarts are most times an annoyance, but all the time a journey deeper in humility and offense-handling for me. Feisty and fiery. I love him in his entirety, and I've been blessed with the grace to forgive things I never thought I could forgive.

During the visit for sister Ronke's funeral, Brother Ayo's wife turned to me to let me know how much my big brother treasured his "Lil sis." Despite the ups and downs of my life, he was always proud of me, never hesitated to shout to the world how clever, how caring, how successful I was. Both of the twins did that. Look at his social media posts, and brother Dele never ceased to announce to the world he was charmed by his "Lil sis."

That admiration is more than mutual. I adored all my siblings growing up, but as I have grown and matured into the woman I am now, I don't see how my life would have turned out without them. They helped me form who I am. They are the best siblings in the world. I wouldn't change them, or the events of our lives, for anything.

By the time I left the UK from Sister Ronke's funeral, all my siblings were in the know of where I stood in my relationship with Bruce. And the renewed love for each other was a need for a time such as this.

***

I am more than happy to say that my children, Joy and Grace, are another beautiful study in sibling relationships. I cannot imagine them not being sisters, cannot imagine one without the other. Nine years apart in age, yet as thick as thieves.

Since Grace was a baby until this day when Joy visits home, they share a bed, and will make do with the tiniest space, enjoying pushing each other. As a baby, Joy would sit quietly by Grace's crib, just staring, enthralled. Sometimes, I'd find her reading to Baby Grace, her voice as soft as a bed of marshmallows. When I found them this way, my heart would skip, do a little dance.

As Grace grew up, she started to trail Joy the same way I'd trailed my sister and elder brothers. She'd join her elder sister in reading chemistry and biology textbooks, even though she did not understand anything they were reading. But how she loved to play pretend with her sister.

Joy wears glasses, and Grace doesn't, but I remember having to purchase a pair of plastic glasses for Grace because she wanted to perch one on the tips of her nose just like Joy did.

***

The nine years between them is the reason they are often at different stages every given time. It is the reason they were never in the same school at the same time, the reason why one was using crayons while the other used felt pens.

An excellent scholar, Joy was done with high school at sixteen instead of eighteen, and ready to go off to college, coming home only for holidays, and in swaths of time she was able to cut out of her busy schedule. As fall bridged the gap between summer and winter that first Thanksgiving away to school, Joy came home.

When she knocked at the door, a small suitcase behind her, Grace went ballistic with joy.

"You came! You came!!" They danced around the kitchen; two sisters enthralled to be friends. I managed to squeeze in a hug of my own.

Thanksgiving was fun, but how fast it went. One day Joy was newly home, and the next, she was packing up to go back.

Grace fell to pieces. "I don't want you to go, please!"

"But you know that I have to. You know I have to be at school." Even as Joy tried to make her little sister see reason, I could also see that she herself was crestfallen. If she had the opportunity and the means to take Grace with her to school, I, without a doubt, knew that she would.

The afternoon after Joy returned, I saw Grace standing by her window. It was a warm and sunny afternoon, just Grace's kind of afternoon, but she wasn't smiling. There was a small crease, a little pocket of a frown at the sides of her mouth.

"You okay?" I asked, knowing she wasn't.

"I miss her, Mom."

"I know, baby. I miss her too."

Grace sighed, "I am sure you do, Mom, but I am sure we don't quite miss her the same. You miss her like a mom misses their child. I miss her like a sister does. You have no idea how I feel!"

I laughed gently. Here was my eight-year-old lecturing me on how you were supposed to miss a loved one. I pulled out a chair and sat beside Grace, both of us staring outside the window now.

"What do you think about paying her a surprise visit?"

Grace looked surprised, then the jubilation flooded her features. "Do you mean it? Really, really? We'll actually fly to MIT? And we'll see her?"

My suggestion had been on the spur of the moment, but after having heard myself say those words and my little baby's reaction to it, I figured why not. Why not, indeed!

We booked the flights for the next day, spoke to Joy that night without giving anything away. But the excitement was back in Grace's voice!

***

"You know she is my best, best friend in the world, you know?" Grace couldn't stop talking as we wended our way through the walkway leading to Joy's dorm room.

"I know." I repeated for the umpteenth time.

"You also know she is my role model, my mentor, right?"

"I know, Grace." There was also a frisson of excitement traveling through my body. Did one ever tire of hugging their child, of holding them in your arms?

"And even though we are sisters by chance, we are friends by choice. You know that as well?"

My child, who had a way with words, had just spoken words that would flood my heart with light. We didn't choose our siblings, who we were born before or after. That was out of our hands, and to genuinely choose a sibling as your friend, even sometimes as your best friend, was a blessing. It was the same kind of blessing I had enjoyed with my sister and my brothers.

By now, we were at the entrance of Joy's door. I left Grace to do the knocking, and there she was, my older baby, her skin as dark as mahogany, her surprise fizzling out of her in nervous giggles.

"What on earth? What are you doing here?"

She whirled around, turned to her roommate, who was watching us fascinatedly, and then pulled Grace into her arms, into the tightest of tightest of hugs.

"I missed you so much already that Mom had to bring me!"

The hug seemed to last forever, Joy kissing Grace on the forehead. Brushing her overflowing hair back. "Hey, there's a mom here looking for some love also."

That was when Joy disentangled herself from Grace and gave me a quick hug. But it was a very quick hug, and Grace was soon back in her arms.

At that point, my knowledge was that these girls would be fine as long as they had each other's shoulders to lean on. They were my pride, my joy, my full-time assignment here on Earth. And they were friends by choice. Hallelujah!

CHAPTER 21

Family Is Everything... The Father Heart Of God In Human Form

D*addy*

You know how much I love you

I need you forever

I'll stay by your side

Daddy oh Daddy

I want always to please you

But I'll never stop trying

To be your number one

You understand me

You teach me how to pray

And you play the games I love to play

I have no fear

when you are near

You guide me through the darkest night

I love you Daddy

You are my hero

and you're always in my dreams

I love you Daddy, oh Daddy

You are my superstar

Daddy

You know how much I love you

I want you to help me

to show me the way

Daddy oh Daddy

Sometimes I might do wrong

But I'll never stop trying

To be your number one

I want to show you

I'll be as strong as you

When I grow up,

I'll still look up to you

So have no fear here

I'm always here

I will be my daddy's boy

I love you Daddy

You are my hero

and you're always in my dreams

I love you Daddy oh Daddy

You are my superstar

I love you Daddy

Oh Yes I do, Yes I do, Yes I do

You are my hero

and you're always in my dreams

I love you Daddy, oh Daddy

You are my superstar

You're one in a million,

and a million in one

Forever I want to,

be by your side

You're one in a million,

show me the way

Guide me through my life

I love you Daddy,

You are my hero

and you're always in my dreams

I love you Daddy oh Daddy

You are my superstar

I love you Daddy

You are my hero

And you're always in my dreams

I love you Daddy, oh Daddy

You are my superstar

I love you Daddy,

Oh Yes I do, Yes I do

you are my hero

And you're always in my dreams

I love you Daddy oh Daddy

You are my superstar.

***

Watching Joy play this song on the piano for Bruce on our wedding day was heart-melting. It made my heart throb with joy for the beautiful future ahead for all. After so many years of missing a father figure, my daughter had now hit the daddy jackpot. I remembered their first meeting; the way Bruce had left his *grownupedness* at the door and laid on the bare floor to play with Joy. I remembered how my daughter's face had been suffused with joy and excitement when she had announced to me that that day was the happiest she had experienced in her life.

The joy still lit her eyes, and when she looked at Bruce, it was with all the adoration in the world. I am firmly convinced these two were a match made by God; not born of a shared earthly DNA, but born to be of shared DNA nonetheless.

Their relationship warms my heart. It doubles my adoration for every single father who sacrificially reflects the Father heart of God to their families and communities amidst the challenges of a mortal world. It makes me exponentially grateful that I myself have been blessed to experience the profound fatherly love in my life. That I have a dad whose eyes light up when I walk into a room. A dad who will climb mountains, kick down walls, and light up shadows to come after me with a love I couldn't earn and that I don't deserve.

✳✳✳

My first indelible memory of my dad are the Sunday services we attended late together.

Waking up to Mom's sumptuous planning for the lunch to come after church, many times I'd want to stay back in bed for just one more snooze. Mom was always a pillar in the church, committed to serve. She'd wake us up early to get to church services on time. But when I knew Dad wasn't ready, I had the most welcome accomplice.

By the time Mom was gone to church, whoever was still home could sit around a little longer. While Mom was so committed, Dad was only a Christian in word and religion; he routinely arrived services late and with just enough time to catch the ending benediction. I didn't really understand the rituals of church at that time myself, and enjoyed the preference of being Dad's assistant for the Sunday lateness.

Those Sundays are clearly etched on my mind. Dad's eyes dancing over the top of the newspaper as he read his favorite weekend columnists, his hands on the steering wheel as he drove us to church, the sound of his pious voice as he said the benediction in chorus with the congregation.

***

It might surprise you that it was alcohol - a story of alcoholism - that would later truly knit my heart and Dad's.

Dad routinely had his dinner with a bottle of stout lager beer each night. The stout was Nigeria's equivalent of other countries' popular beers. It was very dark and bitter, but very much loved by Dad. These were the times before his native hometown, Ilesha, commissioned its own International Breweries Plc., and innovated Trophy Lager. Dad was not a drunk by any means. He could barely even be considered a social drinker. But each night at home, once he was done with dinner, he took a bottle of stout. It was his way of relaxing, of getting back in touch with himself.

As a child, one who was raised in the church and who had picked up some of the unexplained penchants for criticism, I didn't like that my dad drank. I didn't care to explore the matter of drinking alcohol for a believer in Jesus Christ. All I knew was that it was forbidden. There were not a lot of grays in my world back then. Things were either black or white. To me, that Dad drank was bad. It was a sin. And it made him a sinner.

As much as I idolized my father and loved him, his relationship with the beer bottle made me think a little less of him. In many ways, I wanted him to be the definition of a firebrand religious Christian like others I knew. To hold on tightly to the Bible, and to never again touch a drop of alcohol in his life.

I was in my teenage years when Dad's sweet cousin, Aunty Iyabo, and her surgeon husband tapped Dad on the shoulder to join them in the then thriving Saudi Arabia medical careers, in a Muslim country through and through. School was in session when he left and what a joy to know our family's destiny was about to change for the better. Financial prayers had been answered.

I missed Dad a lot in the first weeks that he was gone. And then a letter arrived from him that made him seem closer than farther to heart. The family sat together in the living room, and we all read his letters with excitement. It was a celebration of sorts; we ate popcorn that night, something we rarely did because of Mom's strict regulation of junk food.

It must have been in his second letter that Dad talked about not drinking anymore because it was against the law in Saudi Arabia. That the State had a morality police that arrested and punished anyone found with alcohol. That he had lost his much beloved nightly privilege.

My heart exploded with joy at the thought of my father never touching a drop of alcohol in his life again.

"Did you all read that?" I asked my siblings.

Dad had taken the pain and the time to write a letter to each of his children, and each person was busy devouring theirs.

"Have you gotten to the part where Dad says he no longer drinks?"

Everyone had read that part and were as surprised and ecstatic as I was. We sat and excitedly talked about this and its ramification. We followed that with favorite things we missed about Dad.

The next day, after dinner, I read out a paragraph of the return letter I had written to Dad to my siblings and my mom.

"I am so glad you have stopped drinking, Dad. Now you can be a better Christian and get closer to God. You don't know how happy your not drinking makes me, or how happy it will make God."

I don't recall that anyone called me out on that letter. It seemed we all shared the emotion, and my letter was sent along to be mailed to Dad, along with the others from Mom and siblings.

The way mailing to Saudi Arabia worked at the time for Nigerians, was that we gave letters to someone visiting from and returning to Saudi Arabia. When the person landed in the capital city, they would post the letters to the small town where Dad was located. So, the process took a couple weeks from writer to receiver's hand.

Several weeks after sending Dad my letter, a package of return letters arrived. As usual, the excitement was palpable in the air. I tore mine open, eager to connect with my Dad's remote life.

Dad's tone was furious.

"I am shocked that my own child thinks me a drunk. I am here away in a foreign country; away from everything I know and love; away so that I can gain better living for my family. And you are there, my own child, judgmentally declaring that I was not Christian enough. Don't you think I would have preferred to stay back in Nigeria with my family, living a quiet life than to have gone to a foreign country? Do you realize I came here because of you, my family, to give you a better life?" And he was not done. My siblings received similar rebuke in their letters.

"You mean, none of you read the letter coming to me from Olubusola and none of you stopped her from writing that to me or was this your collective thoughts all the while and she was the appointed or a self-appointed message bearer that had the courage?"

His words tore at my heart. I had not really thought to salt my words with empathy when I wrote with passion. I hadn't realized I was playing judge and jury, litigating his relationship with Christ. But there and then, reading the pain in his letter, it was clear how childish and selfish my letter had been.

As I wrote him a letter of apology, my hands shook and I had tears in my eyes. I loved my dad to the moon and back and would never intentionally hurt him. And yet, I had done just that.

A solo letter arrived for me shortly after the last one, and this was strange. Dad routinely wrote to all of us, mostly in separate letters and sometimes in one long letter with a section for each person. But this off-cycle letter came just for me, me alone.

I was afraid to open it, afraid he was angrier at me, afraid that he had written the final surge of his anger to lay it at rest. I felt embarrassed and scared, lacking the nerves to peruse the content except in the privacy of my room.

But to my wildest surprise, this was not a letter of chastisement. My father had written me of a special experience with a tone of apology.

"You touched a nerve, Olubusola. Yes, you were out of your place to have said what you said, but I need not have had such a negative visceral reaction. I know you meant the best for me as I mean the best for you and all my children."

"And there is good news that I want to share with you in particular."

"Would you believe it, Olubusola? Would you believe that I asked God to reveal Himself to me and He did? I have been attending a home Bible study organized by one of my American colleagues and at this week's session, I prayed God to show me Himself."

"He revealed Himself to me, Olubusola. I awoke in the middle of night with Jesus sitting by my bed. He told me who He is and told me to serve Him. I went on my knees right away in prayer and was immediately baptized in the Holy Spirit. No human hands placed on me, no human ministration or intervention. But Jesus brought His Holy Spirit to me. He did it by himself and He chose to do it in a Muslim country for His own glory alone."

I read Dad's words in bewildering amazement and a heart filled with emotions. Exhilaration at my dad's new and personal relationship with Jesus and newfound respect for this man who was not too prideful to apologize, who was humble enough to make things right with the one he loved.

This is the story of how I fell in love with the man that my father was again. I recognized him as a fallible man, but one who was willing to make right any wrong. A man whose heart now beats with the pure, unadulterated love of our Heavenly Father.

As I have grown, I have had occasions to respectfully, humbly, and privately challenge my dad on a number of things, and he would gladly repent with restitution in tow. He has been and continues to be one of the most humble, brilliant, sacrificial, and honorable men that I know.

***

Dad was also a disciplinarian, especially in matters of knowledge, academics, and career success. He appreciated both the place of effort and the importance of results.

He is now in his 80's, and still works. While not full time, he makes himself available to step in when other pharmacists call in sick for work. He has lived in England for many decades and has built himself quite a network of proteges and referrals. The work keeps him mentally alert and physically fit, he says, as he refers to the Former Chair of the Federal Reserve of the United States, Alan Greenspan's sharp mindedness into old age. I called recently, and he was at work.

"I'll call you back then, Dad. When you get back home."

"No, no. Go ahead. It's always a good time to talk with you. How are you?"

"Great, Dad..." We spoke for about three minutes before I wished him goodbye and a great day ahead, thoughtful to not introduce a lengthy distraction while he worked.

But then, I placed my phone away and had not disconnected the line. Dad also hadn't and I proceeded to hear a background conversation from his end.

"That was your daughter, wasn't she?" I heard a feminine British voice ask.

"Yes," Dad responded, "She's my girl in America." There was undoubtedly that characteristic tinge of daddy-pride in his voice. For the briefest of moments, I wondered if my voice was tinged with the same color when I spoke of my children.

"Your first?"

"No, no," Dad corrected firmly, "my fourth."

"Very brilliant young woman. My girl. She is doing exceptionally well in her field, a male dominated one for that matter. And she gives me reasons to be proud every day. She is one of five children. Although she delayed her doctorate degree, unlike the others that all got theirs early, she is now studying for it and I am so proud."

Tears welled up in my eyes as I listened serendipitously. Even in his eighties, this man whom I called Dad, still summoned pride for me, and could luxuriate in my achievements.

Later, Dad will share of his heart throb as he watched me "selflessly pay your ex-husband's way to a PhD degree and put aside your dreams for his" only to suffer from him later. "But you're at it now...and you can't comprehend just how healing proud that makes me. How proud you and all your siblings make me feel."

✳✳✳

I'm not a fan of cheese.

But one of my fond memories is of devouring triangular cheese quarters Dad brought back for me from overseas trips.

Those were the best cheeses and at least at the time, they tasted different from any other. I cannot explain the science behind that. But I could try and explain the neuroscience with something about a father's love for his children that changes the flavor of his gifts to them, whether such gifts were edible or not.

***

Dad is an investor. A stock market and real estate investor, but much more an investor in humans. There was something my dad did which I've not known another man on earth to practice.

He was blessed with five children, and when each of us was born, he purchased a cow in the name of that child and added them to his growing farm. He would actually name the cow the same as the child's first name and as the child grew, so did the cow. The cow bought for me has since birthed several generations and departed.

But the story does not end there.

My dad has a cow farm, with herdsmen that have been with him from one generation to another of theirs, serving him for all those years. These herdsmen live on the farm and maintain it. The cows are family to the predominantly nomadic northern Nigerians who chose to stay on Dad's farm, and the cows have multiplied many fold. The way Dad ran his business was for the herdsmen to be bestowed with cows themselves every other birthing, and those have now multiplied many times over too. The herdsmen's families gladly cared for their own flock alongside Dad's.

Over the decades, my dad's younger brothers have also invested in cows on the same farm, and together they currently own a huge cattle farm that has become a source of blessing to many, as mature cattle are gifted to family and friends for their celebratory occasions.

Dad would take some of the herdsmen children and train them with us, like they were his. Children who wouldn't otherwise have become educated have become so, changing the stories of their entire progeny.

Those five cows that were originally purchased have multiplied into thousands, and more than one life has been transformed through the power of love and multiplication.

What a model for business and great investment into other humans! And what a man!

***

As a child, I did not understand what it meant for young girls to be said to have daddy issues. My dad was always my daddy with no issues attached. We kissed into my late teenage years and I was safe in his love. I did not have to look for him in another man. Yet God blessed me with the love of more daddies who reflected His Father heart as well - my Uncle Idowu, Uncle Segun, my Papa, Professor Akinyemi, Daddy J.S.A Oladele, Pastor Bodfem, Pastor Adewoye, Pastor Terry Moore, Pastor Aladiran, Pastor Israel, Daddy Odeniyi, Dr. Lawrence Ajayi, and others. Some love mixed with the giver's own human frailties and fallibility, but the language of love nonetheless.

From the very beginning of my life, my dad exemplified to me the person of Jesus, also within his own human foibles. But with no doubt, he has shown me the Father heart of God. Quick to love, and slow to anger. A sacrificial leader who would lay down his life for me, for us. Even now, in his 80's, he is only a call and an ask away. If I was in despair and needed him, gladly he'd hop on the next flight out, without thought for his own comfort.

As a little girl, I would place my hand in Dad's, and all would be all right with my world. Today, my children enjoy the same calm when granddad is on the phone.

Because of my dad, even when I don't understand God, the way I sometimes do not understand my earthly father, even then, I know He is working something out for my good.

He is a good, good daddy. I have known that for a long, long time. And I will know it for as long as I live.

CHAPTER 22

Family Extended...There Is No Fear In <Aslan's> Love

My Aslan is a Lion. He's a Lamb. And he's a German Shepherd dog, all in for exposure therapy.

If you've seen the popular movies of C.S. Lewis' books, or read the books, you'll be familiar with the Lion archetype of Jesus in "The Lion, The Witch and The Wardrobe":

> "Who is Aslan?" asked Susan.
>
> "Aslan?" said Mr. Beaver, "Why, don't you know? He's the King. He's the Lord of the whole wood, but not often here, you understand. Never in my time or my father's time. But the word has reached us that he has come back. He is in Narnia at this moment. He'll settle the White Queen all right. It is he, not you, that will save Mr. Tumnus."
>
> "She won't turn him into stone too?" said Edmund.
>
> "Lord love you, Son of Adam, what a simple thing to say!" answered Mr. Beaver with a great laugh. "Turn him into stone? If she can stand on her two feet

and look him in the face it'll be the most she can do and more than I expect of her. No, no. He'll put all to rights, as it says in an old rhyme in these parts:

Wrong will be right, when Aslan comes in sight,

At the sound of his roar, sorrows will be no more,

When he bares his teeth, winter meets its death

And when he shakes his mane, we shall have spring again.

You'll understand when you see him."

"But shall we see him?" asked Susan.

"Why, Daughter of Eve, that's what I brought you here for. I'm to lead you where you shall meet him," said Mr. Beaver.

"Is--is he a man?" asked Lucy.

"Aslan a man!" said Mr. Beaver sternly. "Certainly not. I tell you he is the King of the wood and the son of the great Emperor-Beyond-the-Sea. Don't you know who is the King of Beasts? Aslan is a lion--the Lion, the great Lion."

"Ooh!" said Susan, "I'd thought he was a man. Is he-- quite safe? I shall feel rather nervous about meeting a lion."

"That you will, dearie, and no mistake," said Mrs. Beaver. "If there's anyone who can appear before Aslan

without their knees knocking, they're either braver than most or else just silly."

"Then he isn't safe?" said Lucy.

"Safe?" said Mr. Beaver. "Don't you hear what Mrs. Beaver tells you? Who said anything about safe? 'Course he isn't safe. But he's good. He's the King, I tell you."

....

Hands flailing, feet pummeling the dusty Bodija street of Ibadan. My eyes were cascading pure water, and the dry air tore my breath from my chest in huge gasps. I was running for dear life, intent, just bent on getting to safety.

If you have never been chased by a daunting German Shepherd dog, let alone two of them, you'll absolutely have no idea what I am talking about. The raw adrenaline fear of being devoured whole, bones chewed to pulp, and the weight of existence in every step, so great that if you didn't take that next step, you'd end up dead.

Somehow, I made it to safety. Barreling into the gate of our home, latching the locks and sliding down the hot metal gate to sit my weary self on the bare floor and recover the very breath of life. That moment sparked the beginning of a phobia for dogs. After the great chase, I would never walk on the same street side with an approaching dog walker, nor would I visit a home with dogs, regardless of the owners' promise of tame gentility. And the phobia would last into three decades.

In my mid-twenties, it occurred to me that I could one day own a big dog of my own. I could be that person who walked a towering canine down the street, my fears gone and my human primacy fully restored.

I lived with and shaped that conviction thereafter. That I would adopt this dog from their puppyhood, I would love him and he would love me, we would build a solid relationship with each other, and we would grow together. Him in maturity, and I in overcoming animal phobia. We would be a family. He will be my friend!

This dog had to not be a small lap dog. It had to be a large breed. Maybe even bigger than the two that had chased me down those dusty streets of Bodija Estate decades ago. I hypothesized that having my own large dog would be the healing therapy for the phobia created in me by the chase.

For years, I did nothing about the conviction, perfectly content to cross the road and walk on the other side upon sighting a big dog.

And then came the year everything went nuts, the season of seven back-to-back-to-back losses. Shortly after my sister passed away, I decided I would finally go for it. Life was chaotic, but with this dog, I would be on my way to healing, reasserting dominion in this one aspect of my life.

As God always so lovingly does, He perfectly orchestrated my meeting with a generational dog owner who'd had this generation of dogs in their family tree for a long time. Pure-bred German Shepherds, who although a breed famed for ferocity, were loyal and could be gentle. They loved to a fault.

That made the drive to Edinburg, Texas a worthy drive when one of their dogs had her litter. Down near the Texas Mexico border, the one of five newly born puppies drew my heart and would be mine to adopt once it could leave its mothers breast in a few months.

I was going to give him a name that meant strength and gentleness. Same qualities that have defined my journey – strength to defend whenever needed and gentleness to nurture champions to accomplishment with love. It had to be a name that showed masculinity. But it had to simultaneously reflect a loving softness to its ring.

Manfred! I chewed on that name for days trying to fit it, but it just didn't sit right. Yet Google wasn't helpful to create other ideas.

And then out of the blue chatting with my husband one day, the name came to me. My dog would be called Aslan. It fit perfectly. Aslan, the C.S. Lewis' allegory imagery for Jesus Christ. Aslan the gentle lover and able protector. What a God-incidence!

So, Aslan became mine and I loved him. Afterall, I chose him.

Yet I feared him, because the effect of a traumatic chase did not wane. But as I fed and cared for my Aslan in love, the fear gradually dissipated and I learned to train him to his maximum potential.

Today, Aslan is my gentle giant. He loves and respects and protects with a loyalty that is incredible! Not the traditional therapy pet, but uniquely my very own therapeutic victory partner, through exposure in love.

When I walk the streets with or without my Aslan, I am no longer in the mind of a little girl that was chased down by two German Shepherd dogs. How things have circled. How things have changed with the power of love.

Truly, there is no fear in love because perfect love casts out fear.

Thank God for His Holy Spirit that enables us to love and to divest all fears.

CHAPTER 23

Lessons The Holy Spirit Taught Me

I attended the Grace to Grief workshop in August 2021, after it felt like my heart was about to break into smithereens. This was after seven back-to-back losses in one year. At this workshop, I would be met with grace, with compassion, and my journey to healing would commence. Another instalment of this workshop would also mark a turning point in my marriage; Bruce would later attend and get further on his healing journey from addiction and childhood trauma.

But first, the devil wanted to stop me from attending.

Snakes! Beyond a deep-seated dislike, I had a crippling fear of snakes. The mere mention of a snake made my skin crawl, like a thousand and one ants burrowing into its crevices. How could a living thing be without legs, slithering around and striking at unsuspecting lives. I hated snakes, and I feared them. They were cursed.

With my Grief to Grace experience just over a week away, I had a terrible, almost-crippling dream about a snake. A huge, slimy thing, and it terrified the life out of me.

Seemingly so real was the curve of the snake's body, as was its ready-to-strike posture. It would be all so real, and then it would fade away.

I woke up, tangled in the sheets, my heart racing and clanging like a thousand bells.

I would have the same night terror twice before morning broke, and by the time the sun made its way across the skies, my nerves were all over the place. At my prayer altar that morning, I was lost for words of prayers, but my spirit communed with God's without words, and I felt a bit more settled when I arrived at work and got lost in the familiarity of it all.

I received a phone call mid-morning from one of the volunteer staff at New Heart of Texas, that runs the Grief to Grace retreat.

"Hi, Folakemi. Just checking in with you. Everything okay at your end?"

"Yes...yeah..." I answered, distracted momentarily by a worksheet in front of me.

"Just calling to let you know that we are eagerly expecting you at the retreat. Also felt it right to give you a fair warning that the devil will try all he can to dissuade you from coming. Now that it's less than two weeks until we meet in person, we are convinced that he'll throw all kinds of mud at you, just to see what sticks, to discourage you from coming. He will want to put fear in your heart, but you need not be afraid."

I was no longer distracted; she now had my full attention.

"Remember that God has not given us the spirit of fear, but a sound mind. You've got a sound mind, Folakemi. Don't ever forget that. Don't let the devil use mirages that aren't really there to scare you."

I sighed, a deep sigh that reached all the way to my belly. When I exhaled again, it was with a gust of hope. God knew what was going on in my life, and He was sending me words of comfort.

"Thank you, thank you! You don't know how much this means."

I would share just how much that phone call meant when I was at the retreat about two weeks later. But not until another layer of *Godness* had been added to the story. The fear in my heart had stilled for the remainder of the two weeks leading to the retreat, although I didn't know that the Holy Spirit wasn't finished with me yet on the topic of fear and snakes.

The third day of the retreat began as usual with an early morning devotion led by lovely Pastor Blake, another volunteer from a local church. He always began with a story that illustrated the scripture shared. He would begin this particular day's devotion with a very peculiar story of an experience he had.

He had returned to his house one day, having picked up his teenage daughter. She in tow, as teenagers do, texting away and inattentive. For them both, it was just a day like every other, except he just happened to lift up his eyes as he made his way into the house, and there on his house roof, ready to slither down and strike, was a perfectly curled-up snake.

As he recounted this story, my body quivered at the mention of a snake. "Not again, Jesus. Not another mention of snakes!" If I didn't hear about snakes again for as long as I lived, I would be perfectly okay with it.

He went on, "I admit I squealed just like a little girl, because you know what? I am an all-Texan man but one who is terrified of snakes."

"Great!" I thought under my breath. "We should perhaps begin a snake-fearers club!"

He told of how his teenage daughter had laughed at him, of how she hadn't squealed the way he did, of how her body shook uncontrollably with mirth. After she managed to catch up with him after he had fled back indoors, on his way to call the exterminators, she steadied him.

"That's not a real snake, Dad! Mom put it there, don't you know?"

He was flabbergasted. "Mom put it there! Why would she put a snake there?"

"Listen, Dad! It's not real! Mom put it there, as a form of a scarecrow, to chase the birds away...the birds always crashing into the windows! That snake is nothing but plastic!"

Before then, he'd never heard about, let alone seen, scarecrow snakes in his life, and he recalled being rooted to the spot for a while, even after his daughter's revelation.

"What I feared wasn't real. What I thought was there to scare me wasn't an actual thing. It was nothing but a mirage. What's that thing staring you in the face, brethren? That looks to be so real, but is nothing but a mirage when you take a deeper look? When you focus your gaze on God and ascribe to Him His greatness due in all situations, when you take a look of faith?"

I was enthralled, but I was more than enthralled. I was struck by his words, felt them tumble into the receiving soil of my heart, felt them lodge there. I had caught a word from the Lord. Fear was a mirage. It didn't exist except in my mind, and if I cared to take a closer look of faith, I'd find that the fear wasn't there in the first place.

I had never before then heard of plastic scarecrow snakes myself, but I want to assure you that I heard plenty about them in the coming weeks. This was not just because I deliberately went in search of them. Conversations about snake scarecrows just seemed to find me. You know how you never know about the existence of something and then cannot seem to hear enough about them after you become aware of them, especially when God is on your case for a work of healing and grace!

What the Holy Spirit taught me in that instance was how to live above fear. He taught me how to go hand in hand with faith to open the door when fear knocks. Fear is often nothing but a mirage.

All in all, my Grief to Grace conference was a lifesaver during a low, low season of life. I went in with ginger apprehension, doubtful that there was anything more anyone could do to show me Jesus. But if there was, I was desperate to find it. Thanks to God, what I was desperate to find did exist in Grief to Grace. The love of Jesus met me in a newer way than I'd ever experienced since dedicating my life to him over 30 years ago. Every component of the retreat opened a new lobe in my heart to heal and deepened my faith. The intentionality and dedication of the staff and volunteers, the soundness of the science behind their approach, every single event was so well orchestrated and heavily marinated in the love of Jesus Christ. And the Holy Spirit was a palpable presence.

Despite our diversity of faces, many people have similar life wounds that only the love of Jesus can heal. I am eternally grateful that He chose New Heart to do just that for me. I am eternally grateful that someone heard the call and obeyed.

***

I learned about the value of prayer and the need to be watchful when I was married to Akin. Unfortunately, it would take the dissolution of our marriage for this lesson to sink in.

A long time ago, it seems, when things between us had not turned so sour or so bad, we laid in bed one hot afternoon. Joy was still very small, and she was at that moment in the living room with Akin's mom, who had come in from Nigeria for a visit. She was preparing to get back on a flight home, and we had spent a long night and an equally long morning saying our goodbyes. I was exhausted, and wanted to catch a few minutes of rest before we began the long trip to the airport.

Not long after I crawled into bed fully dressed (even though I knew it would be hard to fall asleep fully dressed; it just wasn't me), Akin came into the room, yawning himself. He sat first, rubbing his knuckles the way he did when he was bone tired. And then he folded himself onto the bed, beside me, also fully clothed.

I would later realize that we didn't, hadn't slept for long because the sweep of the clock's hand had barely moved in the time that all that was to unfold.

The door swung open, but it was swinging without a sound, like the sound had been sucked from the room. Later, I would realize that I had been sleeping. The door then swung closed, but not before it had let in a little demon. There are no words in my vocabulary to describe that little demon, other than it was tiny in stature but huge in fearsomeness. It was dirty, taloned, horned, fear-invoking.

It made its way, still soundless, to Akin's sleeping form, dug its talons into his chest, and came out with his heart, his still-beating heart. With the second hand, it drew out a small stone from a pouch around its waist and put this stone back into Akin's chest, where his flesh and blood heart had once been.

I woke up to my own strangled cry, beating on Akin, shaking him to wake up. The sound had returned to the room, and my cry seemed to be magnified ten times, and everything now seemed so loud, so so loud.

"Did you not see? Did you not feel your heart taken out?"

He came awake instantly, but he was confused, understandably so.

"Your heart!" I said in a lower voice because the sound of my voice seemed to deafen me.

His hand went involuntarily to his chest, and then he looked at me like I was bonkers, "You okay?"

At that time, looking up at the clock and realizing that we had been asleep for less than ten minutes, I felt slightly off my rockers. I felt crazy.

We took his mom to the airport, and on the ride there, I kept hearing the Holy Spirit whisper a scripture to my heart. "Surely the Lord God will do nothing, but he revealeth his secret unto his servants the prophets." I knew what I had received was a revelation, a foretelling of what was to come, but I didn't know what to do with the message.

For days on end, I would lay awake, thinking about the bizarre events, feeling my heart going into a lurch. But as the days passed, the memory began to dim. It faded away, washed over by the baseness of everyday living.

Until my husband started to misbehave, until he seemed to be filled with nothing but hatred toward me, until he couldn't bear the sight of me, until he started to torture me with the smell of frying oil in enclosed places while I slept, fully knowledgeable of how such caused asthmatic attacks.

Not too long after the event, in a conversation with Akin's brother, he shared that he'd had a similar incident happen to him. He had an open vision, and something came inside his room, and touched his chest, holding his heart. He said he jumped up with motivation to beat up his wife. And he suddenly came to himself, wondering what just occurred. He put himself on a full year fast after that and received deliverance for his family's childlessness on completion of his fast.

He shared this apparently to assert why he had warned me that we shouldn't have shared with Akin's family about my pregnancy at the time. He did not know of my similar experience.

I sank into a chair, my breath gone, my brother-in-law's voice coming faintly but insistently as I sat visiting with him in his ministerial office. Upon leaving his office, I called my sister and brother. "His brother had the same open vision! He did."

There are some things that are forever hidden from us as humans, but fully unveiled before our Lord and savior who knows all things and maps all things together to do us good. We just have to trust Him.

Knowing that Akin's fleshy heart had been replaced with a heart of stone, that he was not himself, this would make forgiveness easier.

***

I have recounted the story of Joy's attempted spiritual kidnapping attempt before, and the way our faithful God kept her and delivered her from the enemy's grip. I have also recounted what the Holy Spirit ministered to my heart when it was all over, His reassurance that we would be happy in Minneapolis.

What I have not yet recounted is my follow-up encounter with Him a few weeks after that bone-jarring incidence.

It was dusk, and because we were still finding our feet in Minneapolis, I was home early. I would never become a social butterfly, the kind that gathered with colleagues at watering holes after work. But it was still early days yet, and I had not yet become as friendly as I would later be with coworkers. So, I was home early and had eaten a lively dinner with Joy, during which she hit me on every side with a barrage of "what if" questions. *What if humans lived to be 200? What if animals lived in houses and humans lived in the wild? What if children made the decisions and parents had to follow through on those?* At her age, Joy could go a mile a minute on issues that fascinated her. She kept me sharp that way. Because I still had enough energy that day, I had met her question for question, and as I said, dinner had been lively.

After dinner was over and Joy had retreated to her room with a book and a Rubik's cube, I went into my room as well, determined to catch up on some Bible study time. I was in the middle of studying the book of Isaiah, written by that prophet who was famous for his prediction of the coming of the Messiah. I found Isaiah to be a book of stark contrasts, one in which terrifying warnings of judgment and destruction are juxtaposed with uplifting promises of hope and prosperity.

I was fascinated.

And then I got to the 49th chapter and was dumbstruck by the 15th and 16th verses. It wasn't that I hadn't read these words before or that they hadn't been the focal point of a preacher's message before. They just struck me differently this time, very differently.

"Can a mother forget the baby at her breast and have no compassion on the child she has borne? Though she may forget, I will not forget you! See, I have tattooed you on the palms of my hands; your walls are ever before me."

I was in the middle of penning down something, but I found I couldn't write. My hand got frozen midair, and my eyes closed for the slightest of moments, and then I opened them because a fire I didn't understand burned behind my eyelids.

And then I heard the Holy Spirit's gentle, soothing voice. It was the most beautiful thing to hear.

"Joy is more my own than she will ever be yours. See, her name is written on my palms. And I will never forget her. Even when you are not there, it is my job to keep her safe. From all kinds of attacks, all kinds of things."

At that moment, with those words, I was transported to that terrifying night, that night that Joy had been unexplainably taken from our room and into the parking lot of the hotel. I remembered the fright in my chest, the initial disbelief at Joy's story, and the way I trembled all night long, in awe and fear.

I remembered the feel of Joy's body in my arms as I held onto her afterward. I remembered it all.

"I've got Joy! And I've got you, just like I've got each of my children."

My vision cleared, but my palms and hands remained sweaty. And then my vision clouded again, and the tears wrenched themselves from my eye sockets. But these were tears of relief, of gratitude, of understanding. Whether I was there or not, whether she was under my roof or not, my child was held in God's hands. Her name was tattooed on the palm of God's hands. As was mine.

***

God is intentional.

We were on our way back from Austin; we had gone to see a chiropractor, one we visited from time to time. I felt straighter than I had been in weeks. Bruce looked better than he had in weeks too, but I knew the way he looked, the way he perhaps felt, was not simply a result of being adjusted. There was a lightness to him that had not been there in weeks, in months even, not since he disclosed his terrible secret to me.

He had just returned from his own session at Grief to Grace, gone for a week, immersed in the cleansing water of the Word, and involved in intensive therapy sessions. I had begun my journey of healing at Grief to Grace, and then it had been my husband's time.

He had gotten back just a few days before our chiropractic appointment but we had yet to really talk. His lightness, his little smile, the way his hand was relaxed on the steering wheel; I knew this had to do with his experience at Grief to Grace.

I prodded him. "Tell me about the anger management activity you guys had at the session."

He took his eyes off the road for the slightest of seconds to look at me, and then he placed his attention back on the road unfolding in front of him.

"What about it? What do you want to know?"

"All about that session. Who were you angry at? Who are you angry at?"

The vein at the base of my husband's neck pulsated, throbbed, but you wouldn't know it if you didn't know to look for it.

He answered me a couple of minutes later with a single word, a single name I wasn't expecting. "Rex!"

I had been bracing myself to hear my name spoken, to hear something along the lines of, "I didn't realize you were doing the right thing for me when you asked me to seek help." The last thing I expected to hear was Bruce's name.

Rex was Bruce's only full genetic brother, and he had died in childhood. I would never meet him, but I knew him so very well. As a wife, I knew the hurt and pain that still throbbed in Bruce's heart when he permitted himself to think of his big brother.

"Why? Why would you be angry at Rex?"

Bruce sighed, "Because he abandoned me. He left me when we were supposed to grow up together, left me to figure out life all by myself."

As he spoke, as I listened, we were both very aware that his anger at Bruce was misplaced. Rex hadn't left this world willingly; he had been taken out of it by a tragedy no one could have ever imagined.

It was in their teen years. Rex had been 16 years old, just a couple years older than Bruce, when Rex had lost his footing on a hike and fell down a cliff. He had been Bruce's best friend, and the only sibling close to him in age.

They had older siblings, born of the same mom but from different dads. My father-in-law had married his best friend's wife after his best friend and fellow air force pilot passed away. He was young and foolish (according to his wife, my mother-in-law). He had no clue what he was getting into by marrying such a woman and adopting all her three kids as his. But he was a man of true honor, the Boaz of our generation. In addition to the three adopted children, they had Rex and then Bruce together.

"I guess I started to pursue some form of justice or the other after Rex died. I felt my brother's death was unjust...and I just wanted to see justice. I felt wronged...it felt terribly wrong for a young child to just die, without having even lived! I wanted answers."

For several minutes, as the car ate up the distance toward our home, both of us were quiet, both digesting the words that hung in the air between us.

And then, a light bulb went off in my head, and as I closed my eyes, I felt the Holy Spirit minister to me.

"Trauma breeds in human beings a sense of injustice that leaves you wanting to fight for justice, that leaves you wanting to correct the balance of things!"

The Holy Spirit went on, "When you experienced childhood abuse, you developed a heart for justice, and that makes perfect sense, right? You want to correct the balance. You want to fight for things. The same thing goes for Bruce...He watched his brother die and grew a heart for justice...

"But here is the thing. God is a God of justice, and He doesn't need you to make it right on His behalf. He knows the world is full of injustice and that you are hurting... but the battle is not yours to fight."

I swallowed as the ministration continued. "When trauma happens in childhood, the devil commissions you into the fight against injustice, and on the surface, this looks great. You are doing the work of God; you are fighting injustice just like He does!"

I nodded, because this made a lot of sense, but the Holy Spirit wasn't done.

"However, fighting injustice can sort of become a prison to the fighter, a prison that doesn't allow you to give God His rightful place. You are so busy trying to fight every evil, so busy trying to right all wrongs that you never let God be God. What happens, then, is that the devil commissions you to do a job that wasn't yours to do in the first place. Fighting the good and just looking to fight against injustice is everything pleasing except that it turns to idolatry. It demonstrates a lack of faith in the God of justice."

"God hasn't commissioned you to be his assistant judge or co-lawyer. He has called you to forgiveness. Are you hurt? Yes! Does the person who hurt you owe you a debt? Yes. But this is a debt you don't need them to pay back. Seeking for justice, by all means, is asking a debtor to pay back a debt they can never have the ability to repay, one that only God can repay. Only God can make whole where there has been trauma. And letting it go with that understanding is a statement of faith and trust in the God that can make it whole. It is not a statement of abandonment nor of minimizing the offense. No. Neither of those. In fact, forgiveness is saying to an offender that: 'you have indeed hurt me. You have hurt me deeply. But you don't have the ability to make me whole again. So, I let it go and give it to the one who has that ability and will make me whole again'."

I turned slightly in my chair to see if Bruce was being ministered to the way that I was, but I saw no indication of it. His eyes were still on the road, and I noticed that the throbbing vein at the base of his neck wasn't as throbby anymore. He was a little more relaxed than he was when we started the conversation.

"The battle doesn't belong to you. It is not yours to fight, never been yours to fight. God is a God of justice. Always leave Him to fight His battle. Sometimes, just trusting in

Him is enough; just resting in His faithfulness and His commitment to making things right is enough."

Later, I would learn that the Holy Spirit had ministered these words to Bruce that same afternoon, on that same stretch of road home, "You were never expected to fight against God, seeing Him as the wicked one who snatched a little child off the surface of the Earth. You were never purposed to explore those Eastern religions that put you in bondage of addiction. You were designed to be loved and to trust in divine love."

On that cold February afternoon, headed back home in a car that suddenly seemed not filled with air but with the very essence of the Holy Spirit, my liberation from the demons from the past, from the ghost of the rape I had endured, bloomed even more.

The peace I would feel, perhaps for the first time since becoming an adult, was intense, overwhelming, tear-provoking. And also, at that moment, I realized that Bruce's seeking for justice for and an understanding of the death of his beloved brother had been the reason he had fallen prey to the eastern religions he had practiced once upon a time in his life, the reason his addiction had snuck up on him and remained glued to him for years.

As the tears, tears of understanding, of release, trailed my face, Bruce seemed to understand without asking because he didn't ask me what was happening, what had happened. He simply slid one hand off the steering wheel and sought mine. The feel of my hand in his was weightless. But everything felt at peace, as it should.

I knew at that moment, that if Bruce would try and do as God bid - that there was power for healing! But I also understood that God will never struggle with the human will. So much of what the future held hinged on Bruce's willingness to allow God heal him.

***

The Holy Spirit would minister to me that God is faithful, even in the hard places. One chilly February morning, sitting and watching, He spoke to me. Times may be hard, but we have the grace to either run through the challenges and fear rather than run away from them. We have been given the grace to run through them.

The Spirit life is like the British education system where you are promoted according to your success, according to the tests you have overcome.

God will never bring us to a place that He hasn't prepared us for, that He hasn't made grace available for. I repeat, we are to run toward our fears to conquer them. We are not made to run! We get to our places of trials because we are ready for them.

I would also learn that the secret to solving our personal problems is to help others solve theirs, so that we do not become ingrown. This is God's formula to seeing that the world remains on an even keel, the way He sees to it that our hearts remain connected and knit together.

Who better to help you through your marital problems than someone who has been through the same problems? Who best to understand your health challenges like someone who has been similarly challenged?

So, what did the Holy Spirit teach me with these two lessons? He taught me that there is no problem I cannot tunnel through; He also taught me that when I tunnel through my life challenges by His grace and mercy, it is in part to equip me to help someone else do the same.

God gives us His abundance because He still meets us with strength, and then He expects me to do the same for my brother.

***

I haven't always been a bold person.

I should have been, but I never was. The very things that were supposed to make me bold were the things that actually made me timid and unsure of myself.

As a young girl born with a supposed silver spoon, I felt reluctant to put myself front and center of things, afraid that I would be labeled as privileged, as entitled. So, I didn't volunteer as much for lead roles or anything that shone the lights directly on me.

Exceptionally brilliant, I had zoomed through school with ease. Being in engineering, where there were so few females you could count us on the tips of your fingers and leading all the boys in class, it was said that I had slept my way to the top of the academic stack. This wasn't a good place to be in, and I made the resolve to try to be as average as humanly possible.

I have always been purposed for great things, but I have also always been afraid of how things would look, what people would say. So, I wanted to be right smack in the middle of the line. Being bright came with its pains.

Today, I am a black woman in the US. And not just a black woman; I am a black woman executive in data analytics. That population is already tiny, and coupled with the fact that I am 5'11, the odds that I will be very different from others when I enter a boardroom are about 100 percent. For the longest time, I struggled with this.

I received my breakthrough into boldness in September 2021.

Papa was invited to minister at a church in San Antonio, and I attended with my family. It was to be an all-night session; a 12-hour stretch of prayers. However, we had to leave early because my husband had work the following morning. We got home around 4 am, but I didn't go to bed with the rest of the family. Instead, I chose to connect with the program online, to partake of the blessings of the saints for as long as I could.

When I joined, Pastor Joyce Sanni, the co-host of the conference, was laying hands on participants for the spirit of boldness. She spoke about how the righteous are bold as lions and how the Holy Spirit fills us with courage. Even though I was not in the same physical space as her, I felt my faith rise. I believed for the first time in my life that I had been timid for far too long and that it was time to shed my timidness for His boldness.

I bowed my head as she prayed, my faith rising that I would rise from that service a changed person, as bold a lion as my Father is.

I can testify that as she prayed, the stronghold of the spirit of timidity was broken in me. I realized that I had been too scared of life and of what people would say to fully, truly take the lead.

All that changed that fall September morning. I am now grateful instead of apologetic for my uniqueness. We are all unique, and there is nothing to be ashamed of who I am, of what I am, of the challenges and privileges I have had. I now understand that I am here with a voice, that I am here with a purpose, and that it is okay not to be understood.

I now value myself. I now appreciate myself.

***

It is easier to run when breathing out than when breathing in.

Running with your eyes closed rather than with it opened is also easier.

One fall day, as my feet pounded the sidewalk alongside Bruce's, as we enjoyed the crisp morning air and the beauty of being able to exercise together, the Holy Spirit spoke to me.

"You must always breathe out. Always, always exhale your sins."

I stopped mid-stride, taking a lesson on the sidewalk, the lesson no less powerful than if it had been delivered from behind a stone pulpit.

When the human race was newly introduced to the world, before sin entered the world, there was no need for remediation. But when sin came, restoration became a thing. As humans, as spiritual beings living in a fallen world, we need to constantly exhale the carbon monoxide of sin. And then inhale the benefits of the Spirit.

To expect to inhale all the goodness God has to give and not exhale and be cleansed of sin is delusional. It is why we hear the stories of men of God who bow to sin, who collapse under the weight of their hidden lives. Who seemingly were filled with inhaled anointing, but apparently, were also filled with the toxic carbon monoxide of sin left unremoved.

We simply cannot manifest divine goodness in its wholeness or for an extended period of time without ensuring that we are sanctified as He intends us to be.

No one lives on inhalation alone. To inhale effectively, you have to become an expert at exhalation.

So, now I inhale. And exhale.

I take on the whole goodness of my father, and then I bow my knees at His throne, waiting on Him, allowing Him to take my imperfections for His perfection, letting Him do the work of purification within me again and again.

Is it always a pretty process? Is it always a neat one? Definitely not! Pain can be involved.

I am a work in progress, reaching onward and upward, yielding my heart to Him again and again. Sometimes, it's easier than other times. And sometimes, it's the hardest thing I ever have to do. But with Him, in Him, by Him, and because of Him, I exhale. And I rise tall. I rise tall, and I bring generations with me!

CHAPTER 24

Family Is Everything... Hear It From My Nieces

Family is a JEM but Life is a Hard Balance (Jemima)

2019 was a hard year.

It would be the year that I'd let it all go. And it was the year that my journey to wholeness and healing also began.

It would be the year that I realized that keeping a balance on life can be hard, almost impossible.

I had a mental health episode, the pinnacle falling on my birthday, the 14th of March.

It had been a long time coming, but I had bottled things up for so long and so tightly that it was bound to happen. It was only a matter of when, not if.

I had been quite hyper the whole week before my birthday. I felt bursts of energy that were unusual. I couldn't sit still, couldn't hold any thought for longer than a few seconds. I wrote messages and then deleted them. I deleted my

Instagram posts, and put up a new one that was bold, brash and quite abrupt.

I was in Bulgaria where I study when all this unraveled. My friends in Bulgaria gave their support as best as they could, as did my friends from back home, who are more like my sisters. Friends are the family we choose ourselves, the loving arms of safety that God hands to us in addition to our natural families. And I would choose my sisters again and again.

I was turning 21 but had finally lost my grip on reality. Things started spiraling and were quickly getting out of control, and I was eventually hospitalized in Bulgaria. It was a very traumatic experience for me. In terms of medical advancement, Bulgaria is quite behind most western countries, and the way I was treated was cruel, as it was based on outdated methods. I was restricted in movement, and had absolutely no control over my health options, had no idea of what was being injected into my body. It was a harrowing experience.

Perhaps for the first time in my life, my words were unfiltered. I was fully truthful, honest, and raw, speaking truths I had never spoken before. Now in retrospect, I thank God for 2019 because that year set me free and gave me the liberty to speak my truth, the truths I thought I would have taken to my grave.

2019 was the year I started becoming honest with myself. Because you can lie to the entire world, to your friends, your family, to the ones you hold close. However, the only person you cannot and should not lie to is yourself. When life happens, as it always inevitably does, everyone needs to be able to check in with themselves and try to understand where they're at emotionally. It is okay to say "I am not okay right now." It is as simple as saying "I don't feel good right now," "I feel insecure," "I feel anxious or sad" or whatever the feeling is. Ultimately you cannot fool yourself, and you certainly can't fool God.

Before 2019, I fooled myself a lot. I had never allowed myself to feel my emotions and truly come to terms with how I felt about anything that was going on in my life - especially about my mom - who had been sick for a long time. And, I truly believed that God was going to heal her, make her completely whole, give me a whole functional mom like other girls had. But that didn't happen.

Mommy was diagnosed with systemic lupus erythematosus (SLE) before I was born. I do remember her being nurturing, loving, business savvy as well as fiercely loyal and defensive of her loved ones. Nevertheless, there were many downturns. There were many lows, so much so that we, as a family, got accustomed to them. Therefore, I had become unmovable by whatever wasn't earth shattering because our norm was not normalcy anyway.

Mommy had the first stroke in 2013, and then the second stroke in 2021. Between the strokes, there was aphasia, needing assistance with daily living, and subsisting on medication.

She braved it all and had faith through it. She walked, even sometimes without a stick or a walker, partly for her stubbornness. She talked and sang new songs but not always coherent. You could tell the thoughts were there. How frustrating it must have been for her. I believed for the longest time that my mom would be able to walk normally and talk normally again someday. That she would be able to get back to what she loved, which was running her own community pharmacy. I believed she was going to be at my graduation event, that she'd be the chief host at my wedding, and that she'd walk me down the aisle someday.

The truth is that she is not going to be. This is something I am still processing, something I am still trying to understand. She has now been gone for more than a year, and I continue to process it all.

But for the longest time, I willed her to be well. I believed she would be healed.

Prior to 2019, I put on a façade for the whole world. I projected that my mom's incapacitation did not affect me so much; that family life, despite its challenges, was great. But the truth is that I wasn't okay and family life was not great. My family wasn't the typical family. Instead of her caring for her daughters the way that healthy and able moms did, it was the other way around for us. My sister and I had to bear the responsibility of caring for Mommy. She did her best. She loved us with every fiber of her being. She prayed for us and gave warm smiles. But the roles were reversed, and we were the ones who had to look after her.

Unfortunately, I believe my sister bore the brunt of responsibility more than I did because when I was in school in Bulgaria, the business of caretaking fell on her shoulders. She helped Mommy with medication, toileting, bathing, and eating. She had to help with everything. This is not something a child should be saddled with. In normalcy, it should not be the responsibility of a child. But my sister did it all, and for that I will be forever grateful to and for her.

All the while, I would smile at the world and say it was okay, that we were fine, but we were not. In my heart, where the little girl who had been me years ago still lived, I wanted to curl up in my mother's lap and have her console me and give me advice on my future endeavors. I wanted her to hold my hand when things got tough. I wanted her to tell me that everything would be okay when I felt like life was stacked against me.

But I continued to smile and said it was okay. This is because I did believe that it would eventually be, that one day Mom would be fully healed and restored, and the order of things would go back to how they were supposed to be. I believed that one day, all would be right in our world.

After my breakdown and subsequent recovery in 2019, I came upon a profound realization. As Christians, especially African Christians, it feels like we are not supposed to or allowed to, say anything negative. We are not allowed or supposed to, lean into exactly what we really feel. It is all too easy to fall into the trap of pretending. We are supposed to have faith and hold on to our faith with all of our strength, or else we could be seen as not having enough faith and therefore are not "good" Christians. I feel that because of this, we often are not honest with ourselves.

As a Christian, having and speaking in faith as well as being transparent and leaning into how you feel is a difficult thing to balance. You want to have and display faith, but you also want to be completely honest with how you're feeling in that moment. Now that I am on the other side of that chaotic year, I know there is no discounting self-honesty. It's always best to be honest with yourself about how you feel. Yet on the other hand you want to lean into your faith in God and not allow those feelings to overwhelm you.

For me, I had buried how I felt so deep that its eruption rocked me. I hadn't been honest about being robbed of my childhood by my mom's illness. The feelings simmered inside until they boiled over and erupted in 2019.

Did I have faith? Yes.

Do I still have faith, even now that Mom is gone? Yes!

But will I continue to allow myself to truly feel my emotions and give myself the permission to be honest? Will I equip myself to try to deal with pain in its immediacy instead of allowing it to simmer? Definitely, yes.

There are still a lot of things left for me to figure out, a lot of feelings I am still getting in touch with, a lot of it revolving around Mommy and some around deep betrayal, but I am happy with who I am becoming today. I am proud of the journey I've had; and of the steps I have taken to get here today.

2019 was my saving grace. My recovery has been excellent. I went back to Uni after taking a year off. 2020 and COVID shook the world, and I had to stay home, doing school online. I cannot express how grateful I am and how much I thank God every day for the opportunity of the time I had with Mommy during the lockdown. Being able to be with her for the last stretch of her life was a great treasure that I'll always cherish. It made my heart knit with hers again in that holy communion of mother and daughter, and I will forever remember the mischievous twinkle in her eyes and the sound of her hearty laugh.

Today, I am proud of the women that myself, and my younger sister are growing up to become. We have been through much adversity, but we are coming out on the other side. We are not victims but victors. We are rising tall in our own spheres. We've got Jesus. We've got our whole lives laid out ahead of us. I have 16 months left at med school before I graduate as a medical doctor. My sister is an aspiring radio show host and media mogul.

The daughters of Adebola are doing exceptionally well. In this way, we carry on the torch for our mother. We will change the world the way she started to do even in her short but impactful life.

Despite it all, she raised champions. Whether it be in her mothering, in our prebirth prayers, or in her heartfelt prayers of faith for us even when she was restricted in her language. I know that she raised conquerors and we rise tall. We thrive, and will continue to do so.

Family is Everything. It is What Home Feels Like (Buyikunmi)

Home is where the heart is, it's where the heart beats to its full potential, and is filled to the brim with the overflowing unconditional love, joy and peace those eternal family bonds bring. There is something so wholesome, completing and fulfilling about knowing you have a place where and people with whom you truly belong. The pure love, safety and unity established within family is unsurpassed, one-of-a-kind, and stabilising.

Certain relationships have a tendency to be sporadic, quid pro quo and rocky. True, undiluted, no-nonsense love, is (thankfully) nothing like that! Family is an irreplaceable, core unit full of people put together to love one another unconditionally, to desire the very best the world has to offer for each other, and to be a rock in all of life's seasons- hills and valleys alike.

Family, in all its glory, is not always perfect. Being human means being capable of making mistakes, having misunderstandings, and occasionally not seeing others eye–to-eye. That, however, is not a debilitating or devastating truth, as the best relationships are not evergreen, perpetually sunny, and with no clouds in sight. The best relationships are the ones where the sunlight always prevails through the storm clouds, where the rain never drowns but always encourages growth, and where the cold births warm huddling together and never leaves room for bitterness.

With family, the walls of defense you might build up with others, are carefully and lovingly taken down, brick by brick. With family, all masks are removed. Family has the unique opportunity to witness every version of you, to be privy to the very essence of who you are, and to be seated in the audience, watching as you experience your mountain-top highs and the very depths of your lowest lows. Despite all this, family is that special set of people who will always take and accept you completely, just as you are, flaws and all.

Loving families provide us with the priceless opportunity to be fully known and utterly seen. For example, a child usually spends a minimum of around seventeen or eighteen years constantly at home, before venturing off into the world. Those years are so formative and give loved ones the chance to study you, to know your passions, your quirks, your pet peeves, what makes you smile and what your hopes and dreams are. These are the people who have meticulously defined and catalogued every type of laugh, translated each particular tone of voice, decoded each of the most micro of facial expressions, and practically have doctorates to their names in the subject of YOU! In other words, nothing slips under their radar!

Family knows when something is wrong, even when the most luminous of smiles tries to mask all other feelings. I can think of countless times when my dad, mum or sister have listened to me, with rapt attention, as I have poured out my heart to them. There are many more times when they have been the perfect sounding boards to hear my aspirations and plans. Every speech, reading and musical performance is listened to and encouraged first, at home. They are my forever cheerleaders no matter how the game is going. Family is your forever team; you will never be left on the bench, and you will always be integral to and included in the game. Family is the harmony to the melody you sing in your heart; it is your built-in choir to sing through the songs of life with.

Love has many forms and if there is one form of love family excels at, it is selfless and sacrificial love. This love sounds like waiting at any hour of night on the phone with you as you navigate a challenge or need someone to love and comfort you. It looks like holding up a rose-gold tinted mirror and proclaiming to you all the wonders about you, that you have yet to discover or believe are true of you. There is no competition with family. Instead, there is actively inspiring, urging, and fuelling you to be the most excellent form of yourself, with validation and honesty at every stage of the process.

Now, putting all those more serious points to one side... Family is FUN!! We make each other erupt into deep belly-laughs that ricochet throughout the house and right down the street. All the inside jokes, loving teasing, and hilarious impressions we do of each other have seasoned our family with joy. Every theme park, cinema, holiday destination, family wedding, road trip, shopping spree, sports day and school concert tells a story of our journey together. Growing up and even now, a cousin (more like sister!) road trip isn't really a road trip if we do not have an entire band in the backseat. I'm talking drummers (for the Afropraise, of course), singers (soprano, alto, tenor, AND bass!) air and mouth guitars and trumpets. Having a sister is wonderful too, sisters are precious, invaluable gems. I have access to two wardrobes and two different styles of clothes, and so does my sister. Having a sister is like always being at a sleepover - talking at any hour of the day, wearing each other's clothes, giggling until your sides hurt, sharing snacks, and watching films together never ends. My sister is my beautiful best friend, and I am more and more grateful for her every day!

Family is waking up on a chilly Christmas morning to a warm cup of fragrant, saccharine hot chocolate with whipped cream and marshmallows. Family is merrily singing Christmas carols and setting the table together in gleeful anticipation of the glorious feast that awaits us. Family is being willing to share your Easter chocolate with a smile, even the Mini Eggs! Family is scanning nervously through the crowd before approaching the stage and finally locking eyes with your people, giving you the encouraging smile, wink or nod you need to go ahead. Family screams your name the loudest as you whizz by in the 100/200 metre sprints and relay races; they're the people bouncing up and down like bunnies.

My family has taught me some of the most valuable life lessons I have learned thus far. My parents were the first people to show me love. Love is an action; it's a doing word. There is no better way to teach love than to demonstrate it to others. My parents are two of the kindest, most selfless, and loving people I know. Through their love for me and my sister, they led us to the omnibenevolent Father, God. My family has taught me to take pride in who I am and has always validated me. My family has instilled wisdom and skills in me to handle various life situations, to be a people person, to be diligent and to take pride in my work, to dream big and how to trust in, seek and serve God wholeheartedly.

My love for writing and expressing myself in words has been nurtured by my dad, who is an amazing author. I have always delighted in a good book, being transported to fictional lands, globetrotting via the pages and walking miles on end in characters' shoes. This comes from my reading enthusiast mum, thanks to her I have an appreciation for a great story. My interest in experimenting with spices and cooking was also sparked by my mum, who makes a mouth-wateringly delicious roast and much more. My love of laughter has definitely been fuelled by my hilarious sister, who is the family's very own comedian, with her witty one-liners and blunt humour! She is also the resident fashionista, who (fortunately!) gives her sartorial wisdom out for free. I don't often choose new glasses, outfits, or accessories without her spot-on guidance.

Shoutout also to doting aunties (who give the warmest hugs), fun-loving uncles (who are always up for a prank or a game), prayerful, caring, and wise grandparents, and finally, honorary siblings and godparents, who take a genuine interest in you and want to see you shine.

I am so blessed, and I am extremely thankful to God for the beautiful family He has placed me in. If your experience of family has been negative or troubling for you, I have encouraging news. God has an open invitation; He is always looking for people to join His loving family and to be His children. Not only do you get an all-loving Father when you join God's family, you also get an awesome brother, Jesus!

To top it all off, you get plenty of brothers, sisters, aunties, uncles, grandparents and more when you join the Christian family. God has a Father's heart and holds his arms out wide open to receive you. He won't reject you; He will never make you feel less than, and He will love you more than anyone else ever has or could love you. A bonus feature of this family is that you will never be separated from God's love, you have always been the apple of His eye. Will you join His welcoming family today?

Family is Everything to a Child Who is not a Child. A Firm Standing Anchor (Oluwatimilehin)

In the middle of France, on a school trip with friends, I felt the dread take me over.

When I left London, things were good. I'd talked to Funso every day. That was the way things had been for a long time. She was in Bulgaria studying, and I was in London, living life the way I had done for a long time. We were separated by miles but remained knitted together in heart, the way two sisters are supposed to be.

We either spoke or texted every day. But then suddenly, I noticed that her responses got shorter and shorter, and sparser and sparser. One day, there was simply no response. I was getting very worried but did my best to keep a lid on the worry. Funso was young and living life, and perhaps she just wasn't with her phone as much these days.

But the heart doesn't lie, and I felt my heart racing in panic each time I thought about her, each time I sent another message to which she didn't respond. So, I went to Dad.

"Something is wrong with Funso. She hasn't replied to my texts in days and I don't like this. Do something!"

He smiled a reassuring smile at me, but there was something a little sickly about that smile. "She is absolutely fine, Timi." He tried calling her there and then, but she didn't pick up either. After trying for a while, he turned to me and said, "If I have to go to Bulgaria, I will. Don't worry, okay? And know that if I do go to Bulgaria, it would have to be an emergency. I won't go if I don't have to."

I was not appeased, but there was really nothing I could do. "Let's hope you don't have to go then. God willing, you won't have to go." At this point, I stuffed my fear and trepidation down into my belly, as far down as I could stuff it.

Two days later, I was in the middle of France on that class trip. We were on our way back to the airport to get back to London when I got a jarring message from my aunt: "Don't worry, but just to let you know that your dad had to go to Bulgaria to go pick up your sister. Everything is good, don't worry. Your mom is with a family friend."

I was the youngest in our immediate family and close to the youngest in our local extended family as well, and everyone felt the need to protect me, shielding me from things they shouldn't be shielding me from. I wasn't blind. I had been Mom's primary caregiver for the longest of times, had grown up way before my time because of the responsibility, so I will never understand the need to shield me. I get angry when things are kept from me because of my age. How was I an adult when taking care of Mom, and yet treated like a child in other matters?

And who was this family friend Mom was with? No one knew how to care for my mom like I did. Mom had a routine, and she liked her routine. And I knew that people would be trying to protect her the same way they were trying to protect me, probably insulting her intelligence, forgetting that aphasia did not stop her mother's intuition. Aphasia did not discredit her astuteness.

Hands shaking, my heart threatening to hammer out of my chest, I dialed this aunt's number. But there was no response. The call kept going to voicemail. Because of the conversation I had had with Dad, I knew his going to

Bulgaria wasn't good. He had promised me he wouldn't go to Bulgaria except if it was an emergency. If he had left Mom all by herself without a caregiver, I knew everything was wrong. Everything had gone wrong. The text may have been well-intentioned to keep me at calm, but it did the opposite.

Who was with Mom? I loved Funso, but I was livid. Funso could take care of herself, but Mom couldn't. What emergency could it be that Dad had to abandon Mom to go rescue Funso? My hands couldn't stop shaking.

There I was in the middle of a massive traffic jam in France, and I couldn't reach anybody. I kept calling the aunt to no avail. I called Funso repeatedly as well as Dad, and couldn't get through to anyone. Prior to reading the text, I had been taking sips from a canned drink. Minutes later, the content of the can was all over my body. I still cannot recall how I spilled the drink, all of it.

"Are you okay?" My best friend, who was on the same trip as me, asked. But I couldn't answer. My words were gone, my throat dry. Gently, she pried my phone from my hands and read the message that had come in. And being that she knew everything that was there to know about me, she immediately knew it wasn't good, that my thoughts were on Mom.

The tears overtook me then. I was someone who didn't cry, and the volume and intensity of the tears that took me surprised me. Still in the middle of the unmoving traffic for the next two hours, I dialed everyone I knew. But either the call went to voicemail, or they didn't answer.

I was crying, hyperventilating, throwing up.

Thank God, the traffic eventually cleared up, and we made it to the airport. Still not knowing what was happening, I touched down in London around 2 am the next morning. Mom was wide awake, waiting up, unnerved that none of her children or her husband were home. No one had told her anything, and nothing had been done right.

But seeing Mom and seeing that she was okay, my heart calmed a bit. Not all the way, but it calmed a bit. There were tears in Mommy's eyes, and she spoke clearly for the first time in a long time. "What's going on?"

Her clear speech and full sentences scared me. No stuttering, no pauses, no sighs. It wasn't her normal.

But I didn't have an answer to her questions, only that Dad had gone to Bulgaria, which was all I knew. Mom, being Mom, started praying. As she prayed, I got her ready and into bed. I tried to fall asleep but ended up tossing and turning for hours until I finally went into Mommy's room curled up on the bed beside her and fell promptly asleep.

My sister came back to London with Dad but I wasn't allowed to see my sister for a month, because I was deemed too young and could be traumatized by seeing her in the state she was in.

I felt a raw kind of anger. I have had to act like an adult for most of my life, but when it really counted, why treat me like a child? To not feel in control, to be an adult and yet not an adult, is disconcerting, and is not something anyone should ever experience.

Because of my experiences, I find that I rely on myself more than I rely on others. Sometimes, I simply do not know how to ask for help, and I barely know how to be a kid. But I am trying to lean more into my inner child these days. I am trying to fulfil the purpose God made me for and to view this beautiful world He made with more gratitude. Is life hard sometimes? Yes. But is it still beautiful despite the hardness? Absolutely.

I still have a lot of things to process, a lot of questions I still need answers to. But I am learning to take the days one at a time. I am learning to allow my inner child and the adult I prematurely became to co-exist within the same body and mind.

If there is something I'd like to remind the world, it would be that children are not just children. They are full, complete, individual human beings with their own feelings and thoughts and motivations. And children do see. We see the things adults hide. We hear the things adults don't say. And we know when adults are lying to protect us. But we do appreciate the way our guardians try to show us how to handle every situation in the way that Jesus would. Sometimes it gets hard but we'll learn together.

Family is Everything. Where Music Rings True. To Live and not Just Exist (Araoluwa)

Imagine your favourite film without a soundtrack. Picture the most intense scene, in silence, the most climactic moment, in musical black and white. There is no denying that every single bit of emotion is built up through music: suspense, thrill, love, heartache. Just the scenes without the music would mean nothing, it would make you feel nothing.

A world without music would be a world without expression, without colour; a world simply in black and white.

Music is a gift from God; it's well and truly the 'language of the spirit'. It's never just been about liking certain genres or certain artists; it's about appreciating each integral part that makes the piece of music what it is, appreciating the way each song makes you feel.

It is amazing to me how one person can look at a piece of music and see random scribbles on a page, endless black lines that don't link up. For another, it's a never-ending story with endless possibilities. It's an empty canvas waiting to be designed.

It's one thing to listen to music and enjoy the lyrics and the melodies but for some people it's about dissecting the different parts and analysing how it comes together to make such a masterpiece. Whatever it may be, everyone finds some sort of enjoyment in music.

Composing is like engineering; it's an acquired skill, yet it comes from the heart and not the mind. It's so personal to you yet other people can still enjoy it. It's a form of modern art.

For me it's more about the expression. Playing an instrument allows me to relieve stress. I feel as if I physically leave behind my worries and problems with each press of the piano key. I walk away feeling so much lighter. There are some emotions that I don't think can be expressed with words. Music is my translation of those emotions. What my words could never properly convey, music has a way of communicating them for me. The saying "When words fail, music speaks," by Hans Christian Anderson has been so true for me.

Everyone in my family knows there's something wrong when I haven't touched the piano in days! There have been times where I go days without even looking at the piano and I've come to realise that it must have been because I wasn't ready to fully feel and express the emotions I was feeling at the time. I did not want them to be real.

However, I have come to the realisation that whatever emotion I am feeling- whether I'm sad or happy or stressed or simply apathetic, music does something to me; it opens up my heart, it heals it, it allows me to feel emotions without having to struggle to put them into words. I lose myself in the melody, drowning out all stress and anxiety.

Just think of the beauty of worship. In the heart and centre of worship, music is found. In this case, it's really not about you, but isn't it amazing how you feel so connected to God, so vulnerable yet protected, so incredibly loved?

Once again, it's about expressing things that simply cannot be expressed in just words. The lyrics speak to your soul whilst the melodies break down your walls, leaving just you and your heart, and your willingness to give everything you have left to God, knowing that even without muttering a single word, he knows exactly what you are going through and he sees you right where you are. Music must be a glimpse of heaven.

It has been my comfort on some of my hardest days. I believe that God uses songs to meet us in our darkest moments. Some of the most comforting songs I know, I discovered on days where singing was the last thing I wanted to do, but the lyrics of the song spoke directly to me, and I felt so seen.

It's no wonder music is a form of therapy. It communicates to the brain and smooths its rough patches. It penetrates through the coldest of hearts and for many people, music acts as an escape from reality.

If music is a language, then surely only some people can understand it. But it does not work like every other language-its universal! There's something unifying about music, it brings people from all different backgrounds together.

I remember days where my sister and I had had a disagreement and she would be singing somewhere in the house and I would automatically join in, completely forgetting that I was supposed to be upset with her! It's disarming- it's impossible to stay angry once music fills the room. In fact, It's an atmosphere changer- you either change with it, or you leave.

My favourite thing about music is that not only is it a memory- maker, but a memory- retriever. The minute a certain song comes on, it sends you back to a specific moment in time. Even if you can't remember the specifics of the moment, you can most definitely remember how you felt. It links up moments in our lives, ties together foggy memories and eventually makes a unique soundtrack.

I pray a day where I stop singing, playing or dancing to music never comes, a day when music no longer speaks to me the way it does now or a day where I stop appreciating the wonder that it is.

If music is what feeling sounds like, I pray we never stop feeling.

CHAPTER 25

Final Lessons
From The Motherland

I grew up in a typical Yoruba household, even though my family was a little less typical than others. But as most people born of Yoruba heritage would attest – my parents' and grandparents' lingua was well seasoned with proverbs. As I grew older, those sayings found their way into mine, too, and now make so much sense for wisdom.

These are the proverbs I shared with my husband routinely, in both their original tongue and their English interpretation, and he was intrigued by them. I share them similarly with my daughters (who have already started to sprinkle some into their own conversations, too). And I share them now with you, with the hope that they will bring you much wisdom and blessing as they have brought to many generations.

Eyin ati ahan ko le se ki won ma ja – Even the teeth and the tongue do fight.

Once in a while, you bite yourself when eating. Your teeth and tongue, who are so collocated and close should be the best of friends, but they conflict in their rhythm too. They won't always have a perfect relationship. As such, there is no perfect relationship without its ups and downs. The hedgehog's quills don't tolerate each other much in the summer seasons when it is hot. But these same quills are the best of friends during the winter, working for the greater good of keeping the hedgehog warm. Cherish your friends and family and don't let little conflicts drive you apart.

Ti a ba nwa owo lo, ti a pade iyi lona, ta ba lowo tan, sebi iyi naa la fe ra – On the quest for money, if you find honor, keep it as destination.

This literally means that someone on a quest for money who finds honor has reached their goal because honor supersedes money. Honor is much more powerful than money. Money cannot buy honor, and honor lasts for generations.

Eni se egusi lo n jobe ede – He who peels the melon seed, and does the hard work, is the one who eats a delicious soup.

E ni ba domi tutu siwaju lon tele titu – He who wets the floor ahead of themselves, will walk on cool instead of hot grounds.

Both proverbs have close meanings. In Nigeria, peeling the melon seed to make *Egusi* soup, a Nigerian delicacy, is arduous. But taking the time and effort to peel means you will have a pot of delicious soup to feast upon later.

Also, it makes sense to pay the price required for greatness. Put in the hard work today and enjoy the benefits later.

Omi eniyan ma mu, ko ni san koja eni – The water destined for me will not flow past me.

This means that we will all accomplish our God-given destinies, that whatever goodness has been ours by divine design will not be missed – God is on our side. Don't allow any present circumstances of life to rob you of this hope.

Ajoje ni mobe dun – Eating together makes the meal more delicious.

It is a proverb that shines light on the benefit of togetherness and collaboration. A meal eaten alone may be delicious, but communal eating takes the taste to the next level. Appreciate the people in your life.

Oju pipon ko ran siga – No matter how red your eyes are, they cannot light a cigarette fire.

This means that no matter how angry you are, you cannot make good use of it by acting it out in the moment. Calm down to solve problems.

Oju to ma bani kale, ko gbodo sowuro sepin – The eyes that will last you a lifetime must not constantly discharge pus from your youth.

This means that you should take care of your property/belongings if you want them to last you for long.

Eni to ba soko loja, ara ile eni lon ba – When you throw a stone in the marketplace, it would likely hit a family relative.

This cautions us to be mindful of our actions because there are always repercussions, especially to close friends and family, that we may not have envisaged when we embarked on an ill-informed course of action.

Ibi pelebe la ti n mu ole je – We begin eating the bean cake from the lowest point.

It is always better to begin tasks with the more manageable ones. There is no hill of tasks that is not conquerable, as long as we tackle it in bits. Don't be overwhelmed by life's unending demands. Take it one day at a time and you'll be just fine.

A pe je kii je baje – Eating late does not mean eating the dregs.

Nigba to Olorun ba ki ni ku aro, igba yen naa ni owuro aye – It is when God calls out "good morning" to you, that the morning of your life actually starts.

Both are used to show that it is never too late for you to accomplish your goals and live your dream. Your morning is when God says it is, not when others say it is. And you could actually be feasting when you eat later than others. Consider Nelson Mandela's latter days were so much greater than his former and his end even greater. Two UN Secretary Generals, both presidents of the EU (Council and Commission), two French presidents, and four US Presidents attended his funeral event - a historic yet-to-be-repeated first. Despite safety issues in South Africa.

Ba mi na omo mi, ko de inu olomo – The person who asked you to help them discipline their child does not really mean it.

Respect designated parents' authority. Discipline without love is abusive and in normalcy none can love a child more than their parents do. Therefore, be cautious with disciplining others.

Gbogbo alangba lo da nu dele, a o mo eyi ti inu n run – All lizards lay flat on their stomachs to crawl. We don't know which one has a stomach ache.

This means that most people dress well and put on their lovely façades. We can't readily know what someone is going through under all that finery. Be empathetic. Be kind. Treat everyone with a little extra gentleness.

Eniyan ko le rin kori majin – You cannot walk without your head shaking.

This means that no one has a perfect life, and it is impossible to go through life without mishaps. But what is important is to keep going after each failure because walk you must. Learn from errors and mishaps and keep moving.

Owo omode ko to pepe, tagbalagba naa o wo keregbe – A young child's hand cannot reach the tall shelf, and an adult's cannot enter the narrow mouthed gourd.

This means that we all have our unique differences, but we are all important the same. A young child might not be able to reach all the way to the shelf to get something, but he is still able to squeeze his small hands through the opening of a gourd to get something out, something the adult cannot do. We all need each other because we all do some things exceptionally well, but we cannot do it all.

Eni ba ma mu obo gbodo sebi obo – If you want to catch a monkey, you've got to act/think like a monkey.

You have to meet people at their level if you are to reach them. People can listen to your viewpoint when you relate with them at their level.

Oruko rere san ju owo, wura ati fadaka lo – A good name is better than riches.

This is a popular proverb across many cultures. A good name will always trump money. Make it generational, and even better! It is worth every sacrifice for it. Exodus 3:22.B.

Ciao!